Once Aboard
a Cornish Lugger

Once Aboard
a Cornish Lugger

PAUL GREENWOOD

AMBERLEY

First published by Polperro Heritage Press as *Once Aboard a Cornish Lugger*, 2007 and *More Tales from a Cornish Lugger*, 2011
This edition by Amberley Publishing, 2015

Amberley Publishing
The Hill, Stroud
Gloucestershire, GL5 4EP

www.amberley-books.com

British Library Cataloguing in Publication Data.
A catalogue record for this book is available from the British Library.

ISBN 978 1 4456 5061 6 (print)
ISBN 978 1 4456 5062 3 (ebook)

Typesetting and Origination by Amberley Publishing.
Printed in Great Britain.

Contents

Acknowledgements

Photographs reproduced by kind permission of Phil Lockley, David Butters, Ivor Toms, Kevin Faulkner, John Southern, Bill Cowan, Mike Pengelly and the author.

ONCE ABOARD
A CORNISH LUGGER

Preface

During the last few years of his retirement, I did my very best to persuade my old skipper, Frank Pengelly, that he should put pen to paper and write his life story. If he had done so, it would have been a fascinating and, I think, historically important composition, because he was the very last lugger skipper left in the port of Looe. His knowledge (common to many when he was a young man) had become unique, and he was the final guardian of it. Frank knew the fishing seasons for the drift nets and long lines, as well as the fishing grounds that covered hundreds of square miles of the channel. Without charts he could navigate the coast from Portland Bill to Lands End, his only aids being a clock, a compass and a tide book.

Unfortunately, by the time he did get around to doing something about it, he was very ill and sadly, he passed on before any real progress had been made.

As a boy I served for 4 ½ years on his lugger the *Iris*. I overcame sea sickness and learned my job on deck working the nets and lines with the other four crewmen. Frank, or 'Moogie' as he was known as, always played his cards very close to his chest. He was the skipper, we were the crew, and provided we did our job on deck, that's all he required; there was very little encouragement given to learn more.

There are now only a handful of us left who remember those days, and as Moogie left it too late, I thought that someone ought to try and record the way of life on those boats before it has all faded from living memory.

Frank's knowledge was vast, and I can't pretend for one minute to be able to write the account that he could have written. He was the skipper, I was the boy, so we are coming at the story from two very different angles. But my memories of the time I spent on the *Iris* are still very vivid, (how could they not be?) and by conferring with the few others remaining from those days, I have endeavoured to keep the account as accurate as possible, although by virtue it is a very personal one.

But before I launch into that tale, I should like to paint in the background history of the Cornish lugger. From the mighty three-masted craft of the smuggling and privateering days of the eighteenth century, to the massive fishing fleets of the late nineteenth century, and the twilight years of the mid- to late twentieth century. So you will understand that the those few remaining luggers I write about, working out their last days around the Cornish coast in the 1960s were not there by accident, they had a long, and a proud history.

Paul Greenwood
Looe, 2007

Introduction

From the seventeenth to the mid-twentieth century the lugger, in its various forms, was the principle vessel of the Cornish fishing industry. The early boats were clinker built double-ended craft, between 20 and 40 feet in length, with a wide beam and deep draught. Contemporary drawings show open boats, stepping two and three masts. They were used for hand lining to catch hake, whiting, pollack etc, long lining for turbot, ray and conger as well as working short fleets of hand bred drift nets to catch pilchards, herring and mackerel.

Marketing was limited to what the local fish jowters could hawk around the villages and farms. The only fish handled in bulk were pilchards. These were salt cured and pressed into barrels, to be exported to Spain and Italy as a Lent food and to the West Indies where the plantation owners fed them to their slaves. The early luggers looked to be slow sailers and must have been heavy to row in a calm, but they didn't work very far from home, and as time was not their master, I suppose it mattered little.

Speed only became important when the revenue cutters had to be out paced in the smuggling days of the eighteenth and early nineteenth century. It was then that we caught a glimpse of what the Cornish shipwrights could really do.

The final form of the smuggling lugger was a splendid fully decked vessel, the largest of them being up to 75 feet in length; both clinker and carvel construction methods were employed. They stepped three masts, allowing a massive press of sail to be set.

It has been recorded that with a 'whole sail' breeze the fastest of them could make the 100 miles from Cornwall to Roscoff in Brittany in eight hours. That's an average speed of twelve knots, very smart sailing by today's standards let alone two hundred plus years ago.

For their size, these craft were very heavily armed and the greatest of them carried twelve to sixteen cannon on the weather deck, and up to a dozen swivel guns, (these, loaded with grape shot, were the anti-personnel weapons of the day) as well as a cutlass and a musket for each member of the crew. When running contraband, 30 men were considered sufficient to work the lugger and her cargo, and if necessary, take on a customs cutter. But when Britain was engaged in one of her many wars against France, Spain, Holland, America etc, letters of marque could be obtained. These documents licensed vessels to go privateering against the enemy. So, as well as running their illicit cargoes, they were also likely to be escorting a valuable prize into harbour. At such times, a crew of up to 60 hands was carried, enough men to fight the ship effectively and put a prize crew aboard the enemy ship, should they carry the day. Looking at the earnings of these vessels, (where records have survived) the money and employment they generated puts them on par with today's tourist industry. Mind you, I suppose there is very little chance of getting killed, imprisoned or hung, for working in a knick-knack shop or a restaurant.

The Cornish smuggling luggers earned for themselves a ferocious reputation, but the crews were well rewarded for the risks they took. For a run to Guernsey or Roscoff and back, a crewman was paid ten pounds, probably more than he would earn in three months working as a fisherman. Any prize money was generously shared, keeping all hands keenly interested in the lugger's success, and at the same time lifting families from poverty to plenty. Meanwhile the venture capitalists reaped huge dividends on their investments, and at the same time kept their hands clean.

Today we can still get some idea of just how big and profitable these contraband operations were because Zephaniah Job, the Polperro 'smuggler's banker' kept detailed accounts of all his transactions, and some of them have survived. For over 20 years Mr Job was agent for, and part investor in, several well-found vessels engaged in smuggling, and if you convert his accounts into today's money the results are quite amazing. He handled some £62 million in transactions of which £37 million was profit to the smugglers, and his was one of two operations active in one small fishing village.

Smuggling was very big business all around the coast of Britain. If ever its true figures could be calculated the results, I am sure, would be truly astounding. These 'Free-traders' as they liked to call themselves, dealt in any imported commodity that the government had seen fit to put a tax on, such as salt, tea, coffee, brandy, silk, wines, perfume and lace. When the French Revolution began, a Polperro vessel, then engaged in loading her cargo at Roscoff, rescued some members of the Trelawny family who had been spending the summer at their villa in Brittany. The skipper of the lugger charged these frightened, rather minor, Cornish aristocrats more for the Channel crossing than the modern ferry charges today. Spies, criminals, aristocracy on the run - the men with the big fast luggers carried anybody providing they had the gold to pay.

After Napoleon's defeat at Waterloo the government of the day then had an opportunity to do something about the massive loss of revenue it was suffering, and they handed the task over to a well-manned battle-hardened Royal Navy. It proved to be well up to the job, setting up a coastal blockade of the Channel, and it was not long before the risks involved in running contraband became much too high to remain profitable. The big luggers (those that hadn't been captured) were disarmed and re-employed as humble coastal traders. Smuggling did continue, but of necessity it became a low profile, small time operation. The glory days were now over.

The fishing lugger meanwhile had remained a slow cumbersome affair. Speed costs money and if it is not essential, then no one will invest in it.

In 1859 the great engineer I. K. Brunel completed his railway bridge over the river Tamar, and that changed everything. Cornwall was now no longer a remote, virtually inaccessible county. Fresh fish (amongst many other commodities) could now be transported to the markets of London, Manchester and Birmingham, and to make the best of these new opportunities, larger, faster and better-designed boats were required. These new craft had to be able to work fishing grounds a long way from their home port, and then return swiftly to land their catches, fresh and in time for the market trains. Prime fish, boxed and well iced for the journey, made top prices on the city markets.

Once again the shipwrights had to come up with the answers. Their forefathers had excelled in the quest for speed in the smuggling days, and now these men had to rise to the challenge of the opportunities being offered by the railways.

But the new class of lugger didn't appear overnight from the drawing board of some genius naval architect. No, the final form of the Cornish lugger evolved steadily over a couple of generations, the fruit of observation, new ideas and experience. A skipper wanting a boat built would discuss with the boat builder of his choice, the sort of craft he had in mind, her length, beam, draught, shape of transom etc. Bearing these instructions in mind, the builder would take a piece of clear pine and carve to scale a half model, then present it to the skipper for final adjustments. Paring a bit off here and there, they would eventually arrive at the final shape of the new boat. This model would then be sawn down at the datum lines, the resulting sections provided the shapes for the frames of the full-sized craft.

A more primitive method used was to build the boat entirely by eye. The shipwright would lay down the keel, put up the stem post, sternpost, deadwoods and transom. Next, three frames would be made and mounted on the keel, battens would then be nailed around fore and aft to give the general shape of the hull. The skipper and the builder would then spend time eyeing things up, fairing the frames in here and there until they got her looking right; 'suant' was the word used to describe it. When both parties were satisfied with their efforts, the build could proceed. This method of construction worked, but a boat could well end up being faster on one tack than the other, for the simple reason that her hull could be very different in shape from port to starboard.

Another peculiarity of some of the Cornish boats was that, when afloat, their stem and frames appeared to be slanting backwards. This was because in the building, everything had been set up perpendicular from the keel, and of course when the boat was afloat she drew around 6 feet aft and 3 feet forward, throwing the keel at least 18 inches out of level, it was a curious effect. Most shipwrights would set everything up from the waterline so as all looked fair when she was afloat, but some of the old men never altered their ways and boats were built with backward raking stems right up to the 1930s.

There were no minimum standards laid down for boat construction. The amount and quality of timber in a hull would vary, governed by the money available to the man having it built. A large budget could mean heavy oak frames set at 16-inch centres, sheathed with pitch pine planking maybe 2 inches thick. A tight budget could mean that the oak frames were much lighter and set out at 20-inch centres, sheathed with 1 ¼-inch red pine planking. But, as Looe shipwright Arthur Collins used to say, "It's not the weight of wood in a boat, it's the way it's fitted," and the Cornish shipwrights could certainly 'fit wood'. Hull planks were cut to such a degree of accuracy that caulking was unnecessary, plank edges were bevelled to fit together perfectly, resulting in even the most meanly built of luggers being well up to the work required of them. And much was required of them, in the days of large families and no social services, where people lived and died by the results of their own efforts. One lugger with a crew of six men could well be responsible for feeding and clothing as many as 40 people. From babes in arms, to dependants too old or too ill to work any more, a heavy burden indeed for the men at sea.

The Cornish lugger was unique and could not be mistaken for any other class of vessel around the British Isles, except for maybe the Manx 'Nicky', but they were based on the Cornish lugger to begin with. Every boatyard had its own 'signature', and every skipper had his own ideas of how his boat should look. Fleets of them were built, (well over a hundred worked from Looe over the years) you could see their pedigree, they were alike, but no two were ever the same. The majority, for all their individuality, were just good working craft providing a frugal living for her people. But there were exceptions at either end of the scale; the odd one would turn out to be a complete 'dog', a slow sailer and an indifferent sea boat, giving everyone aboard a hard time for as long as she was worked. The Looe boats *Dove* and the *Harvest Home* (FY 159), were two such examples.

Equally rare were the luggers whose speed and sweetness of line made them the talk of the coast; in a county famed for such craft they had to be something very special to stand out. The *Talisman* (FY 242) of Looe and the *Sunshine* (FY 222) of Mevagissey were probably two of the finest examples.

This new breed of lugger was between 36 and 45 feet in length, with a beam of 12 to 14 feet, drawing 6 to 7 feet of water. With a straight stem and a long sleek bow for going to weather, they had neat sterns for running, and a graceful shear line to show off their good looks. They were two-masted, setting a huge dipping lug main sail on the foremast, and a standing lug sail on the mizzen; a mizzen staysail and jib could be set in light airs or when on a long passage.

These boats could carry their nets and lines plus a big catch of fish in all weathers, while remaining safe and stable. By the 1890s they had reached their extreme form. In the quest for speed they had gone as far as possible without jeopardising their seaworthiness, and by now even the finest gentlemen's yachts of the day had a job to match the best of them.

For their grace and beauty, the Breton fishermen called them the 'swallows of the sea', and by now fully decked, the final form of the Cornish lugger had evolved. The fish were plentiful and trade was brisk, railway transport and fine new boats had opened up the Cornish fishermen's horizons. As well as working the home pilchard and herring season, they fished for mackerel with their drift nets off the south-west coast of Ireland, while some worked long lines for ray, conger and turbot out as far as the coast of Brittany.

Others followed the herring shoals along the west coast of Scotland and on up to the Shetland Isles and then down into the North Sea ending the season at Scarborough on the Yorkshire coast.

It was while returning to her home port of St Ives from the herring fishery at Scarborough in 1902, that the *Lloyd* SS 5 made the 600-mile voyage in just 50 hours, an average speed of twelve knots. To drive a boat that hard, her skipper must have had nerves of iron. Many of the luggers had made the trip in 70 hours, still a very respectable eight knots average. But the record for long distance voyaging must surely rest with skipper Joseph Nicholls and his crew who, in 1846, sailed the 38-foot lugger *Mystery* from Newlyn to Australia in 116 days. This was several years before the modern design came in, and the *Mystery* would have probably been an open boat in the amidships working area and of the old fashioned cod's-head mackerel's-tail hull form.

By the late 1880s the fishing industry had reached its zenith. 570 first-class luggers were registered in the ports and harbours of Cornwall employing 3,500 men and boys at sea, and probably double that number in ancillary trades ashore. Although their numbers declined continually from here onwards, it would be another 108 years before the last working lugger landed her final catch.

Just before the 1914-18 war small petrol-paraffin engines became available, enabling the boats to leave and enter harbour more easily, and make headway in a calm. An old fisherman told me that when the engines were first introduced they thought they were in heaven as their lives were made so much easier; another bonus was the boats began to last longer. I reckoned the obvious reason for that was oil and paraffin leaking from the engines and soaking into the timber had a preserving effect, but he reckoned it killed off most of the 'sow-pigs' (woodlice) that lived in droves on a wooden vessel, weakening them over the years by eating them from the inside out. I really don't know what to make of that yarn, but he was there so there must be something in it.

The *Undaunted* (FY 393) of Looe, owned by brothers Ness and Johnny Richards, was one of the first luggers to have an engine installed. They used to charge 6d a boat to tow the others in or out of the harbour to save the crew having to row or pay a shore gang to pull them to the pier head. Evidently at slack water she could tow as many as six boats at a time, all that with a 7 HP engine. I think the horses in those engines must have been a lot bigger than they are today.

Those early engines required a fair bit of maintenance to keep them in good running order. The cylinder heads would have to be taken off at regular intervals for a de-coke and for the valves to be ground in. The magneto and spark plugs had to be cleaned and set up with the right gaps, and once a year or so, the big end bearing caps had to be filed down to take the slack out of them. One man on each boat, known as the 'Engine Driver', would be responsible for this work as well as their operation at sea.

These engines had a dual horse-power rating, i.e. 6/7 or 12/14 etc. This was because they ran on two different fuels, petrol and paraffin. Each engine had two tanks, a small tank for petrol and a larger one for paraffin, the pipes from each connected to a two-way tap on the carburettor. To start up, the tap was turned to petrol and the carb flooded, then the choke was applied and the magneto was retarded (this was to stop the engine backfiring and injuring the man cranking the handle). Upon starting, as the engine warmed up, the choke was taken off, and the magneto advanced, it would now be running at the top HP rating. When the engine was judged to be hot enough, the fuel was turned over to the much cheaper paraffin, but the HP dropped to the lower rating.

Initially the engines had no gearboxes or any form of clutch, meaning no neutral and no astern. The shaft was coupled directly to the crankshaft, so that when the engine was started you were away. Therefore, to have any sort of control when entering harbour, the length of time a carburettor full of fuel lasted had to be known to within a few seconds. At the critical moment the fuel would be cut off and if all went well the engine stopped, leaving the boat with just enough 'way' to come along side the quay in a dignified and safe manner, with maybe just a bit of drudging here and there. But if things went wrong, and there was nobody on the quay to catch a rope, then the bow had to be run in between the sterns of the next two boats moored ahead, or scraped up the quay until she stopped. You can just imagine the shouting and swearing, crashing and scrunching that must have gone on at times in the early days of engines.

Thankfully, gearboxes were very soon introduced, giving the boats neutral and a brake in the form of being able to go astern. But the early boxes with their cone clutches were liable to jam in gear, so the 'Engine Driver' always had a lump of ballast iron handy to belt the lever with, should that happen. As problematical as those early engines were, nobody wanted to go back to sails and oars. Through the 1920s and 1930s engines steadily advanced in both power and design. There were many different makes and horse powers to choose from, but by far the most popular with the fishermen were those made at the Kelvin engineering works in Glasgow. By the mid-1930s the ideal power combination for a lugger proved to be the four-cylinder 30 HP, with a straight drive gearbox for the main engine and a 13 HP driving through a two to one reduction gearbox for a wing engine. The maximum hull speed of eight knots could be obtained when the two engines were driving together, and the wing motor on its own was powerful enough to work the boat up to the nets and lines in all but the worst of weather, as well as being very economical on fuel.

These motors were very far from maintenance free, and their performance certainly reflected the amount of TLC they received. But most of the engine drivers on the boats took great pride in looking after their charges, and were genuinely sorry to see them craned out in the late 1940s and early 1950s to be replaced by the more advanced and efficient diesel engines.

Upon the outbreak of the First World War, the backbone of the fishing fleet (all the young fit men and the best of the boats) was called up for service in the Royal and Merchant navies, leaving only the old men and boys to carry on as best they could, working their nets and lines close in, up and down the coast, for fear of U Boats etc. Then with the coming of peace in 1919, the men who had survived those hellish years returned home, and later the boats that had been requisitioned (those that had survived ordeal by matlo) were released by the Admiralty.

When the fishing fleet was refitted and got back to sea, what a surprise the men had. The deep fishing grounds had lain virtually undisturbed for 5 years, and were now teeming with fish. When they shot the long lines, every hook came up with a prime fish on it. When working the drift nets, the resulting pilchard catches loaded the smaller boats down to danger point. Nobody had experienced anything like it. What's more, a hungry post-war Europe needed feeding, so the huge catches that were being landed had a ready market and made good money.

Here then was another massive boom in the fishing industry. The best of the existing fleet was modernised with new and more powerful engines, while the smaller older craft were sold off and replaced by a new design of motor lugger then entering service. These boats carried their beam well forward and were bigger in the bilge than the old sailing luggers. At that time they could also boast two and sometimes three petrol/paraffin engines pushing out as much as 30 HP.

Sails were reduced to a small standing lug mizzen and a leg of mutton foresail, known as a 'marmaduke'. This was enough canvas to stop her rolling when making a passage out and back to the lining grounds, or to help her along should an engine refuse duty. Wheelhouses were now being fitted, doing away with tiller steering. They were bolted to the deck just forward of the mizzen mast, a wheel and gypsy operated chains back to a quadrant on the rudder. Just big enough for one man to stand up in, they were a godsend in reducing hypothermia and exposure in wintertime. All this modernisation made life at sea a lot more bearable and, because of this, the men started to last a lot longer. In the sailing days most were ashore, worn out by their mid-forties through gruelling hard work, exposure and poor nutrition, having started their sea going career at 11 or 12 years of age. But now, although many were still starting at a very tender age, they found they were able to carry on working into their fifties and sixties.

Much longer fleets of drift nets could be worked, as the boats no longer had to be hauled to their gear with a hand-operated foot line capstan. With the introduction of the motor powered line hauler or 'jinny' in the 1920s, it became possible to work 6,000 hooks of long line on a tide, as against 4,000 with a man powered hauler or 2,000 when hauled by hand.

Meanwhile the fish stayed plentiful, market prices were holding up and catch records were being broken. During the herring season of 1920, for example, a Looe lugger, the *May Blossom* (FY 51) shot her nets in Bigbury Bay. She was the only boat out that night because a south-west gale looked to be brewing up, sending the rest of the fleet back into harbour. The skipper, Roger Dingle, and his crew were all young married men with families to support, so it took an awful lot of bad weather to make them turn and run for home. They rode to the nets for just long enough to have their supper then, with the engines cranked into life, all hands donned their oilskins and sea boots ready to begin the night's work. By this time, the rising gale was starting to make life very uncomfortable, with an ugly breaking sea and driving rain. Roger and his crew were in for a hard night. Nevertheless, after several gruelling hours of work, they prevailed and the nets were once more stowed back into the net room, and a huge catch of herring was their reward. The *May Blossom* was now deeply laden, her fish room was full and she was loaded rail to rail on deck. The weather was much too bad to try and get back to land at the fish market on Plymouth Barbican; their only option was to run before the gale and land their catch at Brixham. So, with both engines at full throttle, the mizzen was sheeted away and the foresail hoisted to give her all the help they could. The fate of the *May Blossom* and her crew was now in the lap of the gods; all they could do was to hang on tight and keep pumping.

They shot around Bolt Head, the skipper edging her out to gain a good berth off Prawl Point. The wind was blowing like 'Barney's Bull' and the seas were big and breaking. Several stones of fish were washed over the side, but very little could be done about that.

In a welter of breaking seas they battled around Start Point and then, giving the Skerries bank a wide berth, the course was altered to the north east, right before the wind. Now running bends deep in foam, they surfed up to Berry Head and the welcoming haven of Tor Bay. You can just imagine the jaw-dropping disbelief of those around Brixham harbour that morning as this heavily laden lugger and her weary crew tied up along side the quay to land their catch. They had been the only boat out on the entire coast that night, and the fish merchants were desperate for herring. How many cran of fish they landed has not been recorded, but the amount it made has: the catch sold for £634, not a bad day's work nowadays, but in 1920 it was a fortune. They arrived back in Looe to a heroes' welcome, and the *May Blossom*'s owner, Dick 'Clubs' Pengelly, had a gilded cockerel carved and mounted at the masthead, denoting that she was cock of the fleet.

Back then, 30 shillings to 2 pounds was a week's wage for a working man. Roger Dingle's daughter, Gwen, remembered her father bringing home his wages: for that one night's work he had earned £90, and with this, his wife bought the family a cottage. To earn a whole year's wages in one night, and that enough to buy a home with, the *May Blossom*'s catch can surly have had few equals for its purchasing power.

The Cornish fishing industry was enjoying prosperous times and for some, as in the case of the *May Blossom*, it was exceptional, but it was not to last. The slump of the late 1920s ushered in hard times with a vengeance, boat owners went into debt while their crews were unable to pay the rent on their cottages or the grocery bills at the end of the week. Many well-found luggers were sold off to the highest bidder, while the men who had crewed on them were glad to take jobs labouring on the roads, or any employment at all that would feed the family and pay the rent. Those who couldn't find a job had to live hand to mouth, and hunger was not unknown.

When a vessel was sold, the former owner was then able pay his outstanding debts and maybe put a little money in the bank. But it was the jobless crewman and his family who really started to suffer. Hard times forced Ned Ham, a Looe skipper, to sell his boat the *Adela* (FY 169). Later on when he saw the hardships his old crew and their families were going through he tried to buy her back from the new owner, so that he could re-employ them and try to make them some sort of a living. As poor as it might have been, it would still have been much better than nothing at all. But it was no deal; the new owner would not budge. This played on poor Ned's mind so badly that he eventually committed suicide in the front room of his home at 'Port Cottage' up West Looe Hill, by drowning himself in a bucket of water.

Another former owner tried to drown himself for similar reasons, and if it hadn't been so very sad, it would have been farcical. He made his attempt at oblivion by tying one end of a length of rope to a 56lbs weight and the other end around his neck, then jumped into the river. Fortunately, the rope was too long and so, firmly anchored, he swam around in circles until he was rescued.

Towards the end of the 1920s things did level out a bit, fish prices were very poor, but there was plenty of fish to be caught, so a week's wages could be scraped up if you worked hard enough. Many of the younger fishermen spent the summers crewing on the J Class yachts that attended the big regattas of the day, racing in the Solent, Torbay and the Clyde. Others worked on yachts doing a summer season in the Mediterranean where the wages were poor but they lived 'all found' and were likely to receive a small retainer in the winter. Yet another way a fisherman could boost a meagre and uncertain income was to join the Royal Naval Reserve. A small yearly retainer was paid, and in return, the men had to attend an annual two-week's training on a ship or naval shore establishment, for which they received a naval rating's pay. In fact, most of the men classed that fortnight as their annual holiday.

The 1930s were also very depressing times for the fishermen, but always the hope was that things just had to improve, though unfortunately they didn't. The year 1937 must surely go down as one of the bleakest in the history of the Cornish fishing industry. In that year, the government of the day put an embargo on exports to Italy in retaliation for Mussolini's invasion of Abyssinia. This caused the pilchard trade to all but collapse, because the vast bulk of the Cornish salters' produce was exported to that country to be eaten as a lent food. There is an old rhyme concerning that trade.

Here's a health to the Pope and may he relent
And extend by six months the terms of his lent
For 'tis very well known between the two poles
There is nothing like pilchards for the saving of souls

The embargo was an unmitigated disaster. What effect it had on the Italian people, I don't know, but it certainly punished a lot of people in Cornwall.

The next body blow to the fishing industry in that dreadful year was the complete failure of the herring fishery. Every October shoals of herring used to appear off the south-west coast to spawn in the big sandy bays. Fleets of drifters from all the major fishing ports of Britain would arrive to partake of this harvest. In 1937 the boats appeared, but the expected fish failed to show up. In the previous year's herring season, a number of trawlers had been active in the spawning bays, trying to catch herring in their trawls. They enjoyed a certain amount of success, but every haul they made not only filled their decks with herring, but with spawn as well. The fish they caught were boxed up and stowed down below while the spawn, now dead, was shovelled back over the side, and around the bay they went again to repeat the process.

When there were no herring to be caught the following year by trawlers or drifters, nobody could believe it. Their absence was put down to their just being late, and the boats burnt hundreds of gallons of fuel between them, hunting for shoals that would never arrive for the simple reason that they no longer existed. In the end, the chandlers stopped crediting the boats with fuel that they were pretty sure they weren't going to get paid for, and that was that. The drifters returned to their home ports, the crews were skint and the skippers were in debt.

The Cornish fishing industry had been on a knife-edge for years, but the twin disasters of 1937 really put the skids under it. From then on, the fleet shrank rapidly as boats were sold off for whatever money could be raised on them. The only ones to survive were the most-hard working and frugal of skippers who hung on to their boats, grimly hoping for better times.

With the outbreak of the Second World War, as in the First, every fit and able-bodied man was called up for service in the navy. The best of the boats were also requisitioned for war work, leaving yet again a few old men and boys to carry on as they might. Those who did fish through the war years made a very good living, although the grounds they were able to work were very limited. The country needed all the food it could get, so the government now controlled the fish prices, which meant the men knew exactly what they would be paid per stone for each species of fish and if they all had good catches the price didn't plunge to the floor as always happened on the auction market. Fishing in peacetime is a hard and dangerous occupation, but in wartime the dangers were trebled. Not only did they risk an encounter with the enemy in the form of E-boats, submarines and aircraft, but at night the boats were forbidden to show any lights. This of course greatly increased the risk of collision. Add to that a total black-out ashore, and the wartime fishing skipper was facing some fairly daunting problems. As protection for the Looe fleet, the lugger *Our Boys* had a heavy machine gun mounted on her foredeck. Fortunately they never had to use it in anger, but once a week they opened up with it for practice: "Shooting at the shags," Bill Pye, her skipper, used to say. Two Mevagissey boats, the *Ibis* and the *Pride of the West* were machine-gunned by a German fighter plane but, as luck would have it, he missed both of them. A Plymouth boat was not so lucky however; she was machine-gunned and sunk with all hands while fishing beyond the Eddystone lighthouse.

When peace was declared, and the men were demobbed from the forces, they returned home to exactly the same situation their fathers and elder brothers had experienced when they returned home from the First World War. The fishing grounds had had 5 years' rest, the fish were plentiful, and a starving Europe needed all the food it could get.

The luggers (now numbering about 40 in Cornwall) were made ready for sea, along with their drift nets and long lines. The first boats away returned home with catches the like of which most fishermen only dream of. Fish were teaming, to the extent that some boats had their long lines rendered useless because they were coming up with a mature fish on every hook, and as they circled around the line between the seabed and the surface, the rope backing would become completely unlaid.

Fleets of drift nets were lost through the sheer weight of pilchards taking them to the bottom. Such happenings were now more an inconvenience than a disaster. The fishermen were once more riding the crest of a wave. The county's pilchard works or 'salters' were exporting to Italy again, and six canneries had opened up, tinning pilchards in tomato sauce or olive oil for the home and export markets. During the long line or 'boulter' season, the railways transported many thousands of stone of prime turbot, ray and conger etc, to the fish markets of the major cities.

The boatyards were also very busy as orders came in for new boats, taking out the old petrol/paraffin engines and installing new diesel engines in the existing fleet. These were the first true marine engine, unaffected by damp, virtually maintenance free and running on a very cheap fuel.

A few new motor luggers were built to bolster the ageing fleet, but more favoured for new build especially at Looe, were the smaller, cheaper general-purpose boats now coming off the designers drawing board. Their origins could not be mistaken, a straight stem with a neat transom and sweet sheer line. They were the luggers' younger sisters.

30 feet to 38 feet in length, 9 feet to 12 feet in the beam and drawing 4 feet to 5 feet of water, they were high in the hull as they had no bulwarks; a long foredeck accommodated the engines and cabin, a full width open backed wheelhouse came next and a small tight deck aft covered the steering gear. The main working area amidships was covered with a hatch board deck about waist height down from the rail. They were known as 'quatters' because they weren't considered big enough to work the offshore grounds, but instead earned their living on the home grounds, or the 'quatt'. Four men could make a living drifting and long-lining; two men could work her crabbing, or one man could take day-trippers angling in the summer months. A very handy craft indeed. Fine examples of that class were the *Claire*, skipper Charlie Butters; the *Silver Spray*, skipper Edgar Williams; the *Endeavour*, skipper Fernley Soady, and the *Paula*, skipper Bill Butters.

But the lugger was still the mainstay of the Cornish fishing fleet, be she newly launched or a craft that had first seen service in the middle years of Queen Victoria's reign. The skippers themselves were exceptional men. They would have probably served a minimum of 10 years working under their father or uncle, the then skipper, learning every aspect of seamanship, knowledge of the fishing grounds and developing the steady nerve and great strength of character needed to wrest a living for five men and their families from the sea. In the days before radio you couldn't shout for help if things went wrong, caught in a gale, long lining 60 miles off shore. The skipper's responsibilities must have weighed very heavily at times.

In the long lining season there were many different areas of ground to be worked, with names like 'Klondike', 'Ray Pits' and 'Stone Light Dipping'. The skippers knew how the tide flowed over them at ebb and flood, and the fish to be caught on them: sand and gravel for ray and turbot, rock and rough ground for conger, ling and pollack.

When working the drift nets, they knew where to expect the pilchard shoals and at what time of year. An old saying goes: "When the corn is in the shock, then the pilchards go to rock" meaning that around harvest time the shoals are to be found close in shore. Another says that pilchards were "Food, money and light, all in one night", the light referring to the days when pilchard oil (a bi-product of the salt curing process) was burnt in the lamps. Their knowledge was vast, and very much more than could be accumulated in one lifetime. It was the result of many lifetimes' experience passed on down through the generations, and added to by each skipper. Charts were never used; each skipper carried his own chart in his head and could navigate, fair weather or foul, day or night around large areas of the coast. Unfortunately none of this knowledge was ever written down; the location of the grounds and when to fish them, the compass courses and estimated times to get to them were all committed to memory, and are now lost.

Their methods of fishing were ecologically sound. Drift nets would catch plenty of fish, but never decimate the shoals. Long lines did no damage to the grounds they were shot on, and only caught mature fish. Every generation left plenty of good fishing for the next, and very little (if any) harm was done to the balance of nature. But by the middle of the twentieth century, technology and progress became the watchwords. Why catch part of a shoal of fish when the whole shoal can be caught with a purse seine or ring net? Why try to tempt a few mature fish to take the baited hooks of a long line when, with a modern trawler, you can go on the offensive and catch them hungry or not?

The luggers of Cornwall were considered to be retrogressive, their methods of fishing had hardly changed in centuries and, in truth, it was only the boom after the two world wars that had seen them continue thus far. So, while the Cornish boats were enjoying the good times, progress and politics were lining up yet again to deal them a blow. During the war Belgium, Holland and France had lost nearly all of their fishing fleets and, as they needed food as much as we did, their governments were heavily subsidising the design and construction of fleets of modern trawlers.

These new vessels soon started to become a real headache to anyone working long lines, to the extent that the luggers had nearly as much chance of having their gear towed away, as coming home with a catch of fish.

Over a period of time, the trawlers have reduced the old lining grounds to near deserts. Any mature fish on them now must be suffering from acute loneliness.

Yet another blow was dealt to the industry by our own government when, in 1955, a trade agreement was drawn up with South Africa. A small part of the deal saw Britain importing South African tinned pilchards, retailing on the home market at 2d a tin cheaper than the Cornish product. It wasn't long before the canneries started to feel the pinch and, in a bid to compete, they dropped the price paid to the boats for pilchards from 4/6d (22p) to 3/6d (17p) per stone. However, it did not help. They began to lose orders from the retailers and, one by one, they closed down. The salters were also losing orders. Tastes were changing on the continent, and a new generation of consumers was not as fond of salt fish as their parents and grandparents had been. To crown it all, the pilchard shoals changed their habits for some reason, and were no longer to be found off the Cornish coast during the winter months. Now there was nothing to be earned with either nets or lines from the end of November to March.

Deathblows were raining down on an industry that had sustained itself for centuries, making it only a matter of a few short years before it would be consigned to history. By 1960 many of the once-thriving, bustling harbours of Cornwall echoed more to the ghosts of the past than to the activities of the living. Looe was a typical example. Quayside warehouses stood empty and locked up, the fish market had closed down, fishermen's stores and net-lofts were being turned into cafes or workshops. The few remaining boats seemed to huddle up together for comfort, leaving whole areas of the quayside empty and deserted.

For a few brief weeks each summer the port would come back to life, but the voices to be heard echoed of accents well north of the Tamar. These were holidaymakers going out for a day's angling, or on trips around the bay, and thank goodness they did because for several years it was really only their custom that kept the whole harbour from penury.

The Looe fleet by now consisted of about 15 quatters fitted out with seats and fishing rods for the holiday trade. Most of these boats lay idle from October to May. Two or three of them might take aboard a fleet of nets and have a go for the pilchards in early spring or autumn, crewed by skippers of the other laid-up boats; a couple more worked a few crab pots. Only two boats now worked through the winter months: the two quatters, the *Renee* (skipper Leonard Pengelly) and the *Ella* (skipper Billy Hocking). These two went trawling, and their catches were driven to Plymouth market each morning.

In its heyday, Looe had boasted a fleet of 60 luggers: by the early 1960s only five remained. They were the *Our Boys* (FY 221) built in 1904, skipper Bill Pengelly; the *Our Daddy* (FY 7), launched 1920, skipper A. J. Pengelly; the *Iris* (FY 357) launched 1921, skipper Frank Pengelly; the *Guide Me* (FY 233), built 1911, skipper Ned Pengelly; and the *Eileen* (FY 310), built 1920, skipper Ernie Toms. Two others had survived until 1960 but had been sold off due to the crews retiring and no young men coming into the fishing business to take their place. They were the *John Wesley* (FY 35) taken to Falmouth to be used as a house boat, later to be refitted and put back to sea for another 20 years when the mackerel fishery began, and the *Our Girls* (FY 54), sister ship to the *Our Boys* (FY 221). She went to Portsmouth to be converted to a motor yacht.

The three constructed in the post-First World War boom replaced (in order,) the *Sweet Home* (FY 221), *Olive* (FY 108), and the *Little Charlie* (FY52), three swift little sailing luggers of the 1890s. The *Little Charlie*, skipper 'Watt' Toms, had been a real flyer and used to win a lot of silverware at the local regattas; in fact, after one exciting dual someone composed a rhyme to commemorate it that went.

Old Peter Ferris
He lived up Beech Terrace
He built the Little Charlie
A boat of no size
That went to Mevagissey
And won the first prize.

That was back in the glory days, now long past. A new fishery, bringing all the ports around the coast of Cornwall back to life once more, was just over the horizon, but it would have nothing to do with drift nets or long lines. That ancient fishery was breathing its last in Cornwall.

Those 4 years that I worked with Moogie set me up well for the rest of my sea-going career, because nothing subsequently ever seemed as hard or as physically demanding as the time I spent working on the deck of the *Iris*. As fondly as I look back and write about those years, believe me, I would not want to do it again.

1

Early Days

I was 16 years old and brimming with youthful certainty and optimism. I had just won a three-month battle with my parents to gain their permission to go fishing. Not angling with a rod and line for a hobby or sport, but to join the lugger *Iris* as one of her crew.

As a child I had always played around on the water, out with Dad in his dinghy sailing around Talland Bay, towing rubber eels to catch pollack; expeditions to Looe or Polperro on fine summer afternoons, or rowing into all the little gullies and beaches gathering driftwood for a barbeque.

When I was thirteen I bought a boat of my own. She cost me the princely sum of one pound: a poor worn-out old thing that had lain for years upside down in the withy bed above Talland beach. She was in a dreadful condition and, in truth, her next role should really have been to star at a Guy Fawkes party, not go back in the water. The keel was badly hogged and, having been upside down for so long, the bottom of her sagged in sympathy. In an attempt to cure this, some friends and I draped her over an upended 45-gallon drum. This treatment got rid of the hogging temporarily and, hoping to make her stay that way, we nailed a stout piece of driftwood along the length of the keel. The bottom, both inside and out, was then liberally coated with a mixture of beach tar and cement dust, brushed on smoking hot from an oil drum over a bonfire. Tide line enamel (paint tins washed up on the beach, their contents scraped into one can and all stirred up together with paraffin) was used to paint up the rest of her, finishing up a delicate shade of mauve/brown. She was 14 feet long, clinker built and of an unknown vintage. When out in her we had to bail continually, and the bottom actually undulated when going over a wave. But she was all mine, and with a gang of friends we had endless fun in her. Sails would be rigged and we would skid off to lee, eventually having to row and bail for ages to get back to the beach again.

After a south-westerly gale, a big ground sea would be breaking on the sand bar at low tide and that was when we would go surfing, not with boards, but in the boat. Six hands were needed for this sport, one on each of the four oars, one forward to keep the bows down and bail with a bucket, and myself aft, one hand on the steering oar, the other bailing with another bucket. One thing you didn't need for this sport was any imagination. How we didn't drown, I don't know.

The boat was dragged out into waist-deep water and the person at the bow would hang on while the rest of us scrambled aboard and made ready at the oars; the bow man then hopped in and we would start pulling through the breakers. Trying to hold her steady while riding over a cresting sea, the bow pointing at the sky, the boat seeming to hover balanced on her transom. Sliding down into a trough the other side, the next wave might be breaking, burying us over our heads in white sun-filled foam. Many is the time we were tipped end for end or totally swamped, boat and crew being washed back onto the sand in one big heap. There, laughing at the mishap and wiping the salt water from our eyes and hair, we would gather up the oars and buckets, tip the water out of the boat and launch out again. Given half a chance though, we would make it to the back of the breakers, bucket out half the ocean, then hold station facing the beach, awaiting that big wave. Along it would come, cresting feet above the rest, and half a dozen good strokes on the oars would see us catch the wave as it broke. Oars were then boated and, with myself on the steering oar desperately trying to keep her straight, we would hurtle towards the beach in a mass of spume to be (if all went to plan) left high, but far from dry, on the sand as the wave retreated. Sometimes we would end up skidding down the face of a wave, totally out of control and at a most perilous angle. If we didn't get swamped we would be driven onto the rocks that flanked the sand bar, crashing to halt, then to drag her off and up the beach to inspect for damage. Occasionally a plank would be stove in, but a strip of hardboard generously buttered with tar and nailed over the damage soon had us away again.

Another memory that stands out is of going wrecking after a south-west gale. A friend of mine, Kevin Curtis, rang up one morning to say a yacht had been wrecked during the night under the cliffs at Polperro. As the storm baulks were down, no one in the village could get out and there were loads of stuff for the taking, just washing in the tide line. The gale of the previous night had died down, leaving just a big ground swell. Launching off Talland beach, the boat rode the seas like a little duck as the two of us pulled towards the cliffs where the wreck had struck.

Backing in on the swell, we loaded up with all sorts of treasures: a bottle of gas and a can of petrol, lengths of rope, bits of wood, a rug and loads of other things that we grabbed just because they were there. Being first on the scene, our greed was well up so we decided to row over to a cove where the tide seemed to be taking much of the wreckage. At the mouth of the cove we held station, bow to sea, to work out how we might make a landing. We made a landing alright - a great wave came cresting in and tipped the boat bow over stern, washing us all of a heap right up to the head of the cove. Luckily the boat jammed behind a rock and Kevin and I held on to it as the backwash of the sea scoured the cove clean of everything, including my bottom boards and paddles. The wreckers had become the wrecked; Neptune was obviously not happy with our avarice and had decided to chamfer a bit off our egos. It was Easter time, the air was cold, the sea was colder, and we stood there like a pair of drowned shags, with nothing but an empty boat and lucky to have that.

After dragging the poor old boat up clear of the tide line, Kevin and I then had to scramble up the cliff through the gorse and marram grass to reach the cliff path. There we went our separate ways home, soggy and crestfallen. A couple of days later, when the ground sea had gone down, I returned in another boat to tow mine back to Talland. The wrecked yacht was Norwegian, being sailed back single-handed from the Mediterranean; the skipper's body was washed up some days later and I was told that his watch was still working.

Playing around in boats as a schoolboy led to more adventures, in the form of night trips out pilchard drifting from Polperro on Jack Joliffe's little lugger, the *One Accord* (FY185). This was great fun, working the dip net, pumping out, and helping to land the catch at the end of the night. Mind you, as I soon found out, this was a very soft introduction to the real thing, going out when the fancy took you, and then only if the weather was fine. Even then I used to get seasick occasionally, and my bedroom would be all a-sway when back home the next morning.

The *One Accord* was about 38 feet long and had originally been an open-decked St Ives gig. Jack had bought her when he was demobbed from the navy after the war, refitting her with decks, bulwarks and new engines plus a little one-man wheelhouse. The four-man crew had sailed together for many years: Tom Joliffe, a tall wry sort of fellow who always did the steering; Arkie Pucky drove the engines; Edmund Curtis was chief net mender, while Jacko the skipper kept an overall eye on things and smoked his pipe.

Because the *One Accord* was the only remaining pilchard drifter working from Polperro, she had to land her catches in Looe and then steam back to her home port, a distance of about 3 miles. On more than one occasion, when the sea was glassy calm, Jack would drop me off in Talland Bay to save me the walk home from Polperro. They would be those rare occasions when he actually took charge of his own boat. Nudging her gently into a gully on the west side of the bay under what was known as 'Dickey Bunt's' house, Arkie would be up in the bows looking down into the water: "Rock here, just to port of us, Jack!" he would shout. "Another one ahead of us, and it's not very deep." The skipper would be calmly drawing on his pipe and taking very little notice of Arkie's rock warnings. Giving a touch here and there on the wheel and a nudge on the engine, he would have her along side in the gully. I would await his order before leaping onto the rocks, then turn around to wave goodbye and thank him as they went astern back out into the bay. Scrambling up the cliff to join the path, I was soon home in bed. The first time Jack put me ashore in that gully, Tommy Toms who was out in his crabber, the *Sheila*, hauling pots, looked up from his labours and, for a moment, was convinced that Tom had nodded off at the wheel and had put the *One Accord* ashore.

Mind you, Jacko wasn't averse to scraping the odd rock. The word in Polperro was that if you wanted to know where the rocks were up and down the shore, ask Jack: he had been up on every one of them.

On another occasion, when battling back from Looe to Polperro in heavy rain and a rising south-west gale, I was sent down into the cabin for safety.

Sitting below in such conditions it wasn't long before I was sick all over the cabin sole. For a while I pondered how I was going to explain the mess when we got to the moorings, but I had no need to worry. The old *One Accord* worked a fair bit in poor weather, so it wasn't long before the bilge water was lapping over the cabin sole, washing away all the evidence of my mishap. But seasickness aside, what a wonderful sensation it was to go from all the bang crash wallop and flying spray of a rising gale to escape into the tranquillity and safety of Polperro harbour. Soon we were riding snug on the mooring chains, but it was quite a while before we could scull ashore in the punt and go home. Arkie reckoned we had at least half the Channel to pump out of her.

Looking back now, I can't really say why I decided to go fishing for a living. Maybe it was the freedom and independence that it seemed to offer, or just my youthful need for a tough challenge. If it was the latter, then fishing certainly had all the right ingredients. Leaving school at fifteen, I had started work in an antique shop with a view to learning the trade, but shop life was not for me. I craved fresh air and sunshine and the company of less devious, more straightforward people.

As a hobby I had started to make a collection of old photographs of Looe, and during my lunch hour I used to wander around the quayside talking to the fishermen, trying to get boats and people in these photos identified. That was when I first met Frank Pengelly, the skipper of the lugger *Iris*. Climbing the vertical iron ladder up to his net loft above the old fish market, I would find him there overhauling the drift nets ready for the coming season. Watching Frank at work with the net needle, mending rents and tears in the nets, fascinated me, and it wasn't long before I was having a go, learning to mend 'bars' and 'three-ers'.

In conversation one day, we were talking about the antique trade. I mentioned that I was getting fed up with it, especially being stuck indoors. Having played around in boats most of my life, and having done those few trips out on the *One Accord*, the idea was growing in me that I might like going to sea on a full-time basis. When I told Frank this, much to my amazement he offered me a berth on the *Iris* and from that moment there was no going back.

It was then that a battle royal began with Mum and Dad. I couldn't blame them for being somewhat hostile to the idea of this career change. I was in a job with regular wages and very good prospects, and I wanted to throw it all in to go fishing. Dad gave me the waggly finger, trying to impress upon me the fact that there was no future prospect in fishing. It was a dying trade, the wages were dreadfully uncertain and, what's more, he reckoned that I was never strong enough, or tough enough, to stick the long hours and harsh conditions worked in at sea. He was right on all points of course, but still I persisted, until eventually they caved in.

Permission was granted, but with the final rejoinder that I would be back in less than six months begging for my old job back. I must admit they were very nearly right on several occasions. Working out my last week at the antique shop seemed more like a month, but eventually Friday afternoon arrived, I picked up my last wage packet (£3.10) and cycled home with that wonderful end of term feeling.

Saturday morning saw me biking down to Polperro to buy oilskins and sea boots at Owen Goodland's hardware shop. Owen himself wasn't there, but he had opened his shop and a note on the door informed customers that he had gone out to his garden for the day and if anyone wanted anything, please help yourself, leave a note by the till of what you have had and come back and pay another day. This was typical of Owen; if there was anything more interesting to do than stay in his shop on a fine day, like gardening, fishing or greeting visitors in the street, he did it. His system seemed to work, even if he didn't. Pushing the shop door open, the spring bell jangled and I entered an establishment that seemed to sell just about everything. Clothes, artists' materials, bedding, lamp glasses and lino, carpets and crockery, 78rpm records, shoes, even garden produce, in fact anything you could think of, much of it so out of date or style that there was surely very little hope of ever finding customers for it. At the back of the shop I positioned the stepladder and helped myself to an oilskin jumper off of the top shelf. Next, by ferreting around in boxes and cupboards I found the other items that I needed: a sou'wester, sea boots and an oilskin apron. Leaving my name and a list for Owen, I strapped everything on the carrier of my bike and cycled back home to Talland Bay, feeling on top of the world. It was March 1964 and my new way of life was about to begin.

2

The *Iris* and her Crew

Sunday is the start of the fisherman's week, and four o'clock in the afternoon was sailing time on that particular Sunday. I made sure that I was aboard in good time. It was the long lining or 'boulter' season and Frank was working the Lizard ground.

To be honest, I don't remember a great deal about that very first trip other than, mercifully, it was flat calm. The lines were shot and hauled, and then I was put in the wheelhouse and given a landmark to steer for while the rest of the crew were on deck clearing the lines back into the baskets. Steering the *Iris* meant standing up as there was no wheelhouse seat, and having been awake for many more hours than I was used to, I kept nodding off, only to wake with a start as my knees buckled and my head hit the wheelhouse window.

The catch was landed at Mevagissey as we had missed the tide for Looe. Tying up at the outer quay, the fish were pulled up, maund basket at a time, by a little crane that had been made out of an old line jinny. There it was weighed, boxed and stacked up on the fish merchant's truck, the boat was then scrubbed up from stem to stern before we all went ashore for fish and chips while awaiting the next tide up to Looe.

The catch must have made very good money, because the weather turned poor and we didn't get to sea for the rest of the week, but on Saturday, when the skipper shared the money out, I received £19 and being a learner, I was on half share. This was more money than I had ever had in one lump sum before. I was elated, but Dad was a bit miffed when I told him, as he only earned £18 for a full week as a skilled man.

In the fishing industry there has never been any such thing as a regular wage. The money grossed by the boat every week is shared out after the immediate expenses such as diesel have been deducted. One share for each member of the crew, one for the boat and one for the gear; big grossing big wages, no grossing no wages. When times were good, money had to be put by to see you through the lean times that were bound to come, and this meant a very frugal lifestyle had to be lead. At that time, hardly anyone could drive or owned a car, very few had TVs or telephones and holidays were a very rare treat. It was considered to have been a good year if all the bills were paid and there was a bit of money to spare for Christmas. Some skippers owned their own homes, but most fishing families rented a cottage or a council house where, if they had a spare room, the wife did bed and breakfast in the summer time. The only luxury enjoyed by the men was a pint of beer and a smoke, while the women ran the home and juggled the money.

The skipper of the *Iris*, Frank 'Moogie' Pengelly, was, at 43, the youngest and certainly the toughest skipper in the port. Of medium height and build, he was an amiable enough chap ashore, but at sea, stand back! And if, for some reason, he lowered his head and glared at you over the top of his glasses, you knew you were doomed.

The rest of the crew at the time included Bruce 'Tiddler' Sammels, 55 years old and, apart from one summer away crewing on a yacht, he had been at sea on the luggers all his life. A jovial, easy-going fellow, he could neither read nor write, loved his beer and a pipe of black twist tobacco. It was said that he was the only fisherman in Looe fat enough to fill his oilskin jumper out, wrinkle free.

Next was Clarence Libby, a quietly spoken, gentlemanly type in his early 60s, but to me he looked nearer 80. He was bald, stooped, pale and frail-looking and speed-wise for working he never seemed to get out of first gear, but that gear was a very powerful one and conditions on deck had to be just about life threatening before he would give up and come down into the cabin. Clarence had spent much of his early working life as a sailor on square-riggers, schooners and big yachts which maybe accounted for his premature ageing.

Then came Jack Harris, a slight figure in his mid-twenties. He had served for a number of years in the Royal Navy. A rogue with a great sense of humour, who seemed to live by one very simple creed, money was for spending, beer was for drinking and never, ever overlook an opportunity to get your leg over.

Then there was Harry 'Slender' Stevens, ginger haired and built like a Japanese racing snake. Harry was a baker by trade, but having suffered from TB in his early 40s, the doctors had advised him to get a light outdoor job. Now in his late 50s he had been on the *Iris* for some 10 years acting as permanent 'boy' and ship's character.

Last of all myself, Paul Greenwood, aged 16, tall and skinny, as green as grass, with not an inkling of an idea of what I was in for.

Our good ship, the *Iris* (FY 357) was 44 feet long with a beam of 14 feet and a draught of 6 feet. She had been built in 1921 by the Looe shipwright, 'Young' Dick Pearce (not to be confused with 'Old' Dick Pearce, his father), upon the orders of Frank's father and grandfather to replace their little sailing lugger, the *Olive*. For a lugger she was a great lump of a boat, and carved on each bow and on the transom were the letters I.R.I.S. as she had been named after Frank's four aunts, Ida, Rosie, Irene and Suzie. Originally she had been an auxiliary, but the only sail she now carried was a gaff mizzen, used when working up to the nets and lines, or sheeted away to help on a run home with a fair wind.

She boasted three engines, all Lister diesels: a 45 HP situated in the aft cabin, and a 30 and a 21 HP down in the forepeak. The aft engine had an electric starter, while the two down forward had to be coaxed into life manually with handles and much sweating. All three engines were used when making a passage, but only the aft one was used when working to the gear. This had a throttle control inside the wheelhouse and a gear leaver out on deck for convenience when fishing. All three propellers emerged from the port quarter keeping the starboard side clear for working the nets and lines. She would come around to starboard in her own length, but needed the whole of Looe Bay to come around to port, but as it was considered unlucky to turn against the sun, this didn't matter. When all three engines were running, especially when making all speed to save tide into the harbour and the governors were lashed back, the deck seemed to undulate with the strain, and a turn and a half of port wheel was needed to keep her going in a straight line.

In the wheelhouse (besides the wheel working the chain steering) was a compass, a clock and an echo sounder. Despite having a wheel, tiller orders were still used when giving directions. Hard to port meant hard to starboard on the wheel; the boat went to starboard but the tiller, now only a stump at the rudder head, went to port. It could be very confusing.

The fishing industry in Cornwall at that time was at a very low ebb. Skippers had to maintain their boats and gear on a shoestring budget, and it was all make do and mend. There was nothing to spare to fund any improvements or modernisation and really, apart from having engines as the motive power instead of sails, the job and way of life had much more in common with the nineteenth century than the twentieth.

A lugger's 'safety equipment' consisted of a copper foghorn, usually kept in a cabin locker and rummaged out when needed, dripping verdigris and leaving a foul taste in the mouth of who ever had to blow it. A 'flare-up' consisted of a quart copper mug filled with paraffin which had a tight fitting lid that extended out to the size of a tea plate. On top of the lid was a handle, like the hilt of a sword, and when fitted on the mug a stout piece of wire 6 or 8 inches long wrapped with rag extended down into the paraffin from the inside of the lid. When needed, the lid was taken off and the projecting rag was set alight. I suppose it could have been used to attract the attention of other boats if we were in trouble, but it's main function was to direct steamers away from the nets at night. This was achieved by waving it in a big slow circle in the direction you wanted them to go. In daylight, an oilskin was used in the same way. Ship to shore radios in those days were very expensive and were so big they would have taken up all the room in the wheel-house, which is why there was no radio communication.

First aid consisted of a bottle of whisky (usually kept wedged under the skipper's bunk) and clean engine room rags. A bad cut would have a drop of whisky poured on it before it was bound up. Mind you, some of the old boys would insist on having the tot poured down their neck rather than over any cut. In winter, if any one was 'nipped' by the cold, a tot would be dished out to them as they tried to warm up again, huddled over the cabin fire.

Safety was mainly achieved through years of experience and a high standard of seamanship. If you were in trouble, it was up to you to get out of it. Springing a leak in bad weather was one of the worst things that could happen. It was a rare occurrence, but over the years not a few boats have made it back to the safety of the harbour with one man swinging steadily on the pump, the rest of the crew manning a bucket chain.

I heard a story of one lugger that was making so much water they just could not keep her free so, to try and lessen the inrush, one of the crew sat on the leak and then his backside was caulked around with rags. This staunched things enough for the pump and buckets to deal with it. Leaks were usually caused by a plank end or butt springing, caused by poor fastenings. On the next low tide, one of the local shipwrights would refasten, recaulk and putty the offending area, making her seaworthy once more.

At least with engines you could pretty much rely on getting back to your home port. Adverse conditions just entailed hours of fighting big cresting seas, hoping that the motors would keep going and the fuel last out, but hearth and home were beckoning. In the sailing days, when caught out in a bad blow, the boats would sometimes have to ride to their gear for days, unable to haul it. When the weather abated, the gear was hauled and a course was set for the nearest port, perhaps hailing a merchantman to get a position. Arriving at harbours anywhere from the Isle of Wight to the Scillies, news of their safe arrival would be telegraphed home, the fish sold and some food bought, before making a passage back to their home port.

The *Twilight* (FY 334) of Looe rode out such a gale, eventually making it home to Looe first go, five days after she left port. While anchoring in the bay to await tide into the harbour, a boy rowed out to meet her. Having been away for so long, the navy had been alerted to keep a look out for them, but with no reported sightings, people were beginning to think the worst. After the boy blurted out "What happened to you, where did you get to, and is every one all right?" the skipper looked at him, saying, "Never mind all that, we have been living on boiled fish for days, I thought you would have brought us out a bag of buns or something."

In another incident, the *Kathleen* (FY 297) turned up at the Isle of Wight having weathered a snorter of a westerly gale, and the *Dove*, a misfit of a boat, known affectionately as the 'Sting Bum', took 30 hours to gain the shelter of Torbay, having rode to her nets for two days. That same boat was once blown away in a gale when fishing deep off the Lizard. Three days later she battled in to Falmouth, everyone and everything awash. They didn't even have a dry match to light the cabin fire with and as nobody had a penny on them, they hawked their fish around the windjammers anchored in the Carrick Roads, before tying up at Custom House Quay for some much needed rest and recuperation. The skipper of the *Dove* was Harold 'Nibbs' Butters, and one of her crew that told me the yarn was Edwin 'Snaker' Dann. I knew them both as old men; as characters they were worth their weight in gold, and you could safely say for 'rest and recuperation' read beer. Aboard the *Dove* on that trip was a boy out for the first time. As soon as they hit dry land he caught the train home to Looe and never went to sea again. With an introduction to fishing like that who can blame him.

None of the above trips should have lasted any longer than twelve hours if they were netting or, if lining, 24 to 30 hours. Back in their home port with the rain lashing and the wind howling down the chimney pots, the knowledge that one of the fleet was out there riding a gale must have been worrying in the extreme.

In the sailing days, being caught in a flat calm could be as trying as a gale of wind. The crew of the Mevagissey lugger *Erin* laboured at the sweeps for 20 hours to gain their home port from 40 miles out on the lining grounds. Her five-man crew did 20 minutes on each of the four sweeps, giving each man a spell on the tiller every hour and twenty minutes. By the same token, a Polperro gaffer, the *Mary*, had a man lying in the cabin collapsed with exhaustion by the time she poked her stem into harbour. When engines first became available the fishermen thought they were in heaven, as they made their lives so much easier.

3
Toughening Up

The Channel lining season continued until the pilchard shoals came on to the coast in more viable numbers around mid April. We would know when they arrived because to go long lining you need pilchards for bait and, to this end, a short fleet of nets was carried. Sometimes the nets would have to be shot and hauled twice to catch the 40 stone that was needed to bait up a long line, numbering six to seven thousand hooks stretched out on 7 or more miles of back rope. If you were still short it might be possible to buy a few stone from one of the other boats. But if all failed, it was back to harbour and try again the next night. "With out any bait, you're bate" was the old saying.

On this particular night we went to work hauling the nets for line bait and ended up with about 150 stone of pilchards. Moogie decided that was good enough, it was time to start the summer season. This was excellent news, for instead of ploughing out into the Channel for 24 hours' hard graft, we were bound back to harbour to land our catch. Arriving in Looe just as dawn was breaking, the skipper roused out Gilbert Hocking, the fish canner's agent, to tell him that we had a catch of fish for them and that we were going to haul the main fleet of nets aboard to start the summer season.

The *Iris* was then moored up opposite her net loft above the old fish market. Tiddler and Clarence went up and lowered down bundles of cork buoys and buffs ready to tie on the nets. The buoys were made up of 20 or so cork discs threaded on to a rope, each disc a good inch thick and about the size of a CD. The buffs were a mixture of old and new; the new were like big balloons made from heavy orange plastic, the old were made of canvas, tarred on the inside and painted white on the outside. Looking like monster footballs, the necks of them were fastened around a 4-inch wooden disc in which was set a tapered bung. They were inflated with a big copper pump. Next, the end from the top of a heap of nets, all 'scunned' (tied) together ready to go, was passed down. The boat was slewed off the quay a few feet and we were ready to start. The new end was scunned on with 'tatchins' (short pieces of twine) to the bait fleet and these nets were first hauled through the water to wet them. Two men in the starboard waterways hauled aboard and stowed them in the net room, tying on buoys and buffs as they went. I was put in the port waterways with a deck bucket to throw more water on the skirt of the net to make sure it was good and sodden, and so sink away when shot.

When the job was complete, the lorry arrived with the fish boxes and all hands set to boxing up and landing the pilchards. All hands that is, except me. "Better give her a dig out," said Moogie. So I went back to the pump, a big lead barrel affair with a seesaw handle set back against the aft net room bulkhead on the port side. To work the pump it first had to be primed with a bucket of water. You then jigged on the handle until it 'caught'. Then it was swing away steadily (discharging about a gallon per stroke) until it sucked air, indicating it was 'all out'. There I was, swinging the pump until my back was breaking and my arms were dropping off. I shouted for somebody to give me a 'spell' but was promptly told that, as I had put the water in her, I could get it out. I was learning.

After the fish were landed, and the baskets of line were put ashore, all hands set to with brooms and buckets to scrub the boat down. We were all ready to start the summer pilchard season. It was now lunchtime, and we had been working solidly since six o'clock the previous evening. What a relief it was to get our boots and oilskins off and head homewards.

But our relief was to be short lived. "Five o'clock tonight, boys," said the skipper as we traipsed off, looking forward to a wash, a meal and a few hours kip. We were all aboard again at the set hour and trooped down to the cabin to put our sea boots on, then back up on deck to make the boat ready for sea. Moogie checked over and started the aft engine, while the rest of us unshipped and stowed the leg, likewise the net room and fish box hatches. Harry, the cook, lit the coal stove and put the kettle on. Ropes and fenders were handed aboard, the boat was swung out into the tide and away we went. The good lugger *Iris* began yet another season in her long career.

For the first 2 years that I went to sea, if the weather was a bit unkind, I could spew for England and this was such a night. There was a fresh south-west wind raising a lumpy sea, with sea bobs breaking here and there. The chimney of the cabin fire was sending out a good whiff, as were the engines, while a steady honk of stale fish and bilge was permeating up from below. I was feeling 'cruddy' well and truly, and it wasn't long before I was on my knees paying homage to Neptune over the lee rail. Sea-sickness knocks the stuffing right out of you. After the first bout your temperature drops back to normal and for a while you feel quite recovered. If there's work to be done, you can drag yourself about the deck to do it, you might even perk up a bit and kid yourself that it's all over, and for the rest of the night you'll be fine. Many months later, when I did start to conquer the dreaded mal de mer, that is what would happen, but not at this stage of the game. Pretty soon that old qualmy feeling would return, then it only needed a good lungful of coal or diesel smoke to send me back on my knees clutching the lee rail, eyes streaming and sweltering red hot inside my oilskins, retching fit to turn inside out.

I was wiping my chin with my hat and trying to recover from just such a bout when Jack Harris, ever the joker, suggested that, if I should feel something tough and hairy in my throat when vomiting, I should swallow back quickly. "Why?" I croaked feebly. "Because it's probably your asshole!" he replied. "And if you ever fancy eating again, you're going to need it." The boat gave a mighty lurch and I clung to the rail with the foam in the waterways filling my boots. Jack was sitting on the companionway hatch, laughing until the tears rolled down his cheeks.

The gear was shot that evening without any assistance from me - maybe I tottered around to help scrub down, I can't remember. By now the engines were silenced, the mizzen was set, and we were riding to the nets with a freshening wind. A drifter riding to her gear in a fresh breeze develops a very curious motion, a mile and a half of nets act like a big piece of elastic. The wind and sea drive the boat back and back, stretching out the elastic, until the strain overcomes the sea and she shoots forward with a plunging rocking motion. Oh, what misery.

Harry shouted "Tea up," so all hands went below for supper and maybe an hour in their bunks, but not me. I remember clearly sitting behind the wheelhouse on the cabin hatch trying to sip a mug of tea and nibble on a biscuit. Glancing down the cabin seeing the rest of the crew smoking and yarning, I was convinced that I would never be able to sit down there while at sea.

We rode to the nets for a couple of hours or so, then the aft engine was fired up, all hands pulled on their oilskins and hauling commenced. I was supposed to be helping Tiddler back on the head ropes, but I was completely knackered. I could hardly help myself let alone help Tiddler, and the night seemed to go on for ever. Eventually the pole-end net was hauled over the roller and Moogie came aft to the wheelhouse and squared her away for home.

Oh, the relief when we got into the harbour, and better still when I got home and crawled into my bed. I can still recall that wonderful feeling of peace, safety and warmth after a night of undiluted misery. I suffered many more nights like that when the weather was bad, but gradually the seasickness became less severe and less frequent. Eventually it faded away, until I too could go down the cabin and have my supper on a rolling evening, but the whole procedure took about 2 years. But I knew I had really conquered the 'crud'.

The cabin itself had five bunks, three across the transom and one out each side forward of them. In front of the side bunks were seat lockers in which coal for the fire was kept. The fire was a miniature black lead range with an oven, where pasties were warmed and fish was baked. It was bolted down to the cabin sole over the gearbox coupling of the aft engine which had its own little engine room forward of the cabin but there was no bulkhead in between. In here, to starboard, was a 50-gallon diesel tank with a small leak; the drips were caught in an old cake tin. To port, in their box, were the batteries for the lights, plus the engine oil tank and half a dozen hurricane lamps used on the danns. Under the fore end of the engine was the pump well where the bilge water drained. This was a mixture of oil and diesel leaking from the engines, along with decaying fish and muck draining out of the nets. At sea with the hatch open, the bilge pumped out, the fire alight and the engine running, it was pretty hot down there but the smell didn't seem too bad. It was when working from other ports and the cabin became our home that we had the full benefit of its charms. The covering board in the area of the bunk that I was given leaked so much that the old flock bedtide (mattress) would make a fizzing noise when you hit it. I turfed that out and lined the whole bunk with polythene and then invested in a new bedtide.

When we were all turned in, the weather boards shipped up and the hatch was shut tight, the only ventilation available was the nor'wester. This was a small hatch in the forward bulkhead that slid open to reveal the net room. For five or six hours the aromas would amalgamate and concentrate (like a good stew): bilge water, coal and tobacco smoke, diesel and paraffin, the hot oil smell of the engine, stale sea boot socks plus the anal trumpeting of the sleeping crew.

The first man up always stirred up the fire and put the kettle on for tea, then slid back the cabin hatch to air things out a bit. It's no exaggeration to say that you could have cut the fug in the cabin into chunks and thrown them up on deck. Description does not do the stench of that cabin justice; it's something you just had to experience.

Harry Stevens went into the fishing late in life, which is probably why he never really had the physical strength or quickness of hand needed to work on the nets. But he was as tough as old boots, which is more than could have been said about me at the time. So until I got some sea legs and toughened up a bit, Harry had to go 'out the rail' and toil the best he could, while I did his job, and what a job that was! If there was a decent bit of fish coming aboard you didn't have time to draw breath.

Tiddler hauled and stowed the head ropes; his position was at the aft end of the starboard waterways, just in front of the wheelhouse. My place was to stand behind him, and as he came to a buoy rope he would toss a bight of it over his head. I had to haul the cork buoy aboard and stow it neatly down the net room out the starboard wing, with the buffs going to port, but that was only part of it. The man 'out the rail' would shout, "Go ahead," and I would tug on the lever to put the engine in gear to nudge the boat along the nets. The stower would shout, "Net room," and I had to jump down and pick up a pilchard that had been flipped onto the nets, scrambling up from there just in time to stow the next buoy and work the dip net. This was like a giant prawn net, used to dip up pilchards that had dropped from the nets as they were being hauled. Gulls in their hundreds would be trying to rob the nets, swooping and screaming, wings flapping in your face, feet tap-tapping on your hat as one held station awaiting his moment to dive shrieking into the melee. Scaring them off was also part of the brief, done by shouting and hollering at the top of your voice while whirling a buoy above your head. An awful lot of effort for never more than two minutes peace.

The pump had to be swung regularly as gallons of water were draining out from the nets, then it's time to nip down into the cabin to bank up the fire, appearing back on deck in time to adjust the mizzen and wheel to keep the boat at the right angle to the nets. On and on it went, relentlessly, until the last net was hauled aboard, six, eight or even ten hours non-stop; even the boy's job was tough.

That was my lot for a couple of months, then one evening Moogie told me I was going 'out the rail' and Harry was having his job back. He was more than welcome to it. This was definitely a step towards becoming a fully fledged member of the crew and earning 'full share'.

The men crewing on the drifters were exceptionally strong, and possessed incredible endurance, because everything was achieved by 'Armstrong's patent'. As a learner, it took a long time to gain the strength needed for the job, and much suffering after that to find the necessary endurance. Hauling and dragging non-stop for hour after hour took some getting used to. At times I would feel so hungry I felt that I might collapse. Eventually that sensation would pass off, leaving the stomach feeling red hot. When that stage had been reached I knew I could go on for many more hours with no further trouble; a few boiled sweets tucked in the fold of my hat and snatched into my mouth when chance arose helped a fair bit.

As for thirst, well 'spitting feathers' would not have been an exaggeration. A gallon can of water was kept behind the wheelhouse and passed around when on a long haul, but that was no more than a couple of mouthfuls in perhaps eight or ten hours. When conditions demanded we sometimes worked for 30 or 40 hours straight, kept going with the odd mug of tea and bite to eat when the job in hand allowed.

By now, I was starting to gain some strength. I could swing the pump without my back breaking, shoot my share of nets without my arms turning to jelly, lift 5-stone boxes of fish about, and lay-to on the engine starting handles. Mind you, I was still battling with seasickness. Personally, I thought I was coming on in leaps and bounds, so it came as a great shock when I first went 'out the rail' to haul the nets aboard, helped by the second hand when needed. I got into position, caught hold of the net, braced myself and hauled, and I hauled again and nothing happened. I just couldn't move it. The skipper, as second hand on the skirt, stood behind me and he did the hauling with my arms moving in time, just like a puppet.

The other task was shaking the pilchards out. The net is hauled aboard until the stower shouts stop. He is the last one on the line, so when he has fish to shake out, everyone has. The fish were then shaken, flipped and twisted out of the meshes, preferably without tearing their heads off or ripping the net, and when the stower cleans out his bit of net, up it comes again. Well, I just didn't have the knack and my hands weren't tough enough. When trying to flip fish out with finger and thumb as shown, I either tore the mesh or the twine cut my finger joints open. Trying to twist them out, the heads came off, or the razor-sharp bones just behind the gills known as collar studs cut my hands open.

All the while Moogie was behind me saying, "Rattle your dusters, my sonny, a quick hand for a scabby arse," or else, "Up she comes, John Edward is looking at you". John Edward Hoskin had been the skipper of the lugger *John Wesley* (FY35) and both he and his crew had become a legend on the Cornish coast for the amount of fish they caught and the atrocious weather conditions they would put to sea in.

By the time the pole end buoy came over the roller, my back was breaking, my arms felt as if they were pulled out of their sockets and my hands were cut to raw liver. But I was put there the next night and the night after that, and there I stayed. I suppose there was no other way. Gradually I hardened up to the job, until one night I realised I could do it. "Up!" Clarence, the stower, would shout and when I laid back on the net, up it came, with very little help from the second hand. "Stop!" would come the order, and I could flip and twist the pilchards out of the mesh without an eighth of the damage done to my hands or the fish, and what was more, I was now on a full share of wages.

The money was always shared out on Saturday. All the crew would be down aboard by nine o'clock to get on with any jobs that needed doing.

Someone would push the net cart up to the coal yard on Station Road to get fuel for the fire. Harry scrubbed out the cabin, black-leaded the stove and shopped for stores, the engines were greased up and checked over. Diesel was carried out from the fuel store in five-gallon drums to be tipped into the tanks through a big copper funnel. There were always nets of different mesh sizes to haul in or out of the boat as the season changed. Around midday the skipper would call us up in order of seniority and pay out the share money at the wheelhouse door, having spent half an hour or so working it out on the back of an envelope with a stub of pencil. Then, when all the jobs were done, and the *Iris* was ready for the coming week. A time was set for the Sunday evening sailing, and the rest of the weekend was your own.

4
Teatime

The summer holiday season was now approaching and Clarence, our stower, had left us to work his ferry boat. He was getting on in years and only sailed with us in the spring and autumn to shorten up what would have been a very long winter for him. Clarence had a wonderful collection of sea jumpers from all the different vessels he had sailed on as a young man. Each one had the ship's name embroidered across the chest, and every jumper could bring forth a whole raft of stories.

Tales of when he was an AB on a barque transporting mature trees in tubs to a villa development on a Greek island, the trees so tall they couldn't set the courses (lower sails). Another ship on which he crewed, the mate had a pet monkey which he would send down below to rouse the next watch; the animal would bite and scratch the men out of their bunks, getting them up on deck in record time.

If anyone was feeling poorly, be it a hangover, a cold, 'flu, constipation or the opposite, Clarence had the one sovereign remedy. Looking at the sufferer a bit sideways, eyes twinkling and with the start of a smile on his face, he would say, "What you need, my sonny, is a good drag through with a holly bush."

The thing that always intrigued me about Clarence was his grub tin. It was a work of art. Everyone else had doorstop sandwiches or a pasty, slabs of cake and a packet of biscuits or, in Tiddler's case, yards of boiled tripe and crackers plus plenty of stomach powders. Not so Clarence. His wife packed him immaculate little sandwiches with the crusts cut off, delicate slices of fruit cake and neat wedges of jam sponge, all wrapped in white linen serviettes. He took his tea from a bone china cup and saucer decorated with gold edging and red roses, complete with a silver apostle spoon. When placed alongside our chipped tea-stained pint mugs to be filled, Harry had to squint hard through his glasses and take great care not to wash Clarence's cup into the bilge when tipping the tea from the gallon teapot.

With this in mind, you might easily imagine his wife to be a small, delicate, quiet little person. Not so. May was a big raw-boned farmer's wife type of woman, an ex-rowing champion with probably one of the loudest voices in the town. When we were working on East Looe quay, May would shout to tell her beloved his dinner was ready and we and the rest of the town could hear her loud and clear, and that was from their house which was up behind St. Nicholas' church at West Looe. A damned good shout away.

There was an old sailor man's riddle that Clarence used to put to anybody he thought may not have heard it. Being the boy aboard, I was open to all the old jokes and wheezes, but this was maybe one of the better ones:

The wind was west
And West steered we.
If the sails did draw
How could that be?

Well, I had one hand pointing to represent the wind, the other for the boat, and couldn't come up with an explanation that made any sense and had to give up. The answer was that West was the name of the skipper.

Clarence was a natural gentleman, quietly spoken and always polite. The man who took his berth for the summer was Jack Moore, ex-middleweight boxing champion of the navy. Jack was in his mid-50s and as strong as an ox. His hands were like sledge hammers and his nose was battered all over his face. He played an accordion, and on fine evenings he would bring it to sea, giving us a few tunes while we were riding to the gear. He was of an easy going nature and loved his pint, as did Tiddler, and quite often they would have a few before coming to sea. Then look out. The pair of them could agree on nothing and would be back aft shouting and arguing over the daftest things, until Moogie told them to shut up. Many years later, when Jack was in his mid-70s, he was making his way home, having spent the evening babysitting for one of his sons, when two of the local yobs tried to mug him. One ended up unconscious, having first been propelled by a swift left hook over a privet hedge, and the other was dangled by the scruff of the neck until Jack got him into the light to identify him. The shocked youth yelped for mercy and forgiveness until eventually Jack let him go. I rather imagine granddads were off the mugging list after that incident.

Fishing was good that spring. We worked long hard hours and made some very good wages. The biggest catch of the season went to the *Our Daddy*. She netted 1,500 stone of pilchards in one night - that's ten tons!

The summer evenings were fine and warm and the luggers from Looe and Mevagissey, not forgetting Polperro's *One Accord* were out searching for the pilchard shoals, trying to 'raise a scry' as it was called. If fish were scarce, the boats might end up close together on whatever sign there was; in the light evening air you could hear their crews talking, and the clatter of the pawl on the rail roller as they hauled their nets. On other occasions the shoals could be found anywhere, and the boats would hardly be in sight of one other. When the shoals were located, the boat was steamed up wind of them, then turned around and downwind we would go, with the shooting roller rattling as the nets went over the side, arm over arm at a spanking pace.

Tiddler would be at the wheel keeping the wind fine on the port quarter and knocking the engine in and out of gear to maintain a steady speed. Moogie always shot the head ropes and threw the first or pole end buoy away to the cry of "God speed the plough", tossing the buoy and buff ropes back over his head for Harry to catch and pull out of the net room to hurl them overboard with a splash. The first or pole end net was shot away, then came the dann with its hurricane lamp to mark the end of the fleet for other shipping. The skirt or foot of the nets was the hardest part to shoot, being wet heavy cotton net some eight fathoms deep and a third longer than the head-ropes, so we took turns, shooting four or five nets each, unless of course someone was feeling really perky and they stood there and shot the lot. We all did that at times, why I can't say, it was just how the mood took you.

Towards the end of the last net, the boat would be just creeping along, and as the final buoy went over the side, the wheel was put down hard to starboard, bringing her head to wind. The mizzen was hoisted, and the swing rope (the rope that attached the boat to the nets) was paid out and made fast on the bow kevel. "Stop engine," was the next order, and there we lay peacefully drifting with the wind and tide for the next two or three hours. Before we had our supper, buckets and brooms came into action to scrub down the bulwarks, deck and net-room. The big rail roller and shaking out spars were shipped up, ready for the haul while Jack Harris, as engine driver, greased up the shaft bearings or plummer-blocks as they were called.

Helping Jack to lift up the net room boards (they were 2 inches thick and as heavy as lead) to get at the plummer-blocks, I once remarked on their stoutness and was told that in 1940 many of the Cornish boats had been ordered to assemble at Plymouth's Millbay docks to be made ready to go to Dunkerque. That was when the heavy boards were fitted. But by the time the fleet was ready it was all over and they were stood down. Everyone breathed a sigh of relief and went home again.

When things were all shipshape on deck, it would then be time for supper and a mug of tea. Harry's tea was unique, and very much an acquired taste; on occasions the making of it could be quite a pantomime. Our cook loved a drop of scrumpy and would very often indulge himself before coming to sea. This would make him rather drowsy or, if rubbed the wrong way, very argumentative. His first task on board was to light the fire and put the kettle on to boil. Into the firebox of the range would go paper, sticks and coal, then a good slop of diesel from the engine leak off bottle. A match was applied and away it would go. The kettle was then filled and placed on the range to boil. All was in order, so now was the time to have a little nap. But sometimes he napped for just that bit too long, and when he awoke the fire would be out; everything hot but the fire out. Now it's panic, the tea won't be ready on time and as poor old Harry used to have enough bollockings from the skipper as it was, any extras were to be avoided if at all possible. Into the firebox would go more paper, sticks and coal, plus another really generous slop of diesel. By the time he had fumbled about and put a match to it the range was a mass of diesel fumes, there would be a loud WHUMP sort of noise accompanied by much clattering and swearing. All hands would rush aft to the companionway and, peering down, the cabin would be full of smoke and soot. The range had exploded, blowing off its door and rounders, plus Harry's hat and glasses.

We all knew what had happened - we had seen it all before, as had the skipper who ducked out of the wheelhouse to see if Harry had managed to blow the stern end of the boat right off this time. "Harry, you bloody old fool, you've done it yet again!" Moogie bellowed down into the smoke. Our cook, now as sober as a judge, would go into auto apologise mode, repeating "Sorry skip, sorry skip," as he groped around the cabin for his glasses in order to see to put the wreckage of the stove back together again. Providing you weren't down the cabin when it happened, this was fine entertainment and afterwards, watching Harry's cringe-worthy performance as he tried to act the part of the perfect deckhand/cook, only added to the fun.

Barring explosions, this was how the tea was made. Into the gallon teapot went four tablespoons of tea, and as many of sugar followed by the water (sometimes it might even be boiling). Plenty of condensed milk was then stirred in, and the pot placed back on the range to keep hot until needed. A brown scum always formed on top, plastering the inside of the mug and clinging to your top lip as you drank. The tea mugs were washed once a week when the cabin was scrubbed out, and by then the only clean place on them was where your lip touched the rim.

With daylight still in the sky we sat around the aft deck yarning and enjoying our bit of supper, the wind a light westerly over a tranquil sea, the land aglow, bathed in warm evening sunshine. On such an evening there was nowhere else you would rather be. When supper was over it was time to have a go with the hand lines before it got too dark. This was great sport. These lines consisted of about 50 fathoms of cod-line wound onto a wooden square, a brass swivel joined on a fathom of gut holding four hooks, ending with a 1lb lead. They were baited up with strips of pilchard to fish on the seabed 30 or 40 fathoms down as we drifted along. Whiting was the main catch, fine big fish coming up three or four at a time if we happened to drift over the right ground. We also caught pollack, ling, cod and hake, even the odd conger. Sometimes enough were caught to sell to the fish jowters to make a bit of stocker money; at other times there was just enough for a feed each. If that was the case, the fish were always shared out evenly back in harbour, just before we went home. Tiddler would divide the fish into little heaps on the net room hatches as fairly as he could, one for each member of the crew. Then, appointing one man to turn his back to it, Tiddler would point to a pile of fish and ask him, "Who's shall this be?" and a crewman was named ... and so on until everyone had been named and all had their share of fish. Bait for the lines was always cut up on the bait board. This was an ordinary piece of deal about 18 inches by 8 inches. There was a ritual joke attached to this board which I think held good on all the luggers, and it went like this. If you wanted to cut up some bait for your line and someone had just finished using it, or if you looked about and couldn't see it, you would of course say, "Pass me the bait board," or "Where is the bait board?" and it was passed over, or you were told where it was. But if you said, "Where's the board?" or "Pass me the board," the reply was always "What board?" and the answer had to be "The board the monkey fucked the cat on." With that, it was yours. As far as I can make out, that ritual had continued for generations and never failed to raise a smile.

Another old joke was the lighthouse on the pilchard's head. Slicing up some bait one evening, Tiddler passed me over a pilchard. "There, boy," he said, "can you see the lighthouse on the pilchard's head?" Look as hard as I might, I couldn't see a lighthouse, knowing this was yet another old wheeze, but it was the first one I had come across where the main prop was a dead fish. Admitting defeat, I passed it back to Tiddler who then pointed out a tiny marking on top of the pilchard's head, right between the eyes. Sure enough, it looked just like a miniature lighthouse. Giving the fish back, I was then told to look for the dog. Again, I had to give in. "I can't see a dog anywhere," I said. "No you won't, either," said Tiddler, puffing on his pipe as hard as he could to conceal his growing mirth. "Because he's around the other side of the lighthouse having a shit!" Caught again, to gales of laughter from the rest of the crew.

We had many enjoyable hours with the hand lines, especially if there was a bit of a jape to be played. If someone left their line unattended for a while, that was the time to whip it up a few fathoms, tie on a length of fine black mending twine and lower away again, leading the twine back around the boat where it couldn't be seen. When the angler returned and took hold of his line, the prankster would tug on the twine. "Ha, there they are, I can feel them," says the dupe. Tug, tug, again on the twine. "Come on, my beauties."

Tug, tug. "Right, my lovelies, up you come," and hand over hand, up it comes. If all went well he doesn't notice the mending twine and the hooks come up with only the bait on. "Well look at that," squeaks the victim. "Tugging like fuck they were, and the bastards have all got off!" Meanwhile, in the gloaming, five pairs of shoulders are heaving in silent mirth.

One of the old 5-stone aluminium fish cans hitched on to someone's line was always a good lark. It would shear about very convincingly when being hauled, bringing forth talk of big ray or turbot, and demands for someone to stand by with the gaff. Happy days!

When it got too dark for the hand lines, they were wound up and put away. Somebody might go below to snatch an hour in his bunk, others would remain kneeling on the deck, leaning on the rail quietly yarning, watching the lights along the shore and enjoying a smoke. Moogie was usually in the wheelhouse looking at the echo sounder showing the pilchard shoals steadily ascending to feed in the dark plankton-rich surface water. You could hear them rattling and splashing around the boat. If the signs were looking good our captain would perk up no end, bursting into the odd verse of 'Nelly Dean' or 'Sweet Adeline' and, if he was feeling really great, that might well be accompanied by a spot of tap dancing. In the confines of that tiny shelter, and wearing sea-boots, it couldn't have been easy.

As soon as he judged the time was right we would hear the shout, "Right ho, boys, get ready". The starter whined and the aft engine burbled into life, boots and oilskins are pulled on ready for the haul to begin. Moogie would go forward to the swing rope and order a touch ahead on the engine to take the weight off it, and we would haul away, coiling it down on the net room boards. When the swing rope was up short, it was passed back to the head rope man who then pulled in the last couple of fathoms to the net. The rail man then took hold of the end lining and pulled away to get it all on deck. He got it 'laying fair' then hauled again to pass it back to the second hand, and so on back to the stower.

We were now all ready to start the haul. "Go ahead five," shouts the rail man. Harry shoves the engine into gear and counts five, enough in fine weather. If the fishing is steady and the pilchards spaced fairly evenly along the net, the man 'out the rail' just hauled away steadily and shouted "Ahead five" every now and then to keep the boat up to the nets, while the pawl on the rail roller clattered away merrily. The men behind him shook and flipped the fish out of the net, while the stower cleared out a few scads and mackerel plus the odd conger drill, keeping the rhythm going. We might not make our fortunes that night, but there was a 'little blessing' and it would all add up at the end of the week.

After 5 or so hours of easy hauling, the nets were 'all in' and we would now be heading homeward. Jack Harris and I would nip down forward and crank the '30' into life and give it half throttle, then get back up on deck to help unship the roller and spars, stow the mizzen and box the catch up ready to land. There was no time for another cup of tea, for we would soon be back in harbour.

As we enter Looe bay off Hannafore, Jack would nip down forward and the ease the '30' down and stop as we enter harbour in the soft light of early dawn. At the quayside, ropes and fenders are put out and the leg shipped up. Jack Moore would drag the balance scales and weights out of the shed and set them up. Meanwhile the rest of us would chuck the boxes of fish ashore for Moogie and Harry to weigh and stack up ready for the lorry to take them to the cannery at Newlyn, 120 stone in all.

Buckets and brooms were plied to give the old boat a good scrub up, along with our oilskins and boots. Anything in contact with the pilchards got lagged in scales. When all was clean and tidy, it was time for home. "Same time tonight, boys," said our skipper, as we headed off for breakfast and a few hours' kip.

Hauling away one evening, the conditions were just as I have described. Tiddler was looking down at a bunch of gulls that were fighting over a fish, his 'chickens' he always called them. In his chicken voice, a high falsetto, he clucked and scolded at them for being so ill mannered. "I'll give the missis a telling off when I get home," he announced to the rest of us. "I told her to lock them up at sunset, and now they're out here playing up hell." Then he went back to clucking and scolding. Maybe it was the thought of his wife, the voluptuous Gwen, waiting for him at home in bed, I don't know, but all of a sudden, after a period of silence, he was groping at the front of his oilskin and bellowing loudly to be taken ashore. "What the hell is the matter with you Tiddler?" said Moogie. "Would you believe it," came the reply "Gwenie's pride hasn't stood to attention for 2 years, now he's up like a ramrod, and I'm out here. Get me ashore Moogie, get me ashore!"

5

Sleeping

All the crew except myself lived within a 10-minute walk of the quay in Looe. Talland Bay was 2 ½ miles away and for 18 months or so, until I bought a motorbike, I walked or push-biked there and back. Being young this didn't worry me; the walk took three quarters of an hour; by bike, 25 minutes. The trouble was that the bikes never lasted very long. Because it was much the quickest route, half the journey home was down a very rough lane, deeply rutted and made up with lumps of stone as big as your fist. Going down it in daylight was no problem, but in the dark, guided only by looking up at the lighter sky between the high hedges (lights never stayed working for very long) was a recipe for punctured tyres, buckled wheels and many a spill.

Attempts to sleep during the day were not always very successful. Everyone else was up and about doing their thing, while I was trying to get some rest. Many a time I gave up, going to sea in the evening dog tired and, as Tiddler would say, "With eyes like sheep's cunnie's".

Often it was possible to have a nap on the way out to shoot the nets, and a couple of hours could usually be had while riding to them. When dog-tired, what utter bliss it was to climb into my bunk and lay there dozing, warm and comfortable. But no matter how tired I was, when it was time to turn out you had to be out on the instant, pronto. If someone gave you a shout or shook you, or if steaming and the engine was eased down, there was no time allowed to come to gently and pull your thoughts together. It was out of your bunk and up on deck the very instant of being roused, and woe betide anyone who was slow. I well remember taking time crawling out of my bunk when I first started, to receive one hell of a bollocking. "You idle little bastard, you'll die in your bunk if you carry on like that. The fog might have come down, a steamer might be about to ram us, you don't know what might be happening," yelled Tiddler. "The next time I give you a shake, out of your fucking bunk and up on the bastard deck straight away." It was hard training but it was just. There were one or two men in the fleet who had had some terrible experiences in the navy during the war: they were shaken with a broom handle to rouse them because they would sometimes come out of the bunk fighting for their life.

On the *Iris*, unless you could sleep with one eye open, it was not a good idea to nod off sitting on the cabin lockers - there were too many jokers about. Some poor bugger, utterly exhausted, slumped in a corner of the cabin 'driving the pigs home', was likely to end up with his feet tied together, hat made fast with mending twine to a nail in the deck head and his face decorated with soot from the fire to resemble an Indian on the warpath. It happened to us all over the years. Of course, when the shout goes up to get on deck, there's the victim, only semi-conscious, lunging for the companionway wondering why his feet won't work and what has happened to his hat. The best bit would be if he didn't realise that he had been done up with the soot so that, after sorting out feet and hat, 'Geronimo' would take his place on deck. Sooner or later he would say or do something that, combined with the war paint, would make him look utterly ridiculous. Half an hour or so of pent up sniggering would burst forth in a tidal wave of laughter, and the game was up. Bent over a bucket of sea water trying to clean up a bit, tongue-in-cheek revenge was top of the agenda: "You think that's funny, just wait till I catch one of you bastards asleep. In fact, don't any of you nod off for the next six months!"

At sea one night, we had a bit of unexpected excitement, courtesy of the Royal Navy. It all began with the *Iris*'s electrical system. The wiring for this was not of the best, the lights were operated from a number of old domestic switches, screwed at random to the deckhead of the wheelhouse and joined up with anything from light flex to cooker wire. If a tall man was at the wheel, he had to stand at the stoop or else, as the boat rolled, his hat would brush the switches, turning the lights on and off. On this particular evening we were laying to the nets and Moogie couldn't get the riding lights to work, so a Tilley lamp was rigged forward in their stead.

It was a calm, quiet evening and as black as pitch. We were all sat aft smoking and yarning when presently we heard the thrum of powerful engines but couldn't make out the vessel as she too had her lights out. Suddenly we were in the glaring beam of a searchlight, and a megaphone voice quacks, "Drifter, please display the correct lights, as it is confusing to other mariners," to which someone shouted back, "Where the fuck's yours?" We were being paid a visit by the Fishery Protection boat.

Meanwhile our skipper's third rendition of 'Sweet Adeline' had been hastily curtailed and he was now furiously twiddling wires to try and get some lights working. Eventually on came the riding lights, followed by the working lights and an order to "Get ready". It wasn't long before we were hauling away, but to our great discomfort the fishery boat was still hovering about. Suddenly there was a dinghy at our port side, with two ratings and a young officer aboard. The officer awaited his moment, and as the old *Iris* rolled to port, he nimbly jumped aboard to near disaster. The net room was nearly empty, and the port waterways were very narrow. What he expected as he leaped, I don't know, but luckily he did just manage to pitch in the waterways and not down into the net room; it left him totally unbalanced, gyrating and snatching at the air, like an epileptic disco dancer. When his balance and dignity were somewhat restored, he strutted aft and stood there, full of 'piss and importance'. We carried on working meanwhile, taking no notice of him at all. Forward he came again: "Who's the skipper?" he barked. Frank had to confess that he was, and dropped the net to go aft and give our details. When the officer was satisfied that we were up to nothing illegal, he returned to the mine-sweeper and it departed. Later, Frank admitted he had been very tempted to name Harry as the skipper, but after the officer's undignified boarding he didn't reckon his sense of humour would have stretched that far.

6

Local Characters

Looe was not an easy port to work from, built as it is on a narrow tidal river. On a spring tide the water flows in and out at an alarming pace and the boats have to be handled with great skill if the skippers are to avoid doing any damage and suffer a severe loss of dignity. When the wind is in the easterly quarter, a nasty bar can build at the entrance, requiring deft boat handling to pass safely over it. At neap tides, it's low water in the morning and evening, and the boats had to anchor in the bay.

This is where the 'scruffer' came in. Scruffing was, and still is, the name given to the job of attending to the boats when they are anchored off, and the scruffer was one of a band of retired fishermen who supplemented his pension by working a small boat on the harbour ferry or doing river trips in the summer. In the early 1960s that post was held by Albert the Belgie. He and his family had escaped to Looe from Ostend on his trawler when the Germans overran Belgium in the Second World War. Albert's ferry boat, the good ship *Nancy D*, was not exactly the best in its class; the engine would splutter to a halt on a regular basis due to overheating or the plug sooting up, but he always managed to coax it into life again. It was the same for everyone in those days, make do and mend.

On neap tides when the luggers *Guide Me*, *Iris*, *Our Boys*, the *Our Daddy* and 'Lishy' Soady's quatter *Endeavour* would be anchored in the bay, mizzens set and looking to the west as pretty as a picture, their crews assembling at the sea front smoking and yarning, Albert would be waiting off the pier in his boat, jigging on the pump and hoping that his engine was in a good mood. Moogie would come jaunting out, grub tin under his arm.

"Everyone here?" he asked. "Yes," came the reply, "but hang on a minute, Tiddler has gone for a piddle." With that, Tiddler appeared. "With a gut like you've got you can't have seen the end of your cock for years," comes somebody's kind remark. "I'm going on a diet, then things will be different," he replied as he waddled down the pier with us, having just put five pints of Bass down his neck, his grub tin, as always, stuffed full of boiled tripe and crackers.

Albert saw us coming and poked his boat alongside the pier steps while we tumbled down the granite treads and climbed aboard. The tired old engine was shoved into gear and out into the bay we went, well nearly ... the engine coughed and stopped dead. "Help, help, shipwreck, we are all going to drown," someone shouted in mock terror, "Get the oars out, we'll row her," is another helpful suggestion. "Christ, he'll even want paying in a minute," said Moogie with a wink.

But Albert Diems was 'Mr Cool', and a man of very few words. He had witnessed the horrors of the First World War, he had battled winter gales trawling in the North Sea and finally, in the Second World War, he and his family had been bombed and machine-gunned by the invading Germans and exiled from their country. Nothing that happened here in Looe could even slightly advance his heart rate, let alone alter his facial expression. If he did speak, it was only to answer Moogie who always asked him, "What do you know Albert?" and the reply was always, "Fuck all". End of conversation.

Impassively, he cleans the spark plug and cranks the engine up again. This time we made it out to the lugger, and Albert got his money.

With the aft engine ticking over, the skipper nudged the boat along the anchor road. It was cable laid manila, as thick as your wrist and stiff with tar. I was down in the forepeak coiling it onto the cable tier while the others were hauling. When the anchor was stowed, Jack came down and we cranked up the '30' and the '21' and gave them half throttle. Back up on deck we help the others to unship the net room and fish box hatches, then ship up the shooting roller and drop the mizzen peak. The cabin chimney was billowing evil-smelling smoke, indicating that Harry was having some success with the fire. The four other boats were not far behind us, it was a fine summer evening and the Looe fleet was off to sea once more.

Harry, our little wiry, ginger-haired cook was a widower. He lived in a cottage in the old part of town known as the 'Back Streets'. Nicknamed 'Scrumpy' Harry after his favourite beverage, or 'Harry Slender' because of his slight build, he was the only member of the crew who could drive. His transport was a bubble car, the type where the whole front of the vehicle hinged back, and up to three people could climb in and perch on the bench seat within. It would get you from A to B, but any 'cool' you might have possessed, evaporated the very instant you got in to it. I well recall the time he gave it a coat of paint. No preparation was deemed necessary, he just slapped it on with a hairy cow's tail of a brush. The paint he used was from a jammy old tin of cream-coloured stuff that he had found up the net loft. Textured, I suppose, was the best way to describe the finish, especially after little whorls of wind had liberally coated it with grit and toffee papers.

Regardless of the paint job, Harry was proud of his vehicle, and it played a vital role when he went a-courting. Over the years, he had squired various widows around the area, and when setting forth on one of these hot dates, we would see him resplendent in his best courting rig. It consisted of a white shirt, with a red and blue cravat, blue/green drainpipe trousers, white winkle picker shoes (brogue pattern) and a blue blazer with a flower in the buttonhole, topped off with a green Tyrolean hat with a pheasant's tail feather set at a jaunty angle in the band. A silver-handled cane and gold-framed monocle, completed his raffish air. Thus suitably attired, and fortified with a few pints of the best farmhouse scrumpy, he would board his trusty steed and putter off for a dirty weekend.

We were riding to the nets one evening and everyone was sitting down in the cabin having supper and yarning when the subject of Harry's most recent weekend away came up. Of course we started to tease him a bit: "Come on, Harry, tell us how it went." "Did you rise to the occasion?" and so on. With that, he gets his wallet out of his back pocket and from it produces a tiny wrap of cigarette paper, inside of which, tied around with cotton, was a tuft of pubic hair. "There you are," he said, holding it up to his nose between thumb and forefinger, eyes closed as he savoured the delicate aroma. "Wonderful." With that, it was passed from hand to hand for all to appreciate, while he regaled us with his weekends exploits. At least four more such trophies were produced for our delectation. It was like a surreal wine evening, the vintner passing around his finest wines and telling proudly of their history.

On one occasion, the landlord of the Looe Hotel gave Harry a huge, very over-ripe gorgonzola cheese that would have taken him about a fortnight to eat. Down in the cabin it whiffed away menacingly in his grub tin. With the boat riding quietly to the nets, we would be sitting around the cabin fire enjoying our supper and a yarn until Harry decided to make some inroads into this cheese and took the lid off his tin. The stench was eye watering, breathtaking, instantly causing the crew of the *Iris* to be jammed three deep in the companionway, fighting to get up on deck. Meanwhile the man himself, oblivious to the chaos he was causing, was busy piling mounds of this decaying dairy produce onto cracker biscuits, and savouring every mouthful. He got away with this performance for a couple of nights. Eventually Moogie stuck his head down the hatch, eyes watering with the up rush of ammonia fumes, and diplomatically requested he dispose of it. His exact words being, "Harry, for fuck's sake heave that bloody thing overboard".

Harry was a character extraordinaire, with a mind set all of his own. So many years have passed since those days, but I still chuckle to myself when I recall some of his antics, and the yarns he spun.

7

Sharking

In the days before foreign holidays became popular, Cornwall in the summer months used to be packed to the gunwales with people on their annual fortnight's holiday. Looe would ring to the sound of Welsh, Brummie and a whole variety of other regional accents as different industries shut down for their annual vacations. Most people arrived by train and spent much of their time in the town or on coastal walks, coach trips, shopping for nick-knacks, boozing, beaching and boating. Sea angling, especially shark fishing, was very popular and as a result about 20 boats, both large and small, earned a good living with the rod and line. At the height of the season, during the school holidays, these boats just couldn't cope with the numbers of people wanting a day out so the luggers, to earn a bit extra cash, would take the overflow of people who wanted to go sharking.

To a drifter, sharks were nothing more than a damned menace because they would go for the pilchards caught in their nets and rip them to rags. To counteract this a shark line, made up from a few fathoms of buoy rope, light chain and a big hook, would be baited up and hung off the mizzen backstay while riding to the nets. When a shark took hold, it was hauled in hand over hand and dragged onto the boat. Its tail was cut off, and then it was thrown back again, to be seen last disappearing stern first, one less to rip the nets. A cruel way to kill them but the attitude was very different in those days.

When the luggers first started taking people out angling, it was looked upon as a way to exterminate as many sharks as possible (and there were a lot of them) while getting paid to do it. So away to sea they would go with twelve hapless anglers and, instead of the expected big game rod, they found themselves with a lugger's shark line.

The fun began when a shark took hold. The resulting contest was like something from the gladiatorial games of ancient Rome, man versus beast. An enraged fish, weighing anything up to a couple of hundred pounds or more on one end of a rope, and a terrified angler whose bowels were rapidly turning to water on the other. To lessen the angler's fright, and prevent the skin being torn off his hands by the rope or, worse still, being dragged overboard, the skipper would lend a hand.

While the contest was taking place, the other anglers would line the starboard rail, baying for the shark's blood in a bold and heroic manner ... that was, until the beast itself was boated by the skipper. Having been hauled aboard in fairly short order, the shark was far from exhausted and there it would lie, tail scything the air and beating the deck, rows of razor sharp teeth munching lumps out of the parting boards. On seeing this, the usual reaction from our heroic band of shark hunters was to stampede for the rear of the wheel-house in sheer jaw-dropping terror. Not until the skipper had subdued the shark by beating its head in with a big hammer would their bravado return.

This was not exactly a very sporting or safe way to take people out big game fishing, and after numerous complaints of rope-burnt hands and soiled underwear from the anglers, the committee of the Shark Angling Club of Great Britain called a meeting with the lugger skippers, chaired by its founder and president, Brigadier Caunter. In no uncertain terms it was 'requested' that in future, when out shark angling, they must use rods, and thereby uphold the safety and dignity of the sport. This was duly complied with, and the required rods were thereafter rented by the season from Jack Bray's tackle shop on East Looe quay.

Many years later there was a scheme running to attach a tag to the dorsal fin of sharks that were caught instead of killing them, recording the area and date of capture stamped on it. Released unharmed, the information they carried was used for further research. This shark-tagging scheme was a good thing and ran successfully for many years. Information about sharks caught off Looe came in from all around the Atlantic.

At one of the annual Shark Angling Club dinners, Brigadier Caunter (by then in his dotage) stood up to give his usual speech. He rambled on for a while before dropping a real clanger: "And finally," he drawled, "I should like to thank the skippers for shagging the tarts!" The poor old boy inadvertently brought the house down, and I think it was the very last Angling Club dinner he ever attended.

Shark angling as a sport started in Looe quite by accident. In the late 1940s the brigadier, a keen big game angler, had originally chartered local angling boats to take him out to try and catch a tuna. These fish migrated in schools down the Channel at certain times of the year and, although this particular fish always seemed to elude him, he did catch plenty of sharks. Returning to Looe with one or two of the larger ones on board, fishermen on the quay would pull his leg a bit. "A couple of nice tunny today then, Briggy," was a likely remark. Meanwhile, other anglers who had been out for the day doing battle with pollack and conger began to fancy a go themselves at this rather exciting new sport. Within a few years, shark angling became extremely popular, earning many thousands of pounds annually for the port.

During those busy holiday periods we could not have worked any harder and still remained alive. If the weather stayed workable, the boat's engines never went cold. We were out for five or six nights a week pilchard drifting, and every day with the shark anglers. Returning to harbour any time between three and six in the morning, the fish were landed and the boat scrubbed down. Then, instead of heading home to bed, the two men whose turn it was to go sharking would grab a bite to eat and maybe an hour in their bunks. At half past eight the boat was made ready, another quick scrub around (you could scrub for a week and still not get rid of all the fish scales) and the rods were passed up from the forepeak, ready to take out a dozen anglers at nine o'clock.

The sharking grounds were 10 or 12 miles off the coast, and when we arrived, the day would be spent drifting broadside with the shark lines baited up and paid out on cork floats at varying distances from the boat, while a trail of 'rubby dubby' (mashed pilchards) was shaken from two mesh bags to attract the sharks. The best 'rubby' was salted down in a dustbin, making the fish soft and easy to shake out of the bags and also drawing the oil out of the fish, creating a much more effective trail to attract the sharks with. Its only drawback was the smell, an oily, all-pervading stench of decaying fish.

Many were the anglers who had their days entirely ruined by the lid of the 'rubby' bin being lifted prior to filling the bags. There was just no escaping the smell, and if the poor souls happened to be out on the *Our Boys* when Stan Mutton was in charge, they needed cast iron stomachs not to end up giving their breakfast a second viewing. Stan loved a salt pilchard snack and would select a couple for himself out of the bin; anyone feeling a bit cruddy but had managed to hold on so far despite the dreadful stench was surely done for as they watched in horror at somebody actually eating the stuff!

In those days it wasn't uncommon to catch ten, fifteen or even twenty sharks in a day, and there would be some fairly big beasts amongst them as well. Some of the older crews didn't want to bother with these, so while they were adjusting the clutch on the reel for the angler, a quick and unnoticed touch of a fag-end on the line would soon see the big ones on their way. A yellow flag was flown for every shark caught, and on some days the boats would be flying flags from the mizzen masthead to the stem head, extra flags being cut out from old oilskins.

Returning to Looe at six in the evening, the lugger was hitched up along side the quay to get the people ashore, then it was fish and chips and a mug of tea for dinner. The rest of the crew would be aboard by seven, and away we went for another night's pilchard drifting. A day's sharking meant an extra five pounds in the wage packet, but working 36 hour shifts, with sometimes very little rest in between, is not something I would want to do again. I often wonder what the visitors must have thought of it all when they stepped aboard for their day out. Two weary fishermen, stinking of pilchards and diesel, on a threadbare old boat, herself emitting a different but equally horrible smell from every hatch. It wasn't exactly five star treatment. Nevertheless curiosity got the better of some of them, because it was not at all unusual for one or two anglers from a sharking trip to come out for the night to see for themselves what pilchard drifting was all about, many of them taking photographs and cine film. Some even volunteered their services on the nets. To this end they would be dressed up in old oilskins and sea boots and be put 'out the rail'. Ten minutes was about as long as any of them lasted, the dip net suited them the best. One lad I remember was as keen as mustard with this tool. Tiddler had lifted up the head ropes so as he could get in closer to the fish dropping away from a small meshed net then being hauled. With about three stone in the dip net, the lad launched the long handle back inboard prior to lifting it aboard and in doing so, caught Tiddler right in the bread basket, knocking him down into the net room where he lay winded, like a turtle on it's back. The rest of us couldn't do a thing to help him as we were all crippled with laughing. Luckily we were nearly all in with the catch and he didn't have far to fall; the only thing bruised was his dignity.

If the weather stayed fine for any length of time, we ended up like the walking dead. What a relief it could be to see the gale cone hoisted on the coastguard flagstaff. But every possible pound had to be earned in the summer, because in the winter the dole and a few odd jobs had been the way of things for many years.

The golden rule aboard the boats then, as now, was no drinking at sea. Several men might turn up to go to sea having had a few jars, but there was no more to be had on the boats, and they soon sobered up. Every boat carried a bottle of whisky, but this was purely for medicinal use only. However, there was one area of operation where this rule could not very well be applied, and that was when out sharking. Many of the anglers loved to take a drop of booze with them on their big day out, and some of the old skippers just couldn't turn down a quick gargle if it was on offer. There were a few incidents where it went a bit further than a gargle, but all in all, most of them managed to hold out, at least until they got ashore into the pub. There they could play the old seadog-skipper role for all it was worth, while their admiring audience plied them into near oblivion with free beer.

But those men were great characters, and their like does not exist today. They could tell of the days when they were boys, crewing on the schooners and ketches that traded around the coast under sail, and as young men working on the big J Class racing yachts; of service in the Royal Navy during the war, and of fishing seasons when money was plentiful, and times when they nearly starved. They have all gone now, and the port is very much the poorer for their passing.

8

Barking the Nets

The drift nets we used were made of fine cotton twine and required an awful lot of looking after. There was always mending to be done where sharks had torn into them, or when they had fouled up while shooting or hauling in poor weather. To prevent them from going rotten, the nets that were being worked had to be treated with a preservative every six weeks or so.

There were two methods of doing this; the newest nets were 'barked', while the older ones were 'pickled'. Neither job was pleasant, but pickling was by far the worst of the two. On the day the skipper arranged to bark the nets we would try to get in early from sea, land the catch and then drop the boat back at the bark house. The nets would then be hauled ashore and built up like a haystack outside the bark house door. Buoys and buffs were cast off and stowed on the foredeck. By then Frank Hoskin, who owned the bark house, would have the boiler lit, building up a good head of steam. In front of the boiler was a brick-lined pit about 4-feet square by 3-feet deep which was two-thirds filled with water. Steam pipes would get this pit bubbling hot, and into it the cracked up bark or 'kutch' would be dissolved. This stuff was processed from the bark of a tropical tree and packed in half hundred weight sacks, it resembled dark, dirty-looking amber.

A roller was shipped up at the bark house door and, at a slow and steady pace, two men hauled the nets in, dropping them fathom by fathom into the pit. The skipper stood by with a pole, poking everything well down to make sure it all got a good soaking as well as regulating the speed to make sure that the bark didn't go off the boil. With his hands protected by a pair of heavy rubber gloves, a fourth man pulled the nets out again, and behind him two more of the crew, one on the head ropes, one on the skirt, stowed them neatly by the exit hatch on the sloping floor to drain. Last of all the mizzen sail and the mooring ropes were dumped into the pit to have a soak. The whole process took about three hours. It was like working in very hot fog and we would nearly melt into our boots.

The nets were then left to drain for a few hours before being hauled back aboard. The fleet would now be down in the net room back to front, so we had to shoot head to wind and change ends to put it right. This was important, because the newest nets were always the ones nearest to the boat and therefore likely to suffer least damage. The ones furthest away towards the pole end were the longest in the water and much more likely to suffer shark damage, or be cut up by a coaster going over them. In fact the last couple of nets of the fleet or pole-enders were very often rotten ripe, hanging away in rags off the head ropes, but they always seemed to fish very well in that condition.

Every time a net was barked the heat of the process shrank the mesh a little, so after a few years an alternative method of preservation had to be used to stop them from becoming useless. This method was called pickling, a process that every one hated, but there was no alternative. Harry and I used to get nabbed for this - the boy and the cook - the two least likely to have some other pressing job or be able to talk our way out of it. The nets needing this treatment were piled onto the net cart (an old wooden-wheeled donkey cart) and the two of us would drag it off to the pickling store, a tiny stone built shed in the back streets. Inside this place was an old domestic bath half full of water with a huge draining board attached to one end of it, and on top of the water floated about 20 gallons of creosote.

Wearing oilskin aprons and plastic gloves for protection, I would pull the nets off the cart and into the bath and Harry then dragged them through the creosote and stacked them on the draining board, a filthy job. The nets were then left to drain for a couple of days before being hauled aboard the boat, and until the stuff worked out of them a bit, they were dreadful to handle. Creosote burned your face and stung your eyes, you were black up to the elbows, and your oilskin was covered in it but, as Jack used to say, "If you can't take a joke you shouldn't have joined."

There was a day when Harry failed see the funny side. He and I had dragged a cartload of nets down to the store and were well into the routine of this horrible task when Harry suddenly needed to pump ship so, pulling off his gloves, he nipped outside to relieve himself. Suddenly a howl went up: he had somehow got a dollop of creosote on the end of his 'old man' and, with eyes a-water and burning member in hand, he dashed to his cottage to gain some relief. His speed on the straight was very impressive, and I don't think anyone wearing hobnail boots has ever cornered so fast; the sparks fairly flew, it was as if he was going down the road full throttle on an invisible motorbike. I know it sounds cruel, but I now know exactly what people mean when they say they nearly died laughing.

As the fishing season progressed, so the size of the pilchards changed and to match this, small or big meshed nets were being hauled in or out of the boat all the time. When nets were finished with for the season, they were put onto the cart and hauled up to the net spars, there to be hung up in the wind to dry before being stowed up the loft. If they were put away wet, or even damp, they would heat up and rot just like a compost heap. There was even a danger of spontaneous combustion. For this same reason, if we were weather bound for more than three days, the fleet of nets had to be hauled up out of the net room and stacked on deck to cool and air it, then hauled back down again three days later, the process repeated until the weather improved. If the fishing had been heavy, the nets would be soaked in pilchard oil and full of scales, heads and quite a few whole fish. This would really speed the heating up process, making the nets nearly too hot to handle. Towards the middle of the fleet there would be a steaming miasma of rotting fish billowing out over the hatch coamings, a good lungful of which could send you retching to the rail.

Another danger to the nets was rats. The rich oily smell of pilchards would attract them aboard the boats in search of a meal. Inevitably they would end up in the net room, burrowing from morsel to morsel through the nets. Then the next time the fleet was shot there would be dozens of rat-sized holes, entailing hours of work with the net needles to repair. The answer to the problem was 'Scamp', Moogie's Jack Russell terrier. Put aboard a boat and given the magic word "rats", he would go into action like a canine version of the avenging angel. After a sniff about to get the scent, he was off snuffling and yapping, with the crew stood by to shift anything that might be standing between him and his victim. Coils of rope, fish boxes, fenders and boards were all cast aside for this small dog, who was worked up into a pitch of fury by all about him shouting "Rats, Scamp, rats!" and "Where is he? Tear the bastard to shreds!" etc. Suddenly he would make a lunge, there would be a terrified squeal from the rat and Scamp would appear with it in his jaws to the cheers and praise of the boat's crew and any others who had gathered around to watch the fun. I don't think I have ever seen a dog looking so completely and utterly pleased with itself at that moment.

9

Herring Fishing

Our sharking season ended with the school summer holidays. It was a nice extra in the wages, but we were all glad when it was over. With autumn approaching, it wouldn't be many weeks before the pilchard season also ground to a halt. The boats would chase the migrating shoals up and down the coast for ever-diminishing catches, and by November they would be gone. From then on there was very little to be earned fishing until the following March when, hopefully, enough pilchards could be caught to bait up the long lines.

After a hard summer season the autumn fishing was very pleasant. Because the sun was setting much earlier, we would leave the harbour just after lunch. Shooting the nets at teatime, we would be hauling by about seven o'clock and very often be back in the harbour again by midnight, sometimes even earlier. If we were working close to home and Neptune had decided not to let us have any of his fish that night, Tiddler, back on the head ropes, might take a look at the wheel-house clock, do a quick calculation and then announce that if we got our fingers out we could save tide in for a pint. If that idea took hold then look out: we went from jogging along steadily on an easy haul, to working as if the Devil himself was after us. The pawl on the roller would go from a steady click, click, to one continuous clatter. Clearing the nets out, water and fish would be flying everywhere, and the old engine was in gear more than it was out, driving the boat along the fleet. Arriving back into harbour with maybe only minutes to spare before closing time, everything was done for speed. Ropes and fenders were put out, the leg shipped, boxes of fish thrown up on the quay to be weighed. Moogie, who wasn't a drinking man, would be shaking his head and saying, "If only you bastards could work like this normally, we would all be rich," as he watched his crew rip off their oilskins and stampede for the pub.

Although the wages were tailing off rapidly, it was easy work, and we were usually home for the best part of a night's kip. The married men would joke about getting home 'under the lee of bum island' and if they were lucky, 'catching it with the dew on'.

At that time I had somehow been given the job of boat's fish jowter, so when we returned home with only a small catch of mixed fish, herrings, mackerel and pilchards, it was my job to sell them. By nine o'clock I would be back aboard the boat to lift up the hatches and drag out the boxes of fish that represented our night's work. Loading them onto the net cart, I would go to my pitch under the arch in Fore Street, and sell them at 6d a fish. Stan Mutton off the *Our Boys* had a pitch by the town clock. Whatever I made was always shared out as stocker, i.e. divided equally among the crew, but no share for the boat. It was very often cold and draughty standing in that alleyway flogging fish, but luckily an ancient retired butcher by the name of Dick Wickett, (known to the local lads as 'Old Dick Fuckit') lived in a cottage nearby and he used to bring me a mug of cocoa and a sandwich in exchange for a couple of herrings.

By late October 1964, the fishing had dwindled away to nothing and the luggers had hauled their nets ashore to begin the long winter's lay up. But rather than do nothing, our skipper, along with Bill 'Pye' Pengelly and his crew on the *Our Boys* decided to haul a fleet of herring nets aboard and work out of Brixham, trying our luck on the 'silver darlings' around Torbay. For generations the Cornish luggers had gone to Brixham in October to fish the herring shoals that came in to spawn in the big sandy bays, but that was now only a memory. The ministry of 'Ag and Fish' still paid a small trip subsidy to herring drifters, so if we only caught one herring to prove we had been to sea, the subsidy was paid, which meant at the very least the boat would not go into debt. It was better to try and earn something than tie up with a certainty of earning nothing.

So, on a fine Sunday morning in late October, with ten herring nets stowed in the net room and a few baskets of line on deck, we headed for Torbay in the company of the *Our Boys*. As we would be living on the boat, each of the crew had a bag of spare clothes and washing kit. When fishing away, the skipper provided bread and jam and a big slab cake, and each evening a meal of some description was scraped together. Anything else, you got it yourself. It was a fine run up the coast, catching the flood tide around Start Point and arriving in Torbay during the late afternoon. The two boats scouted around for any sign of herring as well as keeping a lookout for the *Bluebell*, owned by the Fry brothers, and the *Hopeful*, skippered by Peter Easton. They were two little inshore boats that also fished for herring, working moored nets around the bay, and we didn't want to get afoul of them as we would be working right in the shallow waters. Because of this, the buoy ropes had been shortened up from three fathoms to one; sometimes we would be so close to the shore that the buoys had to be flung in under the head ropes, and still the nets would touch the sand. We had to be careful when hauling because of weaver fish, tin cans and 'gooseberry bushes' - spiky little bushes that got tangled up in the nets, though what they really were and where they came from I have no idea.

A likely area in the bay was selected and the nets were shot. Then, after a quick scrub around, the spars were shipped up and we all went below for a helping of stew that Harry had cooked for our supper. He had made enough to last us for two days and kept the big dixie lashed to the engine to make it quicker to warm up the next day. Working a short fleet of nets in shallow water didn't take much time or effort to haul, so we would usually shoot three times a night. The only disadvantage was for the man out the rail where, instead of laying back and hauling the nets over the roller, he had to stand tight out to the rail and lift them over because herrings didn't hit into the net very hard. They seemed only to poke their noses into the mesh and then give up. To us this was very easy work; instead of picking, twisting and thrashing the nets to get pilchards out, all the herrings required was a little flap and out they fell, lovely plump glittering fish, slithering down the deck.

After a night of shooting and hauling around Torbay, we went into Brixham to land in time for the fish auction. Mooring up in the inner harbour, we then carried the few stone of herring that we had caught, up to the market in maund baskets. It had been a long day and night. The *Our Boys* tied up along side us and we helped to put her catch ashore. Afterwards it was smocks and overalls off and climb into our bunks for a few hours kip until lunchtime. Then those who liked their beer went ashore for a few pints, while others had fish and chips and a stroll around the harbour, followed by a couple more hours in the bunk before it was time to go to sea again. Dinner would be dished out while riding to the nets on the first shoot of the night. A couple of times a week it would be Harry's famous stew, at other times baked herring was dish of the day or, if someone had scrounged around the trawlers, we might have a boiled plaice or a bun crab each, all bulked out with plenty of bread and butter. 'Afters' was a slab of cake and a mug of tea to complete the meal.

I once made the mistake of asking Harry what we were going to have for dinner that night. "I'll boil up a Feenock," came the answer, and of course I fell for it. "What's a Feenock?" I asked, right on cue. "A donkey's cock stuffed with onions," came our cook's reply, grinning from ear to ear, tickled to bits by his own wit. Another dish we were always threatened with was 'half a leg of a sheep's head'. Having been a baker for many years Harry had one golden rule: when it's brown it's done, and when it's black it's buggered. TV chefs, eat your hearts out.

If the wind was blowing too hard to go to sea, we would all have a wash and brush up before going ashore to either the pub or the cinema. A deck bucket full of fresh water was heated up on the stove, and then placed on the cabin sole where we could all sit around it. First it was out soap and flannels and we all had a wash. Then everyone lathered up and the razors were employed. Lastly, with a drop of water poured into our tea mugs from the kettle, teeth were cleaned (false or otherwise) with everyone spitting into the wash bucket. When the ablutions were completed, Harry would take that same bucket of water and scrub out the cabin.

There were no toilet facilities of any kind on the luggers. If you needed a pee, you did it over the rail; the other call of nature was dealt with in the same manner. Perched on the rail with your bare arse hanging over the water, shirt tail flapping in the breeze, you clung to the mizzen backstay with one hand, a sheet of newspaper in the other, and a far away look in the eye. If it was very cold or rough, a drop of seawater was dipped up in a deck bucket and you retired with it down forward. Tiddler, our champion beer drinker, used to really suffer, sometimes having to hang off the backstay several times a night as he didn't dare pass wind in his trousers for fear of an accident.

When going for a run ashore, smocks and overalls were taken off, and a coat or jacket was worn instead. But working and sleeping in the same clothes all week meant the smell of fish, diesel and BO must have been fairly overpowering and although nobody in the pubs seemed to mind, we could clear a fair area around us when we went to the cinema.

Going to the cinema was a farce. I don't think anyone ever managed to watch a film right through. Because we worked by day and by night, in fact anytime at all, the wheels and springs of our body clocks were scattered far and wide, and we became adjusted to snatching an hour or so whenever we could. Being warm, dark and comfortable, the cinema was the ideal place for a kip and it wouldn't be long before we all started nodding off. Every now and then you would come to and try and work out what the film was all about, glancing around to see who else was awake. But after ten minutes or so the heavy eyelids would get the better of you and off you went again. It was only the stampede of the rest of the audience trying to get out before 'God Save The Queen' was played that roused us to make our own exit.

The last fishing night of the week was Friday, and after landing our catch on Saturday morning, we would then go home for the weekend. 'Skips' Ransom, a retired RAF officer living in Looe, drove us back and forth in his car, a big black Humber Hawk, while Freddie Lewis, a Looe boatman, chauffeured the crew of the *Our Boys* in his Bedford van.

Moogie always sat in the front with Skips, while the rest of us bunched up in the back. Our skipper had never driven a car in his life, but on this particular morning he was being rather observant. Suddenly he pipes up, "Here, Skips," he says. "There doesn't seem to be a hell of a lot of difference between steering a boat and driving a car. You've got a wheel for hard to port and hard to starboard and a lever for ahead and astern." "Well maybe you'll have to have a go one day," said Skips. "Fucked if I won't," said Moogie. It was probably fortunate for us all that he never did.

Upon our return to Brixham on Monday afternoon we would climb down aboard the old *Iris*, pump her out and make ready for sea. Then another week of shooting and hauling the herring nets around Torbay would begin. Thus we passed the time until the two luggers were steamed back to Looe for the Christmas break. We didn't catch a lot of herring, but the little money we did make, combined with the subsidy and a bit of dole money for bad weather days, made us a wage of sorts, five or six pounds a week, maybe ten if we had been lucky. It kept the wolf from the door, but only just.

10

April Gales

The intention had been to return to Brixham after Christmas, but the weather took a turn for the worst, completely wiping out January and February. The herring nets were hauled ashore, dried and stowed back up the loft. I managed to get a few weeks' work labouring for a builder, Jack worked on a coal round, while Moogie, Tiddler and Harry passed the time up in the loft overhauling nets and lines.

By mid-March the weather was settling down a bit, so the skipper decided we should haul in a short bait fleet of nets and put the lines aboard. But, as the saying goes, 'Everything in our favour was against us'. When the weather was right, we couldn't catch enough pilchards for a bait up. When we caught some bait, the weather was too poor to go out in the Channel, so the lines were shot along the shore for black conger. These sold for next to nothing per stone because much of the catch was small stuff known as 'arse worms'. After a winter spent scratching about, everyone was desperate to get some money coming in. We were all skint.

One night in early April we found ourselves with plenty of bait, but yet again the weather was shaping up to be pretty grim. Moogie could stand it no longer, however, so away out in the Channel we had to go, 'shit or bust'. Harry cut the pilchards up while the rest of us were on our knees beside the baskets of line, baiting the hooks with pieces of fish taken from a washing up bowl resting on top of the line. Hook held in the right hand, a piece of bait in the left, to be hooked through twice, heads down, tails up, all hanging down neatly from the rim of the basket. Four baskets of line per man, 250 hooks per basket, unless you had a box, and that could contain up to 400 hooks.

Before we were many miles out, the wind and sea started to make down Channel, and by the time we reached the lining grounds 40 miles out it was certainly poor enough. But the lines were all baited up, so they had to be shot. The old *Iris* was squared away before wind and tide, then shooting commenced. Over went the first dann, with its black flags and two hurricane lamps, then the dann line, ending with a grape anchor to which the end of the first basket of line was tied. Tiddler was at the wheel, keeping her on course, with Moogie shooting the line, right arm swinging as he threw the 7 miles of rope away tight and straight. Clarence stood behind him with a sharp knife to cut any hooks away should they catch up on the boat or shooter. He was also ready to knock the engine in and out of gear, to Moogie's orders.

Jack, Harry and I dragged the baskets of line to the shooting platform at the aft end of the starboard waterways, to bend the end of the basket of line then being shot to the top of the next one. Then pull the empty basket away and lift the next one up in place, and so on, to make one 'long line'. The middle dann line, with its brick sinker, was bent on with a rolling hitch and shot away from the port quarter, followed by its dann. Hooks were now flying over the side at a great rate, engine in gear in the troughs, and out when we surge ahead on a sea. 7 miles later, away went the end of the last basket of line, with its anchor and dann line, followed by the boat dann, hurricane lamps flickering, big black flags crackling in the wind.

Down went the wheel and as we came up head to wind, the mizzen was hoisted and sheeted home; the skipper took the wheel and proceeded to stay in sight of the dann for the next couple of hours until the tide turned and the haul could begin. Empty line baskets were stacked and lashed and anything that might move was secured - it was now time for a mug of tea and a bite to eat. The wind was freshening up all the time and by now some really big lumps of sea were starting to build. Moogie kept the old boat riding head to wind; thankfully she didn't make hard work of it.

At slack water the jinny was started, the dann was gaffed aboard and we went to work, the seas by now big and breaking. Regardless, the old jinny chuffed away, the skipper was hauling behind it, and the line was steadily coming aboard. Tiddler was coiling, Jack was gaffing, I was unhooking the fish, while Harry worked the wheel and engine. Clarence was waiting for the first length of line to come aboard to start repairing and clearing it back into the baskets. I don't remember how much line we had hauled, two or three baskets at the most, when suddenly a huge sea reared up, the boat pointed her bow at the sky and surfed away stern first, and the line parted. Here was a problem. To haul the rest of the line, we would have to battle our way up to the other dann and ride around until the tide turned again. The skipper looked around at the weather and, as tough as he was, he knew when he was beaten.

"That will do, boys, we're going home," was his decision. He stopped the jinny and strode back to the wheelhouse. Labouring head to wind, anything and everything that might move or be washed about was secured, including the hatches which were spiked down with nails. When all was ready, we stowed the mizzen and Moogie awaited his moment to bring us around on a course for home without the seas sweeping the deck. Once safely around, the two forward engines were cranked into life, then the forehatch was spiked down as well.

There was now nothing more to be done, so we retired below, shipped up the weather-boards and slid the hatch shut to prevent gallons of seawater cascading down the companionway ladder. We climbed into our bunks, but there was precious little rest to be had in them. The *Iris* was rearing and plunging so much, that no matter how you tried to brace yourself, you were still flung about. Being thrown about down the cabin like that was dreadful for seasickness, especially with the hatch shut tight building up heat and fumes from the range and the engine. I know for sure that I wasn't the only one to throw up on that trip home.

Every so often Tiddler would lift a board in the cabin sole and peer down into the bilge to see how much water she was making. Then, with the shout of, "Whose turn is it?" one of us would have to dress up in sea boots, oilskins, sou'wester and muffler to go up on deck to pump out. One blessing was that the pump didn't need priming, the deck was awash and the air full of flying spray. Braced against the bucking and plunging of the boat, you swung away at the pump, stopping every now and then to hang on tight to the mizzen jump stay as a big cresting sea made her lurch violently, causing the props to race and thrash up foam. Eventually the pump would suck dry and then, thankfully, you could slip back down the cabin to your bunk, knowing four others had to go through it before it was your turn again.

How long it took to get back to Looe, I can't remember, but I do know we were all very glad to arrive. It had been a hard, wet, miserable trip, we hadn't caught any fish and to add insult to injury, the weather had driven us back into the harbour, leaving most of the gear still out in the Channel.

Three days later, the sun was shining and the sea was sparkling calm, so away we went again to see if we could retrieve the line. This was long before anyone had Decca or GPS. The only navigation aids a skipper had were a clock to tell him how long he had run for, a compass to steer a course by and a tide book to work out the tidal flow. Moogie had set the course and timed the run out, then he started to box the area. Down to the west for so long, then turn, out a bit and up to the east again. We boxed around like this for several hours and had no joy whatsoever, all eyes straining until we were seeing danns everywhere. The skipper had almost given up hope, but decided on one more run before we turned for home.

Thinking that would be it, I nipped down the cabin and put a steak and kidney pie in the oven for dinner. It was on that last run, pushing a bit further to the east, that the shout went up, "There it is!" and away in the distance we could all now make out the black flags of the pole end dann, 40 miles out in the Channel. All was made ready and when we arrived at the dann, it was gaffed aboard. With everyone at their stations, the haul began.

Unlike the last time we had been out there, the weather was perfect and, with the old jinny on full throttle, the line fairly flew aboard, arm over arm. All the gear was retrieved, but we didn't have much of a catch of fish, just a few stone of poor looking ray and conger (they had been on the hooks far too long); any other fish had either worked their way off or had been eaten by their mates. By the time the end of the gear flipped over the jinny wheel, my forgotten pie was a charred ruin. But, not to worry, a mug of tea and a bite to eat was enjoyed before we set to work again, clearing and repairing the lines back into the baskets as we steamed back home to Looe.

As an old man, 30-plus years later, Moogie still talked about that trip. He had experienced many hard times, but I think that one stood out in his memory.

11

The Engines

Between the ending of the lining season in early May and the start of the summer pilchard drifting, the *Iris* was treated to her annual paint up. This wasn't a very elaborate affair. She was taken over to West Looe where she would dry out at low water. When the tide had ebbed enough for us to wade about in our sea-boots, all hands would set to with deck scrubbers working the tide down to clean the weed and barnacles off the boat's bottom. Then at low water, with the sun and wind drying the planking, cans of anti fouling, or 'patent' as it was called, were stirred up and lapped on with 'long tom' brushes. Black bitumastic paint was slapped on the sides and outside bulwarks. The inside bulwarks were painted white, while hatches, coamings and covering boards were painted blue after a quick rattle about with some blunt scrapers. For quickness the paint was a mixture of half undercoat and half gloss. The last thing to be painted was the deck, for which all the leftover paint was tipped into a deck bucket and stirred up, then paraffin added to bulk it out. On some paint ups, the wheelhouse would get a coat of its own brown and cream, but as for down below, I never saw that painted at all. I think fish oil, diesel and smoke preserved her below decks. The skipper used to take great care cutting in the name and fishing numbers on the luff of each bow. I can see him now, balancing on the top of a set of steps, brush in hand, making faces fit to win a girning contest in his concentration to get it neat. If the weather was kind to us the whole job would be completed in just two days, then it was back to East Looe to haul the fleet of nets aboard to begin the summer season.

The 1965 season started bleak, and continued to be so. There were plenty of pilchards and because of this, the cannery tried to reduce the price paid per stone to the boats from 3/6d (17p) to 3/- (15p), so we all went on strike. After three nights ashore, they relented and agreed to pay 3/6d again; considering they were paying 4/6d per stone 20 years before, we weren't exactly being overpaid.

No sooner was this business settled than the main engine, the 45 HP in the cabin, died on us. It had been running very badly for months, with the exhaust stack above deck glowing red hot in the dark, leaving a trail of sparks and flame behind us. Because of this, Frankie Oliver on the *Our Daddy* nicknamed her 'the old black dragon'. We were a fortnight ashore while the engine was being repaired, but it wasn't all bad - I had two weeks blow out on sleep and attended plenty of parties and barbeques, a welcome change from hard labour.

The forward engine room was the home of the 30 and the 21 HP Listers. It was entered via a small deck hatch at the luff of the port bow, a four-rung ladder took you down into it, the only place below decks with near-standing headroom. An ordinary domestic switch operated the lights which consisted of two small bulbs dangling from the deck head by their wires. Aft from the ladder were the two dark-green painted engines with their open fly wheels and belts. These engines were dry sump, so beside each a brass 5-gallon tank piped lubricating oil to them, while fuel was gravity fed from a couple of 30-gallon tanks under the deck head to port and starboard, secured on stout wooden beds.

Right in the forepeak was the cable tier, a heavy plank shelf supported by battens fastened to the port and starboard frames, about 2 feet down from the deck head and extending back from the stem 5 feet or so. Here, lashed down hard and fast was the anchor and its tarred cable.

The engine room had once been painted grey or white, but the overall colour was now black from the smeech of the engines. Occasionally somebody was sent down there with a deck broom and a bucket of diesel to give it a scrub out – another choice job. The deck head had never been painted and from it, foot-long fronds of black pluffy wood used to dangled down, brushing your hat as you moved about. These fronds were caused by sea water soaking through the deck over the years and being crystallised by the heat of the engines, the expanding salt pushing the wood fibres apart, then to hang down like soggy rope ends. To cure this problem we nailed strips of hardboard up over the worst areas.

One summer the exhaust pipe on the '30' cracked and, as the weather was fine, the boat continued working 24 hours a day so there was no time to fix it until the weather turned. Meantime, to stop the forward engines the hatch was first lifted to allow billows of hot brown exhaust smoke to escape, then down the ladder you went, taking a deep breath of fresh air that hopefully would last you until you emerged again. It was like descending into a small compact version of hell: you couldn't see anything, the noise of the engine was deafening, there was nothing to breath and the heat had the sweat pouring off you in seconds. Groping through the oven hot blackness, the throttles were first eased back then the engines were knocked out of gear, next the engine stop levers were held back allowing the fly wheels to slow to a leisurely halt. By that time you were turning purple and spluttering on the fumes, going for the hatch and fresh air as if your life depended on it, which I suppose it did. We were more than pleased when that exhaust was eventually repaired. There were no fire extinguishers, sprinkler systems or safety equipment of any kind in the engine room, only an assortment of ancient spanners kept in a wooden box lodged behind the ladder which, because of its location, was usually full of water.

The '45', being the newest and most-used engine, was treated to 5 gallons of new oil every year; the '30' got the old oil from the '45', while the poor old '21' had to make do with the two-year-old stuff from the '30'. Getting rid of the stinking dregs from the '21' was not a problem, it was simply drained straight down into the bilge.

By the season of 1967 the '21' needed so much 'easy start' to get it going that the two men winding the handle were nearly rendered unconscious. Eventually it was abandoned on its bed, never to run again. With the 45 HP Lister back in good running order it was back to business. The fleet had been catching plenty of fish, not only in Looe but in Mevagissey and Newlyn. This was more than the cannery could handle, so we were put on a limit of 120 stone per boat. Unfortunately, you can't regulate how much fish goes into a drift net; you can shorten up the number of nets you work, shoot, then haul more or less straight away, but when the pilchard shoals are running you are going to catch them. And so we did, coming into harbour with the decks loaded, scooping up 25 five stone cans for the lorry, then shovelling the rest over the side. It was a heartbreaking and wasteful thing to have to do. The five Looe drifters carpeted the bottom of the harbour with unwanted pilchards, slocking in hundreds of bass and mullet for a free meal.

Coming in from sea one morning in late October, we landed the catch and the last drums of diesel were tipped in the fuel tanks. It was time for a refill. We were working out the last of the pilchard season, the wind had been south-westerly for several days, not blowing hard enough to keep us in from sea, but enough to make life wet and uncomfortable and never able to get out of our oilskins. All the rest of the empty drums were brought out from the store and loaded on deck, and Jack Harris and I were the lucky pair to go with the skipper on the run to Plymouth.

Diesel in those days was 1/3d (7p) a gallon and the local marine engineer, Ken Newton, and his son Robert would bring it to the boats in 5-gallon drums on their hand cart. However, the depot at Plymouth sold it for 1/- (5p) per gallon for a minimum order of 300 gallons, so Moogie had 60 or more 5-gallon drums kept in a ground level store, and when they were empty all hands would load up the *Iris*'s decks and he and a couple of the crew would steam to Plymouth for a refill. The amazing thing about these drums was that originally they had held treacle, and great dollops of the stuff used to fall into the funnel when we were pouring fuel, but this extra in their diet never seemed to worry the engines.

We rolled away up to Plymouth Sound in a lumpy sea and drizzle rain, made fast along side the jetty in the Cattewater where a big hose was passed down and fuelling up began. Filling 5-gallon drums from a hose designed to refuel coasters was a ticklish task, but eventually the last drum was topped up and we were on our way for home. Bashing around Penlee Point the old *Iris* was throwing back the spray and Jack and I were sheltering behind the wheelhouse with a mug of tea in our hands when suddenly I remembered the date. "It's my birthday today," I mentioned to Jack. "How old now then?" he asked. "Seventeen," I said. "Happy birthday," was the reply, and we chinked our tea mugs together.

Arriving back in Looe, all hands stowed the diesel drums back into the store, and away we went again for another wet rolly night at sea. Happy birthday indeed.

12

Working Big Shoals

A big shoal (or 'scull' as it was called) of pilchards would give its presence away no matter how deep it was swimming. The first sign looked for was the black water: whether the fish turned the water black themselves, or the plankton they fed on had that effect, I don't know, but either way pilchard water looked as black as pitch. The next sign would be very fine, light hints of fish oil coming to the surface from the underlying shoal. Downwind we could smell it from a fair distance away. Feeding off this oil would be the stormy petrels, 'Mother Carey's chickens' was the fishermen's name for them. These little birds looked like swallows with tiny hooked beaks and webbed feet, flying low over the surface of the sea, tiny feet tip-tipping the water, their heads bobbing up and down dipping up droplets of fish oil. Keeping them company would be the guillemots, scattered around above the shoals in twos and threes. These sharp-beaked, black-brown birds about the size of a small duck are the champion deep divers of the sea bird world, able to swim down as deep as 30 or 40 fathoms to feed off a shoal of fish.

If there were no sharks, whales or dolphins harassing the shoal, then the fish would stay down deep, it being too dangerous for them to come near the surface in daylight. The drifters would shoot their nets above these deep-laying shoals and as darkness crept into the water so the fish would rise up under the safety of its cover to feed on the plankton, (their natural predators can't see to operate at night), only to run into miles of drift nets laying in wait.

If a large shoal of fish was being harassed by something a little more serious than guillemots and Mother Carey's chickens, then we would witness the most amazing drama. When the big predators go into action they drive the fish up towards the surface, and as soon as they rise to within reach of the gannets and gulls, a feeding frenzy of near unbelievable noise and magnitude takes place. Gannets, so numerous that you just couldn't begin to guess at their numbers, circle up in the sky over the fish, then suddenly go into a vertical crash dive, wings folded, powering into the sea like aquatic fighter planes. They utter a deep harsh quack, quack, quack noise just before hitting the water, making a crisp thudding sound when they do so. 30 or 40 feet is about as deep as they go before bursting back up to the surface with more harsh quacking, flapping vigorously up into the air, rapidly gaining altitude to repeat the process. It's truly baffling how the hundreds diving down don't get tangled up with those climbing back up and how those circling above pick their moment to dive. They display a degree of precision and skill that makes the best human aviators look utterly ham-fisted.

Add to this, myriads of herring gulls screaming, squawking, fighting and scrounging for anything they can get hold of, regardless of who caught it first. Any bird with a fish in its beak gets unmercifully mobbed until it either swallows it, or is robbed. Gulls can't dive, but they do try if the fish are driven right to the surface. From a height of 40 feet or so they fold one wing and hurtle down broadside at the water, hitting it with a splash, instantly bobbing to the surface again, having gone down all of 6 inches. A useless pursuit, at the wrong angle and depth, but they must think it will come good one day. While all this mayhem is going on the real pirate of the air, the skua, (or the 'Tom Harry Shit Bird' as it's known in Looe) is swooping about awaiting its chance. The 'Tom Harry' is about the size of a gull, but leaner, meaner and much more streamlined with brown-black plumage. They live on fish but never catch any of their own. Instead they wait for a gull with a full crop to take to the air, they then chivvy and panic their victim until it throws up its catch in order to escape this unwanted attention. With the gull's dinner now plunging seaward, the 'Tom Harry' crash dives to catch his ill gotten gains in mid air, as smart and as neat as can be. A bastard of a bird but you have got to admire them.

The drifters from Looe and the luggers *Erin*, *Lindy Lou* and *Snowdrop* from Mevagissey would be motoring about with their echo sounders operating, trying to get an idea of how extensive the shoal was and in which direction it was moving. All the while, the squawking and screaming of thousands of over-excited seabirds is nearly enough to drive you insane, you feel as if your brain is going to come loose on its holding bolts. But as the sun drops low and the light gradually goes out of the water, the daytime predators pack up and all goes quiet once more. We are the night watch, it's our turn to have a go now. "God speed the plough," says Moogie as the pole end buoy goes over the side, then we're off downwind with the buoys and buffs splashing overboard, the shooting roller chattering away to itself. We shan't ride to the gear for too long tonight; we could be in for a hard haul.

Heavy fishing meant hours of hauling and dragging which, in turn, led to sea-boils and poisoned hands. The sleeves of your oilskins would chafe your wrists raw, rubbing in all sorts of muck as it did so. Pretty soon you would end up with a ring of yellow-headed sea-boils each about a quarter of an inch across, and they stung like hell. To relieve the pain you rolled your oilskin sleeves up a bit to get clear of them, then a second ring would appear and again you would roll your sleeves up to a third position. By the time boils appeared there, the first lot had healed a bit so down went the sleeves, and it started all over again. After hauling for an hour or so the pain wore off a fair bit, and so if you didn't look you wouldn't notice that your oilskin sleeve was chafing them to a patch of raw flesh which was bleeding steadily. When your wrists got really horrible, bandages were tried, but wet bandages don't stay in place for very long. The forearms of a drifter-man were always a mass of sea-boil scars.

Because you were twisting and flipping fish out of the nets all the time, your fingers and palms of the hand went black from hundreds of tiny fish bones embedded in the skin. The short fine bones were no problem, it was the longer ones piercing into the flesh that caused the trouble. The end result was puss-swollen fingers and the backs of the hands red and puffy. Saturday was poisoned-finger day; you sharpened your penknife and squeezed the offending digit to find where the poison lay closest to the skin, then lanced it. If you couldn't face doing it yourself, you got somebody else to lance it while you looked away.

But the fish that really tore our hands to ribbons were scads (horse mackerel), totally armoured up with razor sharp spikes and prickles. After picking a yaffle of them out of the nets it was agony to even catch hold of the mooring ropes to tie the boat up in the harbour.

Some men really suffered, getting a red line up their arm and a lump under the armpit. When that happened it was time to see the doctor. Trying to think of ways to lessen the pain, I once bought a pair rubber gloves, the sort used for housework and washing up. We started the haul that night, me with my bright yellow hands, delighted with myself, poisoned fingers, cuts and sea boils all protected. What a relief. The only drawback was that it was going to take a while to get up to speed shaking out the fish while wearing them. Moogie meanwhile (before the muck off the nets fogged his glasses right over) had his eye on me, and it wasn't long before I heard him say, "Greenwood, get those fucking gloves off," and that was it, back to the agony.

Another real bastard was the twine of the nets cutting your finger joints open. 'Sea c**ts' they were known as and, like all the other things that plagued us, there was no chance of them healing up until the weather turned poor and we had a few days in from sea. Cuts took a very long time to heal because they were opened up every night as the nets tore the scab off. When the fishing was heavy we all suffered these things, but you had to grin and bear it because the share out would be good on Saturday morning. That summer the money fell well short of the pain, however, because of the quota. It was only the sharking that made our money up.

Our bookings for sharking used to be done through Jack Bray's tackle shop, but he eventually became so exasperated with the luggers that he refused to have them on his books any more, and we all moved to Frank Hoskin's tackle shop further up the quay. This was the same chap that operated the barking boiler. The biggest problem arose when the pilchard catches were big. There, alongside the quay, shaking out their nets would be the four luggers and there was no chance they would they be finished in time to take out the anglers Frank had booked for them. He would be in his shop surrounded by 48 irate and disappointed people on a lovely summer morning, their flasks and sandwiches packed but their day out has just been cancelled. Frank must have been able to talk faster than a Philadelphia lawyer to smooth down the ruffled feathers of a mob of that size.

We came in from sea one morning ahead of a rising south-west gale. This time the catch was small and was soon put ashore, and it was Moogie and Jack's turn that day to take the boat out sharking. So just before nine o'clock our skipper jaunts into the tackle shop only to be told that because of the weather everybody has cancelled their trip. Frank was curtly informed that everybody had not cancelled their trip, and he was to round up a dozen hard asses because the *Iris* was going to sea. And go they did. The weather was atrocious, so bad in fact that Moogie and Jack had to shoot a couple of nets to ride to as a sea anchor. Meanwhile ashore, the other sharking skippers were fizzing with indignation that anyone should take visitors out in near life-threatening conditions. They were going to report the *Iris* to whatever higher authority they thought might take action in such cases and when, indeed if, he got ashore they were going to tell Moogie exactly what they thought of his greed for gold, etc. Just before six that evening the *Iris* arrived back in harbour safe and sound, and not a word was said or any action taken. Moogie may have done wrong to take people out in such weather, but none dared tell him so to his face. Mind you, the anglers he took out that day probably holidayed for the rest of their lives in the Yorkshire Dales after that experience. Thankfully we didn't go to sea that night.

Many of the nights spent out drifting were no fun at all, but at other times it was nothing short of enchanting. Still calm nights that were totally silent, a big moon turning the sea to silver, with the fish shining in the nets, deep down in the clear dark water. Clear moonless nights, the sky studded with countless stars and the nets aglow with millions of tiny bright green jewels, flashing and sparkling as we hauled them. These 'jewels' were a form of luminous plankton that the drifter men called 'briming', and it was these tiny sea creatures that helped us to locate the shoals of pilchards.

A typical briming night would see the boat held back off the nets by a gentle breeze, the pawl on the rail roller rattling away as the head-rope and rail man haul steadily on the gear. Fish are scarce, just a few here and there along the bottom of the nets. The stower unbuttons the odd scad or mackerel from the meshes, mutters "Up, up," while the rail man shouts, "Ahead five," for a five-second burst on the engine to keep the boat up to the gear. The night is very dark and our world seems to extend only as far as the working lights could penetrate into the blackness. Seagulls paddle around the boat hoping to snatch a feed, but there is precious little to be had, so even they are quiet; others on the wing enter our world from the darkness like ghosts. After 4 or 5 hours hauling, the smell of hot paraffin from the hurricane lamp on the dann marking the end of the fleet of nets wafts downwind. We will soon be 'all in'. With the last, or pole end, net stowed down the net room, the skipper glances around the deck. We have caught about 70 stone of fish, hardly enough to make a wage but enough to make him think there might be more about if we look around for them. There was still time, with dawn several hours away yet. So as the cook stirs up the fire to brew a pot of tea we drop the mizzen peak, the rail roller is unshipped and the shooting roller shipped up. Moogie shoves the aft engine into gear and opens up the throttle, all lights including the 'nav' lights are switched off. The echo sounder in the wheelhouse, sparking away as the rotor scorches its trace onto the paper, is now the only glow of light aboard. Two men go forward to the luff of each bow to kneel on the deck, then lean on the rail to stare down into the dark water.

The old lugger bullies her way through the sea, disturbing the plankton, turning the bow wave and wake into bright green fire. Down in the water the noise of the boat scares any fish we pass over and they would panic off out of our way, activating the plankton as they go. A shark clearly outlined makes haste to clear us, mackerel dart away like miniature torpedoes, a small shoal of herrings bunches up close and dives for safety, appearing to roll as they do so. Our quarry, the pilchards, burst away in all directions looking like an under water firework display. On seeing this, the men at the bow give the skipper a shout, who confirms this sighting with the marks on the sounder paper. For a while we box around the area locating the pilchard shoals. Eventually the skipper decides it's worth shooting the nets again so around before the wind we come, the bearings of the shooting roller start to clatter as half of the fleet of nets go over the side again. Then it's hard to starboard on the wheel, and hoist up the mizzen peak, the net is dragged forward and we ride from a mooring rope made fast around it with a rolling hitch. For an hour or so we lay to the gear, the eastern sky going from black to dark grey; the night is ending and it is time to haul away again. If justice is done, another 40 or 60 stone is added to the catch, which means we have at least secured a small wage as a reward for our night's toil.

When working the drift nets, the hardest hauls we experienced were either in a dead flat calm, or a gale. In moderate weather, the motion of the boat helped us to haul the gear. As she rose on a sea, you would lay back on the net, and when she dropped away again you hauled in the slack it created. 'Let the boat do the work' was the motto. But the combination of a flat, windless sea and a spring tide guaranteed hard louster. We would be ready to shoot the nets, but in which direction? There would be nothing obvious to go by. "Put a bit more coal on the fire, Harry," says Moogie, hoping the resulting smoke would give a clue to a likely wind direction. No such luck, the smoke drifts skywards undisturbed. Now it was all guess work, maybe a breeze would make off from the land when the sun goes down.

A decision is made and we shoot away to the south. With the last net over the side, we come around on the swing rope and still not a breath of wind. With neither wind nor waves to make the boat pull back on the gear, the tide starts to carry the nets into big bights and whorls. This is bad news. After a quick supper the skipper decides to start the haul before things got any worse. We go to work and before you know it, the nets are leading across the bow to port. Tiddler turns the head-ropes around the aft kevel (cleat) and grinds astern on the engine. After a while we come clear of the gear and start to haul away again. There is no movement in the water to help, so it's a dead haul, the rail man and the second hand on the skirt are sweating like bulls. We haul away for a net or two and things go fairly well, then they are leading down the port side again, so the roller has to be shipped up on that side and the next few nets are hauled from there. All change, and the nets are looking away from the starboard side, and it's back to working from there again. Sometimes you could have the nets right around the boat, in which case the engine was stopped for fear of wrapping the prop up. A sweep (big oar) was then shipped up on the starboard quarter, and a man had to row the lugger to her gear. It could be a long, tedious, fathom by fathom haul, and by the time the pole end buoy came over the rail we had nearly melted into our boots.

The exact opposite of that was a haul in a gale of wind. We didn't get caught out in those conditions very often because there is very little to be gained trying to work drift nets in really bad weather. The nets go up and down with the waves, making their presence known to the fish and warning them off, plus a lot of damage can be done when hauling fine cotton nets in poor weather. But anyone who goes fishing, no matter how experienced they may be, will get caught out occasionally.

It's late on a summer afternoon, and the wind is fresh south-west with an angry looking sky. The shipping forecast gives better weather coming in, so this was reckoned to be the last of it. The drifters are tied along side the quay, their cabin fires lit and chimneys belching thick, yellow coal smoke. The crew men are stood around yarning, waiting to know if they are going to sea that night, but nobody is very keen; in fact most of them seemed quite intent on going home or to the pub. But the decision is taken by the skippers who were at that very moment in a huddle discussing the situation as the tide was ebbing. All of a sudden the knot of skippers splits apart, each man striding towards his boat, waving and shouting to their respective crews, by now scattered up and down the harbour: "Come on, get her ready, lets go and have a look at it," is the shout.

Many of the men aren't very happy with the decision at all. "What the fuck do they want to go out on a night like this for?" says one. "I went out the sea front, and it's looking bloody awful," says another. "Better be tied to a bull's arse and shit to death," comments another. Despite all the grumbling, the boats are quickly made ready for sea, steaming out of the harbour before the ebb tide strands them. Once out clear of the shelter of the bay there's a lot of sea running, backed up by a fresh breeze: in fact, if there was water to get back into the harbour most would have returned. But as we had scraped out on the last of the tide, there's no chance of doing that, so on we go. Perhaps the wind will decrease as the sun goes down?

Steep angry seas smack the side of the boat sending spray sweeping across the deck and all hands are dressed in oilskins, sea-boots, sou'westers and mufflers. The skipper at the wheel tries not to bury the boats head as we plunge along. All of a sudden a shout goes up: "There they are, down towards the Dodman, going down like spikes!" Somebody has seen the gannets working a shoal of fish, so we're off to investigate. Sure enough, as we approached the gannets are going crazy and there are good marks on the sounder, but are they pilchards? The gannets might have been diving on sprats or mackerel. There was one way to find out.

A gannet will swallow fish until it is too heavy to fly, then along with others in the same condition, they sit on the water paddling gently about until the meal is digested. If they have to fly, they spew up their fish to lighten themselves enough to take off, and that is when we would take advantage of them. Spying a bunch of gannets on the water, the skipper headed the boat right for them, all hands on the foredeck and as we approach the birds everyone starts screaming and shouting and waving their hats in the air. That does it; panic ensues and the birds spew up to make their escape, leaving their hard-won meal slowly sinking away. Bad news for the gannets, good news for us … it's pilchards.

Moogie boxes about for a while before picking his spot. Then downwind we go, the old lugger surging on the waves while the nets are flung over the side, the shooter's arms going like pistons, buoys and buffs splashing down astern of us. Riding to the gear we have a bite of supper while watching an angry looking sunset. The wind shows no sign of dropping, in fact it seems to be doing just the opposite. As soon as it gets dark the haul begins, the engine is hardly ever out of gear driving the boat up to the nets. She rises on a sea, we lay back hard on the net, then she swoops down the back of it and we haul like mad. Up she rises on the next one, and we lay back again.

The wind freshens and the seas are getting bigger. By now the aft engine throttle can't be opened up any more for fear of damaging the gearbox when working the gear leaver. So two of us nip down forward and crank up the 30 HP, the gear leaver for which comes out by the shaking boards so the stower could operate it. Away we go again, the 30 HP keeps her up to the weather, while the aft engine pushes her ahead when needed, and it's back to the routine. Up on a sea she rises. Hang on tight. There's a crash as a breaking sea bursts around us, then we slide down the back of it, bundling the net aboard while it's easy to get. The next few waves aren't so bad; the 30 HP is out of gear and we push ahead on the 45 HP, then it's ahead again on both engines as a monster sea rears up and the man out the rail yells, "Let go!" Everyone drops the net and hangs on and, despite the best efforts of both engines, the boat surfs off stern first on the wave, with the hard-won net whipping back out over the roller. The big sea roars past us, and the hauling resumes. There is no respite and, for however long it takes to gain the fleet of nets, the crew keep battling, 6 or 7 hours non-stop, maybe longer if there is any weight of fish to be shaken out. All our strength and endurance are needed on such a night. But the drifter crews had plenty of that, and combined with pure dogged persistence the pole end buoy would eventually come over the roller.

The skipper then dodges the boat head to wind, the catch is scooped into boxes and lashed down, any left over is shovelled down into the fish room, the hatches shipped up and the mizzen stowed. When all is made ready, the skipper brings her around to shape a course for home. By the time the night is over and we eventually get home to bed, I feel as if I've gone ten rounds with a heavyweight boxer.

12A

Superstitions

When I first went to sea, there were old retired fishermen on the quay who remembered what life was like when they were boys at sea as far back as the 1890s. But in all their accounts of gales and hard times, none of them could recall any disasters happening to the Looe luggers. It used to be said that "God has got Looe under his wing" and I think that must have been true.

Regardless of their good record, if today's safety standards were applied to the boats of 40 years ago, none of them would be allowed to cross the harbour, let alone fight a gale, long lining 60 miles out in the Channel. One cursory inspection would have been enough to give an M.C.A surveyor apoplexy. Yet go they did, for generations, and in many cases, much further than our modern fleet goes today. But despite all today's emphasis on safety, there have been many more casualties and sinkings in the modern fleet over the past 30 years than ever there was in a century of the old fleet. So what has gone wrong? I think anybody in commercial fishing will have his own theory on that.

One thing that was rife then, and hardly exists today, was superstition. There was loads of it and it was all taken very seriously. The foremost being never to mention the word r*bb*t; for some reason they were considered to be the most unlucky of animals. Skippers have turned their boats back to harbour and tied up rather than continue at sea after that word had been mentioned.

If a net room hatch was turned upside down while being unshipped, it had to be put back the right way up immediately, spat on, and then spun around three times with the sun to undo the bad luck. After the nets were shot, the chances of a good catch could be greatly increased by throwing a coin over the side to 'buy some off Neptune'. Whistling was not allowed, for fear of whistling up the wind. Green was an unlucky colour, so no green hats, jumpers, tea mugs or even socks, nothing green at all ever. Vicars and ginger-haired or squinty-eyed women seen before going to sea were also looked upon as a bad omen. Sailors and fishermen consider the sight of a clergyman on the quay or standing near their boats very unlucky. Many will refuse to sail in the face of such an ill omen and will try to lead the minister away from the boats. Several years ago an old Polperro fisherman, Edmund Curtis, was alarmed to see a new minister to the parish had strolled innocently down to the quay to have a look round. Horrified at the thought of all the bad luck that would follow, he firmly led the minister off the quay and down Lansallos Street before he considered the danger over, politely advising the man not to return!

In some ports it is considered a bad omen to say the word 'church' or 'chapel' while at sea. I once heard about a debate on religion that once took place in the cabin of the Looe lugger *Our Daddy*. Alfred John Pengelly, the skipper, was a staunch teetotaller, a gentleman in the true sense of the word and a devout Christian. Alfred's uncle, Dorman Pengelly, was one of his crew, a curmudgeonly old chap who was rather inclined to say what he thought, when he thought it and to hell with anyone who disagreed. One fine evening when the *Our Daddy* was riding to her nets and all hands were below in the cabin having a bite of supper and a mug of tea, the topic of conversation that evening touched on religion. By all accounts it got a bit heated. Dorman had not said a word until there was a momentary silence and he had a chance to air his own views on the subject.

"Anyway, when I die I want to be buried face down," was his opening line.

"Why's that then, Uncle Dorman?" said Alfred John in all innocence.

"So as the good Lord can kiss my arse," came the reply, to stunned silence from the rest of the crew. I rather think at that moment they were expecting a bolt of lightening to come through the deck striking him dead where he sat. Fortunately for Dorman, God didn't hear or chose to overlook this little outburst and he went on to live to a ripe old age, dropping dead on the quay one day while on his way to inspect a new wheelhouse being bolted down on the *Daddy*'s deck. And as far as I know he didn't get his burial request.

A superstition at Plymouth has it that if two or more things happen to go wrong while you are getting the boat ready for sea, that was it, your luck was out and you had better stay in and try again the next day. Veteran fisherman Bill Cowan related a yarn to me that took place just after he had been demobbed from the navy at the end of the last war. Bill was fishing with his uncle on the Polperro gaffer *Vilona May* working out of the Plymouth Barbican. Getting ready to go to sea one evening they had one hell of a struggle to get the engine started only to see the bow rope foul up on everything possible when it was let go. When finally they put to sea and were trying to set a bit of sail to help the old *Vilona* along, the mizzen sheet wrapped itself solidly around the outrigger. "That's it," said Bill's uncle Alfie. "We've had the warnings, our luck's out and we're going back." With that he put the tiller hard over and turned for home. Bill was wild at Alfie's decision; another nights work lost, but there was no arguing so back they went.

Back in the days when seagoing was very much a male preserve, it was considered in some ports to be a bad omen if a woman set foot aboard a boat. I rather think money cured that one however. With the growth of tourism and pleasure boating, no boatman was going to turn away a booking because the wives and girlfriends wanted to come along too. There are also many accounts of wives and daughters sailing on the ketches and schooners that traded around the coast, and I have only heard stories of how good they were, pully-hauling on deck, taking a turn at the wheel, even doing the navigation. As for cooking aboard ship, I do believe that was a male preserve. Certainly nowadays if some macho sailor or yachtie trotted out any slack-mouthed banality about women being bad luck on boats I rather imagine he would find himself going cross-eyed with agony as his knees buckled towards the deck after an indignant female foot had made firm contact with his trousers.

Going to sea in the fishing trade to earn a living is a dangerous occupation and anyone who has spent any length of time at it has had friends and acquaintances who never arrived back in harbour to land the catch that they had been so earnestly hunting. And all fishermen are well aware that every time they go fishing they are as likely as any of those that went before them to join the casualty list of men lost to Neptune. They just hope and pray that no matter how dreadful the weather they get caught out in, or

how ever hair-raising and perilous the accidents that can befall a fishing
vessel at sea, they will always arrive back in their home port safe, if not
always sound. And thanks to long experience, good seamanship and many
a silent prayer, all but a very unfortunate few do just that, trip after trip,
summer and winter, year in year out.

Some boats can be unlucky, if not downright cursed, no matter who is
running them or how well they are looked after. Engine trouble, electrical
problems, leaks, gear loss, towed in yet again with the prop wrapped up,
with them the bad luck never ends. Two such vessels spring to mind, the
Sparfell and the *Golden Dawn*. They broke the hearts and bank balances of
all the skippers who tried to earn a living with them.

Whenever and wherever folk face danger and take risks earning a living
on a regular basis, superstitions abound. Last of all there is the number that
comes between twelve and fourteen, as bad as those animals with the floppy
ears and bobtails, so I shall say no more on the subject.

*

At the end of the 1965 pilchard season the herring nets were once more
barked up and stowed aboard and, once again in the company of the *Our
Boys*, we headed around Start Point for Brixham. Jack Moore had gone
ashore for the winter, jowting fish around the town from our old net cart. It
was the same story as the year before, shooting and hauling around Torbay
and Babbacombe, mostly for very little, but persistence seemed to be the
answer because we always ended up with a modest wage at the end of the
week. One night we caught a few stone of pilchards, just enough to bait up
the baskets of line that we carried, so Moogie shaped a course up across
Lyme Bay to Portland Bill where we shot the lines off Chesil Beach to catch
rays. Weather wise it was a fine, clear starry sky with a light offshore wind,
but it was bitterly cold. The lines were freezing in the baskets, and we were
dipping up buckets of seawater to throw on the lines and to warm our
hands in. Nevertheless all went according to plan and we had a good catch
of fish, landing it at Brixham fish market the following day.

Brixham was like all the other fishing ports around the south west at that
time, 'out on the bones of its arse'. Its fleet of trawlers was made up of a

number of ex-admiralty MFVs, a few old Belgian trawlers that had come over with refugees during the war, one or two ancient motorised sailing smacks and other ageing tonnage, all rigged as sidewinders. Our interest in them extended only as far as their coal lockers, situated on deck behind the wheelhouse. In the darkness of an early morning, we would come quietly chuffing in on one engine and, going along side two or three of these trawlers, we would 'borrow' a bucket or so of coal from each of them.

One particular morning we were hitched up alongside a brand new trawler called the *Spartacus*, a pretty little craft, paintwork shining and everything in tip top order, a very rare thing in those days. On her deck were several large lumps of steam coal that had been trawled up with the catch the day before. No-one was about and the temptation proved too much for Moogie. "Quick boy, nip aboard and pass them over," I was instructed. In no time at all those fine great lumps of coal were cracked up and in our locker. About an hour later the skipper of the Spartacus was aboard with a sack in his hand, muttering and cursing.

"What's up?" Moogie shouts across.

"Well," says the skipper, "I had some nice nubs of coal on deck that I was going to crack up and take up to mother, but some bastard's had them away."

"You can't trust any bugger nowadays," said Moogie. "Anyway, Harry has just made a pot of tea. Come down in to the cabin and join us for one."

"I don't mind if I do," said the skipper climbing aboard, trying to dodge the smoke swirling around our decks. It was an economical, but not a very honest way to keep the cabin stove burning (my apologies to any Brixham men reading this).

One Friday afternoon, a fresh wind was blowing right into the bay making it much to poor to go to sea. So we had fish and chips for our tea, then the five-men-and-a-bucket ablutions were performed, ready for a run ashore. Jack and I, fed up with the charms of Brixham, caught a bus to Paignton a few miles up the coast and spent the evening rambling around there for a change.

Returning to Brixham well after pub closing time, we climbed down aboard the boat and turned in, merry and well pleased with our night's adventures. Moogie and Harry were already in their bunks, but there was no sign of Tiddler. This was a very good thing, because if you could get to sleep before him you had a night's rest; if not, you were doomed because he snored fit to rattle the deck planks.

We were just dozing off when the man himself clambered back aboard and stumbled down into the cabin, well pissed. There was much muttering and grunting as his jacket and shoes were taken off prior to climbing into his bunk, then he decided that he needed a piddle, so up on deck he went to ease his bladder. Once relieved, there was more muttering then he started to shout and bawl that the wind had died down, the stars were shining and we really ought to be putting to sea. Harry got out of his bunk and stood in the companionway trying to coax him to come down and turn in, but he would have none of it.

"Come on, Moogie, are you afraid to go to sea or something?" he bawled loudly.

"Now, now, Tiddler, be a good boy and come and turn in," cajoles Harry.

"Turn in be buggered," says Tiddler. "There's twenty stone of herrings up in the bay for us tonight, I can feel it in my water."

"Stop being such an old twat, and let's get some sleep," shouts Jack from the depth of his bunk.

"Come on, Moogie, let's get going," came the beer-soaked retort from up on deck.

This went on for about ten minutes, and all the while the skipper lay in his bunk not saying a word, but his pride would only stand so much goading no matter who was doing it, drunk or sober. Suddenly he was out of his bunk and starting up the aft engine and, to quote the old Looe shipwright, Arthur Collins, "Our hearts sank that far, you could have scooped them out of our backsides with a spoon." Away we went to sea, it must have been about one o'clock in the morning and we were all several pints the worse for wear. Of course the *Our Boys* wouldn't be left behind so out they came as well. Steaming around the breakwater, we shipped a big sea. I was forward coiling down ropes, and got soaked. Tiddler meanwhile had gone down forward to put on his oilskins, and was emerging again on deck just as the boat took it into her head to fall off a sea (she was an old cow for those sort of tricks). Tiddler, in his beer-soaked state, lost control and came hurtling aft, plunging onto the shaking boards, one of which promptly unshipped, and with a squawk he disappeared from view. Moogie ducked out of the wheelhouse to see what had happened to him. On finding the great beer drinker down in the fish box unharmed, the skipper told him in no uncertain terms to stay where he was. Loud honking snores soon started to issue from that part of the boat.

We shot and hauled the nets twice that night and came back into harbour on Saturday morning with a miserable three stone of herrings, having suffered a cold, wet, rolling night. To add to the misery, Jack and I had been feeling very cruddy due to the stale beer sloshing around our stomachs. Tiddler meanwhile was keeping a very low profile. One word from him and we would have throttled him, that is if the crew of the *Our Boys* hadn't beaten us to it.

While waiting for Skips to arrive in his car, we decided to treat ourselves to breakfast of scrambled eggs up at the café. We were served up a ghastly, greenish-yellow slime on flaccid toast, ideal for the way we were feeling. While trying to eat it, I happened to mention just how bad we were going to feel on the ride home. Jack heaved and very nearly lost what he had so far managed to stuff down his neck. We were not a very cheerful bunch that morning. The ride home with Skips exceeded all expectations for car sickness; twice before reaching Looe he had to pull over to let us all have a stomp around in the fresh air. Home never, ever seemed so inviting.

Returning to Brixham on Monday afternoon, we shot and hauled for another week. Thus we continued, trying to scratch a living, until the boats were steamed home for the Christmas break. Once the Christmas and New Year celebrations were over, we awaited some decent weather to allow us to return to Brixham and resume our herring drifting. It was now early January 1966 and the weather, as always at that time of year, had been boisterous to say the least. South-west gales sweeping in from the Atlantic were building up a massive swell ending in a screaming nor'westerly wind as the depression passed over, only to be followed by the next one shouldering its way in from somewhere west of Ireland. But eventually a winter anticyclone started to build and we bundled our bags down into the cabin and made the *Iris* ready for sea. A lovely winter's morning greeted us, the sky dark blue with a brassy sun shining low in the sky and, at last, a tranquil sea under a light offshore breeze. Torbay was once more our destination, but the trip was broken by a stop off at the trawling grounds south of Plymouth known as 'sleepy valley' to try for some mackerel. We had heard rumours of the Plymouth boats catching big mackerel in their trawls and so we made up a twelve-hook feather line apiece to see if we too could catch some. A couple of boxes of mackerel would be a nice boost to our herrings on Brixham market the next day.

On reaching the 'sleepy valley' grounds, the skipper proceeded to motor slowly about with the echo sounder running, looking for any signs of fish. He didn't see very much, but there were some tiny marks close to the bottom, so he stopped while we gave them a try with the lines and, much to our surprise and delight, we hauled aboard some fine big mackerel. Every time we drifted off the mark, Moogie would steam slowly about until he located it again, then with the prop thrashing hard astern to stop the boat, it was away lines again, and we would soon be hauling up a fine big fish on every hook. They were so voracious, some were even dragged aboard having swallowed the lead. All day we carried on fishing in this manner and by late that afternoon 100 stone of jumbo mackerel were boxed up on deck. Moogie now decided to land our catch back at Looe and try our luck out there again the next day. Torbay could wait a while. Little did we know that the herring nets were never going to be shot again.

For the next three or four days the weather held fine, and we landed a nice catch of fish each day. Come Saturday, when the money was shared out, we were very pleased with our efforts. The fish merchants had paid us £1 a stone for our mackerel, big money compared with the 3/6d we had been getting for pilchards and 6/ for herrings.

News of our success had got around, and the crews of the *Our Boys* and the *Our Daddy* also made up hand lines and joined us at sea on the next fine day. Nobody was disappointed, everyone caught prime mackerel that made top money on the market. Never had fishing been so easy or so lucrative. No shooting miles of nets or lines, nor battling for hours on end in poor weather to get the gear aboard before we could run for home. Every man simply worked a twelve-hook feather line with a 1lb lead on the end and if the weather came on too poor, it took only minuets to wind the lines back on to their wooden squares and we were ready to head for home. It was truly a revelation and, in the famous words of Harold Macmillan, 'we had never had it so good'. No one knew it then, but the beginning of one of the biggest revivals that the Cornish fishing industry had ever known was under way. But by mid-March the mackerel shoals had deserted us so it was back once more to hard labour, out in the Channel with the long lines, a world away from mackerel catching.

Our old shipmate Clarence Libby died that spring. One night he was very poorly indeed and had to leave his place on the nets. He looked dreadful, yet wouldn't go down below and lie in his bunk, insisting instead on staying in the wheelhouse, working the wheel and engine lever. When we got back into harbour he went straight home, and I never saw him again. All of us on the *Iris* attended his funeral, decked in our best sea jumpers and dark trousers, and as Clarence was originally a Polperro man he was buried in the cemetery at the top of the hill above that village. We stood with his family and friends, bare headed at the graveside, trying to blink back the tears as his coffin was lowered down. Harry gave up that struggle and just stared ahead with the tears rolling down his cheeks. A good man had passed on, and we were going to miss him a great deal.

A couple of days later we were once more out in the Channel, shooting away the lines on the 'Klondike' ground with big grey seas rolling and the gulls wheeling around us. There's a saying that when a fisherman dies he comes back as a gull, so just maybe our old shipmate was swooping by, keeping his eye on us. It's a lovely thought, returning as a gull, providing of course that you managed to keep clear of Andy on the *Endeavour*.

14

Fog

Being caught out at sea in gales of wind, battling to retrieve the nets and lines, and fighting the weather for hours to get home to port could give us some very anxious times and were exceedingly uncomfortable to say the least, but the weather we most dreaded in those days was fog.

To the fishermen of today, fog is no big deal. Radar reveals what shipping is about and where it is. A GPS linked to a track plotter shows on screen a chart of the coast and your position to within 10 feet. Take the cursor and draw a line (clear of all obstacles) from your position to your home port and steer along it, and you arrive back safe and sound. It's all good stuff, and nobody should be without it. So unless the man at the wheel makes a real hash of it, the dangers and inconveniences of fog are minimal.

The navigation methods in the 1960s were exactly the same as the 1860s, only in fog it was probably more dangerous for us because of the steamers. When putting to sea the skipper always noted the time that we cleared Looe bay, the course steered and for how long. While working the gear, if the land was visible, the compass course for home was checked regularly in case fog did close in. If the land could not be seen, the drift from wind and tide had to be estimated so that a fairly accurate course for home could be picked off. In reasonable weather conditions, any deviation could be corrected when land came in to view, or the loom of the Eddystone or Start lighthouse was sighted.

But when fog really closed in and the stem of the boat could hardly be seen from the wheelhouse, it was a very different story. The skipper would know we were so many hours steaming off the land, and the course back to harbour should be 'X', but that was the only information there was to go on. When making a passage for home in such conditions, the crew all stayed on deck, ears and eyes straining to see or hear anything that might mean danger, hands cupped to ears tracking the course of a steamer by the blast of its foghorn. A shout from the man at the stem and the skipper would wind the wheel hard down to avoid, perhaps, a trawler hauling her gear. Like a blind man crossing a busy road, we would work our way across the shipping lanes. Sometimes there was the terrifying moment when the thumping sound of a big ship's engine close at hand starts to engulf us, though often she was so near that it was hard to tell which way to go to avoid her. The tension at that moment was almost unbearable until someone shouts out, "There she is," and all eyes are suddenly riveted to the ghostly outline of a large merchant ship bashing along at a good fifteen knots only yards away as she passes, leaving us wallowing in her wake, engulfed in the thick oily smoke of her funnel. There but for the grace of God ... Stemming the wash of a vessel we had neither seen nor heard until the last moment, the danger passed, did little to soothe the nerves or the imagination. Hour after hour we stood on deck, taking turns blowing the old copper foghorn, oilskins glistening and hats sparkling with dewdrops while the cold wet fog ate into you until every bone ached.

Timing the run in, the skipper would switch the echo sounder on and when it climbed from a steady reading of 40 fathoms up to 25, we knew we were getting close to the land. The two forward engines would then be stopped, and we would proceed carefully in on the one motor until the sounder showed ten fathoms. The aft engine would be knocked out of gear and stopped. With the boat now laying still and silent on the water, everyone would cup their hands to their ears listening for any sounds that might give a clue to our position, sounds such as another vessel's engine or foghorn, waves breaking on the rocks, a dog barking on the land or, best of all, the blaring of the Looe foghorn.

If we were fortunate enough to make such a good shot of it, a couple more manoeuvres would get the foghorn bearing north-west of us, then all we had to do was steer towards the welcoming blasts to reach the harbour, safe and sound. When that happened the mood on the boat changed instantly, the tension lifted; the ordeal was over, we were now out of danger.

On other occasions we might not be so lucky. Stopped on the ten fathom line in perfect silence, closely wrapped in a world of cold wet vapour with nothing to indicate direction but the compass, it almost made you dizzy. Are we east or west of Looe? That was the question. If there was a hundred yards or so visibility, the skipper might gently nudge the boat in towards the shore to get a glimpse of the rocks, their strata telling us where we were. The Oar Stone, a big rock to the west of Looe Island marks a boundary in the rock strata, looking out to sea to the west of it and back into the land to the east of it. To find Looe after that meant steering along the ten-fathom line, stopping the engine every ten minutes and listening until eventually the foghorn was heard. It was a time consuming, tedious way to gain port after a hard trip, but there were no other options. That was how it had to be done. Occasionally a boat would get totally lost and confused. The only answer then was to drop the anchor and wait for the fog to clear.

Be it gales or fog, Moogie always seemed calm and collected, totally imperturbable. Later, many years into his retirement, I asked him if he was always as cool as he looked and his honest answer surprised me. "Greenwood," he said, "sometimes I was terrified!" I'm so glad I didn't know it at the time.

An accident ended our lining season early in the spring of 1966. Moogie was shooting the lines away at a spanking pace when suddenly he was being dragged aft with a hook through the palm of his right hand. Tiddler threw the engine hard astern and Moogie managed to catch a turn of the strop around the mizzen backstay and hang on tight. The surge of the lugger still going ahead parted it. Without a second glance he ripped the hook out of his hand and carried on shooting the gear with blood going everywhere as he did so. If the turn on the backstay had been missed, our skipper would have been dragged overboard and drowned, the weight of the sinking line already shot would have ensured that. This all happened in an instant; Harry, who was standing by with the knife ready to cut away any such foul-ups, was flattened as Moogie hurtled aft. His hand must have been giving him absolute hell. A 3-inch conger hook, ripped out barb first, does an awful lot of damage. But 'never say die', with his right hand wrapped up in engine room rags, our skipper hauled behind the jinny for the 7 hours or so that it took to get the gear in, and we finished the trip. The next day his hand was puffed up like a balloon and he had to have some time off. As it was getting near the time to start the summer drifting season, a decision was made to finish the boulter season a little early and take the old *Iris* over to West Looe for her annual paint-up.

Mike Faulkner then joined us as sixth hand. He was nicknamed 'Bushy' because of his head of curly hair. In his mid-twenties, he had started fishing when he left school, but the prospects back then had been so poor he had gone ashore to learn a trade and became a mason. With everything now looking on the up for the new winter fishery, he had decided to come back to sea again.

15

Heavy Fishing

The spring season of 1966 was one of very mixed blessings. There were plenty of pilchards up and down the coast, but we couldn't really earn any money because the canners had yet again imposed a quota on the landings. The weather was pretty blustery as well, lows coming in from the Atlantic giving us fresh south-westerly and north-westerley winds. We were making a wage each week, but everything seemed to be conspiring to prevent us making a real go of it.

During July of that summer, one of the worst sea disasters in recent times occurred off the Cornish coast. A pleasure boat from Falmouth called the *Darlwin* took guests from a hotel on a day trip to Fowey. The weather had been fine enough when they had set out but, by the late afternoon, when it was time to return to Falmouth, the wind was south-west and freshening up rapidly. Nevertheless the boat proceeded on its return voyage and was last seen bashing her way around the Dodman … and that was it. She was never seen again, all 29 people on board were drowned and the poor, sad remains of these once happy holiday makers were brought into harbours up and down the coast as the local pleasure and fishing boats came across them. Six were brought into Looe, a very grim and haunting experience for those involved.

That dreadful disaster was the start of all the regulations for boats taking paying passengers being tightened up. Initially this meant that, for the sharking season, a life raft had to be carried. Those first rafts had copper tank floatation and were wooden slatted with a life-line around the edge, measuring about 6 feet by 4 feet and 18 inches deep. We could never find anywhere to stow it on the *Iris* where it wasn't in the way. Later, proper inflatable life rafts packed in an oilskin valise became available, but they were still big, heavy, awkward things to find stowage for. After dragging their liferaft around the deck and finding nowhere suitable to lash it down, the crew of the *Our Boys* eventually solved the problem by squeezing it down through the cabin hatch and stowing it in a bunk. Ideal!

That season we worked a fleet of 22 nets, and some of them were very long nets indeed. The average drift net was 90 fathoms long, kept afloat by twelve buoys and three buffs, but some of the nets Moogie put together required 18 buoys to keep them afloat. The hurricane lamp lashed on the pole end dann looked to be nearly out of sight when we came around on the swing rope. The other drifters worked fleets of between 12 and 15 nets of a standard length. Many is the night I have watched them get underway for home when we still had half our fleet to haul. By the time our last net came over the roller most of the other boats had landed their fish and their crews were home, snug in bed. One big annoyance of being the last boat out was ending up with all the gulls. The air around every drifter used to be full of them, screaming and fighting for fish. But when a boat put its working lights out to steam for home, they soon realised there was nothing more to be had and would flock to anyone still working. So the last poor buggers hauling (and it was usually us) had to work in a blizzard of screaming, shitting birds.

Andy Andrews, the head rope man on the *Endeavour*, devised a method of keeping them at bay. It was effective, but it remained unique to Andy. He would snatch a gull out of the air and throw it down on the deck beside him. The *Endeavour*'s bulwarks were high and the working area for the head rope man was narrow, so there was no way that a gull could make its escape. But seagulls are very bold creatures and, after recovering from the initial shock of capture, a few ruffled feathers would be preened back into place and it was soon gorging on fresh pilchards. That was until it was time for this unfortunate bird to star in its new role. When the other gulls started to make too much of a nuisance of themselves, Andy would snatch this poor creature up off the deck and, brandishing it aloft in his left hand, the gnarled index finger of his right was inserted firmly up its little feathered jacksy. The squawk of pain and terror it let out was enough to keep the rest away for quite a while. By the time the *Endeavour*'s crew hauled their last net over the rail, Andy's victim of the night must have had the sorest bum of any bird in the world, proving conclusively that there really is no such thing as a free lunch.

Anyone who crewed on the *Iris* really knew the meaning of hard work. She had a long established record for being a workhorse. 'Moogie' Frank, as with his father 'Moogie' Tom who was skipper before him, always pushed the limits of what could be achieved. If a younger, stronger man joined the crew such as Mike Faulkner, filling the gap once held by an older, slower man, then the nets or lines would be lengthened out to keep everyone at their limit. If you could stick it, there was a big difference in the money shared at the end of the week compared with some of the other boats. Mind you, big catches didn't always mean big money.

Pilchard fishing up and down the coast had been heavy, so the cannery once again put us on a 120 stone per boat quota until they had cleared the backlog a bit. One evening aboard the *Iris*, riding to the nets deep off Fowey, we were looking forward to a quick mug of tea and going to work before too many fish poked their heads in the meshes. Jack and I had taken people out sharking during the day and now, on our second night without any sleep, we were hoping for an easy haul and an early night in. Moogie had gone forward to make the swing rope fast on the kevel when he noticed the buoys nearest the boat had started to bob, indicating that a shoal of fish had hit in hard. There was no time for our supper, we donned oilskins and started the haul there and then while the sun was still up in the sky over the western land.

This first shoal went from the top to the bottom of the boat net. The head ropes and skirt were put together, the whole thing being about as big around as a dustbin, and all hands on the foredeck hauled until our eyes bulged to inch it over the rail. Spreading the net, foot by foot, the pilchards were shaken out, then we strained to haul a couple more fathoms aboard and do the same again. There was to be no let up, the shoals were hitting in hard all along the nets.

The tea that Harry had brewed when the nets were first shot was eventually drunk some time in the early hours of the following morning where we stood, up to our knees in pilchards, attached to the deck as firmly as if we were standing in wet concrete. Eleven nets were cleared and stowed, the remaining eleven were 'boarded in', which meant hauling as fast as possible and shaking out what fish you could without breaking the rhythm. The nets, fish and all, were then piled into the net room to be run out and cleared once back in the harbour. It took 10 hours non-stop to get the pole end buoy over the roller (the sun was now well up over the eastern land), the nets and fish were piled up like a haystack and we had to wrestle them about so that the skipper could see over the top to steer. Then, with the governors on the engines lashed back to make all speed, we just managed to save our tide back into Looe. The *Iris* was the only boat that night to have heavy fishing. The *Endeavour* had even shot a second time to try and make her quota up, steaming along a berth off our port side with us shouting that we had plenty and not to bother. However, her old Bolinder engine made so much noise it was like being in the company of a Shackleton bomber, so it was hardly surprising that her crew didn't hear us.

With the ropes ashore in the harbour, we boxed up and landed our 120 stone of fish. It was then time for a much-needed breakfast in one of the quayside cafes. Revived by a good fry up and a couple of mugs of tea, it was then back to work. We had caught a huge catch of fish but unfortunately we had no market for it. To clear the decks a bit Henry Dunn, one of the local farmers, arrived and took a trailer-load away at a knock-down price to use for fertilizer. Then, with the roller and spars rigged athwartships, we proceeded to 'shake out'. It was mid-afternoon before the last fish were shaken out and the nets salted and stowed back down the net room. To get rid of the deck-full of unwanted pilchards, the boat was steamed out into the bay and there, with the wheel lashed hard to starboard, they were scooped over the side as she motored in circles. By this time even the gulls weren't interested; most of them couldn't even fly, let alone swallow any more fish.

We scrubbed the old *Iris* from end to end and, just before the hatches were shipped up, Moogie rather lamely suggested that we go out and shoot away again so as not to miss that night's quota and wash the nets out. I rather think he knew what our reply would be, because within 10 minutes we were in harbour tied up.

On that trip we had hauled by hand 2 miles of net, 9 fathoms deep, containing an estimated twelve tons of fish. Every single fish had been flipped, twisted and shaken out of the meshes, and we had worked non-stop for over 20 hours to do it. The cannery had taken three quarters of a ton, the farmer had taken about two tons, we had dumped over nine tons out in the bay and for all our labours we had earned about £4 each.

We were all toughened up to hard physical work and had become used to going without any real sleep for long periods of time. But there was definitely a limit to how long anyone could keep going for. It varied from person to person, but once that line was crossed, wherever it may lie, you were venturing into very uncertain territory. We could all work for 36 or 40 hours at a stretch without any apparent ill effects. You looked haggard and felt worn right out, but a good kip and a decent meal would soon put you back to rights. It was on the occasions that even those hours were exceeded that strange things could start happening. Hallucinating was one effect.

Steaming out one evening, Tiddler rushed down forward and jammed the engines hard astern, stopping the boat dead, before emerging back upon deck in a real sweat, shouting, "Don't any of you bastards keep your eyes open? Did none of you see that?" The sea was glassy calm, the sun was shining and there was nothing around us for miles. Nobody said anything more than, "I think its gone now, Tid," and he went below and put the engines back into gear and opened up the throttles again. I clearly remember driving home one morning and slamming on the brakes to avoid a rocking chair that leaped out of the hedge in front of me. It was all very weird.

The zombie effect was another result of staying awake too long. When that happened, your brain just went on strike; someone had to pass you your mug of tea and then make sure that you drank it, otherwise you just sat there staring out with it in your hands. When it was time to haul, whoever was suffering had to be helped on with their oilskins and put to their place on the nets. Working at a steady pace he would be fine, but if a splat of fish come aboard and the rhythm was broken while it was being shaken out, he would be unaware of it and try to carry on in the same way until he was brought too by a shout. Some men were tougher than others, but I think most of us experienced that sort of thing once in a while when the going got really hard.

My poor mother used to get quite upset at the state I used to arrive home in, and many is the time that I didn't get home at all. If the fishing was heavy it was just too much effort to get back home to Talland for a few hours rest before going back to Looe again in the evening. It was much easier just to collapse into my bunk aboard the boat. If we had managed to land the catch in time, a couple of the crew may well have taken the boat out again with a load of anglers. If that was the case, I would go up to the net loft and crash out on the nets; after so many hours on my feet it was utter bliss just to lie down, close my eyes and sleep regardless of the surroundings.

The combination of fine summer weather and good fishing meant we had to go for it while the going was good. After one such spell, when we had seen every sunrise and sunset for a fortnight and I hadn't been home for nearly a week, we were alongside the quay shaking the nets out when Mum arrived at the quayside having caught the bus in to Looe to search for her long lost son. She was not happy: "Where the hell have you been for the last week? I have cooked dinners for you that have all gone to waste, you haven't phoned to say what has been happening. I didn't know if you were alive or dead". That sort of performance from your mother in front of everyone makes you feel about 2 inches tall. But she did have a very good point, so I apologised to her and explained about the heavy fishing and that I wouldn't be home that day either, as another catch had yet to be landed and we were away again on the next tide. It was after that incident that Mum gave up; she expected me when she saw me, and hoped for the best when she didn't.

When I did arrive home, the whole family knew about it because the stench of pilchards and diesel was strong enough to very near clear the house. In addition, fish scales drying and falling off my clothes left a trail wherever I went. Because of this odour and litter problem, I was given a bedroom with its own door onto the courtyard and forbidden from entering the house in my work clothes.

The summer of 1966 was the first time that radio communication was tried out by the Looe fleet, only to be silenced later by due process of the law. It all started with a chap called Bill Breeze. Bill owned an engineering works at Bakewell in Derbyshire, but lived in semi-retirement in Looe. A sociable type, he would stroll around the quay chatting to one and all, and he loved to go out on the boats. Day trips, angling, out by night on the drifters and, to avoid his mother-in-law, he even went long lining. In return, if any skipper had trouble getting parts for an engine, he would have them made at his factory at no charge - a very useful man to know.

One Saturday he came jaunting down the quay with a couple of hand-held walkie-talkies of Japanese manufacture. He demonstrated them over the length of the harbour and everybody was duly impressed. They had a range of 5 miles or so, and their usefulness on a boat didn't need spelling out. As Bill offered to supply them at a very reasonable price, all the lugger skippers and most of the shark boat skippers ordered one there and then. A couple of weeks later the new toys arrived and, as radio communication was something few had experienced, the airwaves were red hot before the novelty wore off. Alfred John of the *Our Daddy*, who had a lovely singing voice, serenaded us one evening with 'Lower Lights' and 'Will Your Anchor Hold', two of the fishermen's favourite hymns, while other singers in the fleet warbled some old music hall favourites with much banter and chit chat in between. All in all, those little radios were a great hit.

But the bubble was soon to burst. The Post Office, then in charge of radio communication, started picking up all this chatter and sent letters to all concerned, warning them that they were broadcasting without a licence, and even if a licence was applied for it could not be granted as the sets were broadcasting on an illegal waveband. 'So be good boys and pack it up right now, or else' was the gist of the warning. Several such warnings were issued, but all to no avail, the radios remained as popular as ever. However it all came to a head late one afternoon as the angling boats were coming in from sea. Each one was boarded and the offending radios were confiscated in a James Bond-style raid. Later a summons was issued to all the skippers to attend the magistrates' court at Liskeard. On the appointed day and hour, the radio pirates of Looe stood before the man on the bench who gave them the waggly finger, and fined them ten pounds each.

Silence reigned once more over the airwaves, and it was to be another 7 or 8 years before the small, and legal, marine VHF radios started to be come available.

That summer I had the job on the nets as stower, not generally a popular berth. You had to be very quick handed, unmeshing mackerel and scads, clearing conger drills and anything else that the other crew members had passed on rather than break the pace of the haul. These drills were caused by the conger swimming up from the bottom to help themselves to supper. Their calling card would be about 4 inches of net wound up tight and covered in slime. The stower was also responsible for the boat's trim, which meant stowing the net evenly across the width of the net room to prevent an unwanted list. Working such a big summer fleet, one net stowed incorrectly meant the hatches wouldn't ship up. 'Bushy' didn't want the job so he took my place out the rail and I went as stower. I stayed in that berth until I left the *Iris* three seasons later. It was a job I quite liked. Whereas the rail berth was all muscle and louster, stowing required a fair bit of skill, swishing the net evenly out the port and starboard wings of the net room as flat as a billiard table. Shirking up the rest of the crew with "Up, up," when your bit of net was cleared, getting the timing right and there was a bit of fun to be had at the expense of our poor cook. When a fish was flipped down the net room I would shout, "Net room," and Harry would have to jump down and get it. Before leaping, he momentarily balanced on the coamings, steadying himself with the engine gear lever. If the timing was right, then a split second after he let go of the lever to jump 'Bushy' would shout, "Go ahead". Harry would attempt to turn in mid air to snatch at the lever, but always missed it, and would land in a heap down on the nets. If I thought I could get away with it then I would 'accidentally' throw a fang of net right over him, pretending not to have seen this. There he would be, cursing and swearing, having lost his hat and fag all soggy, trying to get the fish and crawl out from under the net all at the same time. On deck we would be silently splitting our sides at his antics. Moogie, staying deadpan, would add to it by bellowing, "For fuck's sake, Harry, what are you pissing around at? Chuck that bloody fish up and get out the way". The poor old bugger, we had to treat him nicely for a while after that.

The downside of being the stower was when there was a heavy plankton bloom in the sea, 'cow shit water' it was known as. Plankton washing through the nets on the tide would stick to them in their billions, making the twine look about three times as thick. When hauled, the nets were a mass of green-brown slime and with all the flapping and shaking, the air would be full of it. The stower, who stood down on the fish box shaking boards about a foot lower and a bit aft of the rest of the foredeck crew – and, of course, working up head to wind – was in pole position for anything airborne.

By the time the last net came aboard on a night when the 'cow shit water' was about, my oilskins and hat would be running with this slime, and my face set rigid behind a claylike mask where my body heat had dried it on. Everyone had their share of this stuff, but the stower had double. Mind you, when it came to green slimy hats, everybody on the drifters had one, 'cow shit water' or not. Because we all wore long oilskin jumpers it was nearly impossible to get to your hankie so if you needed to wipe your face or blow your nose, the easiest thing to hand was the inside of your hat (because the outside was always wet).

During the summer months, swarms of jellyfish would drift up-Channel on the warm Gulf Stream and there were many different types. Brown umbrella-striped ones the size of a large mushroom, transparent purple-tinted ones the size of a tea plate, and white opaque ones, the bodies of which could be as big as a dustbin lid. They all pulsated along in an aimless sort of way, each one towing behind it several feet of sting-laden, jelly-like tentacles with which they caught their prey. Of course when they came up against our nets, an awful lot of the tentacles got caught in the meshes and the jellyfish would swim on leaving them behind. By the time a few thousand of these creatures had all suffered the same accident, the nets would be liberally coated from end to end in what we called stingers, and sting they did. In clearing the nets of fish, every shake and flap sent these still active tentacles flying about. A single sting was not very startling, it felt like a very mild nettle. But repeated hundreds of times over several hours and your face, hands and forearms began to feel as if they were on fire.

16

A New Fishery

By mid-October the pilchard season was drawing to a close, so the nets were hauled ashore, dried out, and stowed up in the store for the winter. The herring nets were left where they were, as we didn't intend to go to Brixham. Mackerel fishing was the new winter occupation, and all around the harbour boats were making ready. Shoals of mackerel were coming on to the coast from Plymouth to Newlyn. Where they came from and why, nobody knew, but come they did. After years of stagnation and decline the fishing harbours along the south Cornish coast were coming back to life. From barely scratching a living in the winter, we were now earning good money. Moogie even got so keen that we went to sea on Boxing Day.

This was a brand new fishery and there was much to be learnt about it. We started off using 1lb lead weights and a dozen feathers on a hand line. Hauling the line up in a fresh wind, it would get blown around the deck and tangle up, bights of it would wrap around your boots or mackerel flapped around in it. Either way it was the devil of a job to keep clear. Hauling it into a fish box helped, but it wasn't really the answer. A line full of big mackerel could swim around with your lead weight, sometimes leading to every one of the crew tangled up together in a real 'bunch of bastards'. The hydraulic gurdy and line stripper were still way off in the future. There were also big shoals of pollack about at that time, and if we dropped our lines into them everything was parted away in an instant. Do that three or four times and it was time to go home as there would be nothing left to tie on the lines. Sharks were another menace. But despite all the frustrations, those first couple of winters laid the foundations for one of the biggest revivals the Cornish fishing industry had ever seen.

The gurdy (a wheel of 18 inches or so in diameter clamped to the rail and turned by a handle) was one of many improvements introduced: the line was wound on to it, doing away with all the tangles. The sets of feathers became 24 hooks long made of heavy-duty gut, and the leads to sink them with now weighed 3lbs each. Catches started to exceeded 100 stone per man instead of per boat, as when we first started.

With so many boats fitting out in Looe for the winter mackerel fishery, the old fish market truck driven by the market manager, 'Shakes', could no longer handle it all. It was going up to Plymouth market perilously loaded, sometimes doing two or three runs. To ease the situation, Ray Pettier, the local coal merchant, stepped in with his lorry. After a day on the coal round, he would hose it down to get the coal dust off before loading up with boxes of mackerel to take to the market in the morning.

Young men were starting to trickle back into the industry and boats that hadn't had a fish on their decks in 20 years were being refitted and sent back to sea. Hippies, Spanish waiters and even farmers were getting in on the act - one lot used fertiliser bags cut up as oilskins and even had their dog with them. Initially they caught few fish, but they did provide a lot of entertainment and suffered much ribald commentary. To be fair, some of these more unlikely characters did stick it out, and several of them became damn good fishermen. Mackerel fishing on the *Iris* was like any other form of fishing on the boat, it was done to the maximum. If the fish were biting, then we worked non-stop right through the day; the gallon water-can would be passed around but that was it as far as refreshment was concerned. We used to feel quite envious watching the other crews belaying up for 10 minutes or so, enjoying a mug of tea and a sandwich. But we were usually the top boat and in our skipper's eyes, that was what it was all about.

The Christmas holiday lasted all of two days that year and we were back to sea again on Boxing Day. New Year's Day 1967 was celebrated with a deck-full of mackerel. If the weather was workable and the fish were biting, there was no let up. Moogie was the ultimate fisherman, and I think that if anyone had tried to work in worse weather or longer hours than he did they would have either sunk their boat, or dropped dead from exhaustion.

We carried on in this manner until the mackerel shoals left the coast in early March. Then, in a more or less seamless change over, ten drift nets were stowed down into the net-room as a bait fleet, and the decks were jam-packed with baskets of line. It was time once again to do battle out in the Channel, after conger, ray, ling and pollack.

Nowadays the fish room of a modern fishing vessel is well insulated and the catch is gutted, washed and iced to ensure it stays in prime condition for the market. That, however, was not the way of things on the luggers. The fish room or fish box, as it was called, was beneath the shaking boards where the unhooker worked. It was divided into three pounds, one for conger, one for rays and one for white fish such as ling, pollack and whiting. There was no insulation of any sort on the *Iris*; the top section or the forward bulkhead was open to the engine room, so for the 6 or 8 hours of the return trip with the hatches shipped up, the engines chuffed away keeping the temperature up nicely. But ray and conger take a long time to die, in fact, some would still be showing signs of life when being landed, so maybe that was how we got away with it. Nevertheless that sort of treatment can't have done much for the quality of the fish, but nobody seemed to worry; it had always been done that way.

As the line was hauled, the gaffer hooked the big fish aboard, telling the man behind the jinny to ease up as he did so. With smaller fish, he just caught hold of the strop and passed them over the hauler heads. The unhooker then dangled the fish over the appropriate pound and with his T-hook (an unhooking tool), flipped it off the hook and down it went. Mind you, a 70- or 80-pound conger could take a bit of dealing with. Sometimes they weren't even hooked but were caught because they had swallowed a smaller hooked conger. Once gaffed aboard, they would spit out the smaller conger and then go ramping around the deck in a really evil temper. After a bit of a fight we would get them below where they would slither about barking and swallowing whip congers that would wriggle around in their guts and then pop back out through their gills. Occasionally, one of these big eels would lever its tail under the parting boards and unship them, with the result that all the fish would then be mixed up and someone had to go down there and sort them out again. This had to be done with care, because if a big conger got a grip you were in trouble. They could drill a finger off at the knuckle very easily, and there was nothing you could do that would make them let go. Severing the head from the body with a sharp knife was the only answer.

On one trip a couple of bottom boards unshipped and all the congers escaped down into the bilge. What a state they were in by the time we had gaffed them out from amongst the ballast and under the engines. They took a fair bit of scrubbing up before they could be landed.

Back in harbour, the catch would be tossed up on deck where it was gutted and washed, then flung up on to the quay to be graded, boxed and weighed ready for the market. After landing, the fish box had to be scrubbed out, a filthy job because bucketsful of slime mixed up with shit and old bait had to be scooped and passed up before the scrubbing out could commence, and the stench was eye watering.

That season I was given the dubious honour of looking after the line hauler, or jinny as it was called. Like the rest of the boat, it was pretty much clapped out. Lurking in a box beneath the hauler head was its 'Brit' 3-HP petrol engine; a magneto provided a spark for the plug, and a brass oil chest provided lubrication to the bearings through wicks and pipes. It had been bolted to the deck on the luff of the starboard bow sometime in the early 1920s and in its time it had been a good old servant, but had now grown rather cantankerous with age. It was what was known as a one-man engine, because all its little foibles had to be known and catered for if it was to start and, hopefully, stay running. When it was primed and ready, a handle was engaged to the very worn dogs in the centre of the flywheel. There was not a lot of compression to worry about, so you cranked away, going faster and faster. It would begin to fart and splutter, but still you had to keep winding until, if it fancied the idea, it would eventually pick up and chuff away, emitting clouds of sickly exhaust fumes laden with unburned petrol. Sometimes it took three or four goes to get it running and as many changes of spark plug, each one heated up and pencilled.

Stopping dead while hauling the line was one of the jinny's more exasperating habits. Two men would then have go to the rail and haul by hand (the strain of it nearly glazing their eyes over) until it could be coaxed back into life again. Backfiring on one occasion, it bounced the starting handle overboard off my forehead, giving me a tidy gash. Luckily I was only giving it a test run in the harbour and I managed to retrieve the handle at low tide. I suppose a new set of piston rings and reseating the valves would have cured most of the problems, but that didn't seem to be the way of things in those days.

We said goodbye to the *Guide Me* that summer. Ned, her skipper, had passed on and after the funeral his widow put the old lugger up for sale. A local publican bought her, and the crew continued to run her, skippered by 'Waller' Pengelly. But it didn't work out. Her engines were worn out, her nets were in rags and she was leaking badly. Without massive reinvestment (and that was out of the question) she could not continue, so she was put up for sale again. Amazingly she soon found new owners, and one fine afternoon in late August we watched her steaming out of the harbour, the decks cluttered with all her gear. She was on passage to St Peter Port in the Channel Islands where she was refitted to work as a crabber.

And so the seasons rolled on, long-lining in the spring, pilchard drifting in the summer and back to mackerel fishing in winter. Moogie's son Mike left school and joined the crew, keeping up a family tradition that had gone on for generations. Poor Mike suffered with seasickness as bad, if not worse, than I had but his father showed him no mercy. It was the same old treatment: "Come on, my sonny, up off your knees and catch hold the nets, work it off." "A quick hand for a scabby arse," "Rattle your dusters," and "John Edward is looking at you," etc. When I think about it now, a 15-year-old kid being goaded along through seasickness, trying to work and stay awake sometimes for 20 or 30 hours on the trot is almost unbelievable by today's standards, but back then there were men at sea who had gone through the same thing when they were only 12 years of age, a tough start to a hard life.

Steaming out to shoot the nets one summer's evening, we were on deck making ready when something, I can't remember what, went wrong. There was an awful lot of effing and blinding going on and our skipper obviously thought that this was not suitable language for his young son to hear. With a face like thunder, he poked his head out of the wheelhouse window and, glaring at us over the top of his glasses, bellowed, "And you lot can stop that fucking swearing!" Nobody laughed, we didn't dare, but he knew and we knew that our captain's attempt to capture the moral high ground had nose-dived to earth. The swearing continued unfettered and the subject was never raised again.

In the spring of 1968, with the good prospect of the winter fishery, and his son's future to think about, Moogie ordered a new boat from Curtis & Pape, a boatyard situated up the West Looe river. Designed by Alan Pape, the yard boss, she was to be 38 feet long, with a forward wheelhouse and a hatch-board deck working area. Packing two powerful modern diesel engines and a top of the range echo sounder, plus radio and autopilot, she proved to be a fine craft. I was supposed to be joining her as one of the crew, but that was not to be.

I had always fancied the idea of doing some time under sail in a big sailing vessel of some kind. So when the opportunity arose, I jumped at the chance of a trip on the newly launched STA vessel *Sir Winston Churchill*. She was a three-mast topsail schooner, 150 feet long and 300 tons. Operated as a youth training ship she took young people between 16 and 21 years of age on two-week character building cruises. Sailing as a trainee on her maiden voyage in March 1966, I thoroughly enjoyed myself and was asked back again to sail as watch leader for another two weeks in 1967. In early 1968 I sailed once more as watch leader, this time for a five-week stint. But that was going to be it; financing the trips and taking time off from the fishing was costing me too much money.

Then, out of the blue, I received an offer to sail as full-time bosun on the *Churchill*'s newly launched sister ship, the *Malcolm Miller*. This was much too good an opportunity to pass up, so in October 1968 I left the *Iris* and joined the STS *Malcolm Miller* at Millbay Docks, Plymouth. My drifting days were now over. Most people sailing aboard these schooners considered themselves to be leading a fairly tough life. There were no winches, everything was haul and drag, there was plenty of sea time, and both vessels were as wet as hell in bad weather. But after 4 ½ years on the *Iris*, life on the *Malcolm Miller* seemed like one long holiday to me.

The first skipper I sailed under was Glynn Griffiths, a quietly spoken Welshman who ran his ship in a happy easy-going manner. He never overlooked the fact that sailing was the first and foremost object of the exercise: but birthdays were remembered and celebrated, there would be drinks all round for the permanent crew after battling a gale of wind and fancy dress parties and musical evenings were held on fine nights at sea. The rigours of sail training were leavened with good humour.

I well remember my 21st birthday, the 30th of October 1968. We were crossing the Irish Sea from Dublin, making to round Lands End and then up the Channel to Portsmouth. It was the sort of day that, on a sailing ship, you just let pass and hope tomorrow will be better; the wind was blowing south-west force six to eight, with decks awash and plenty of spray and rain. As for it being my birthday, I thought maybe I would take a run ashore and celebrate it in our next port of call. But the day suddenly took a turn for the better. To my surprise, I was called up to the chartroom where, to the popping of champagne corks, the captain and officers wished me a happy birthday and presented me with an engraved tankard and a card signed by all of the crew. Braced against the Atlantic rollers that were flooding the deck as they passed us by, we drank champagne, ate nibbles and made small talk. It was a very memorable party, and I treasure that tankard still.

Captain George Shaw was the second skipper I sailed under. He ran his ship in a very different way. A dour Scot and as hard as nails, who believed that life was not to be enjoyed, it was to be endured. He was a first class sailor, of that there was no doubt, and providing the kids understood that they had come for two weeks sail training and not for two weeks fun, then they were okay. The maximum sail was always carried in the conditions then prevailing. He never sought shelter in bad weather, and we always left port on the appointed hour, no matter what the conditions were at sea. Double-reefed mizzen and staysail was the rig of the day for force nine and above. In those extreme conditions we worked the ship with water up to our waist and breaking over our heads. Big seas would smash aboard, forcing gallons of water through the vents and hatches turning the companionway ladders into waterfalls. The galley fire would be out, and we lived in our wet clothes and oilskins. While the gale lasted all would be dank and miserable. But to be honest, those conditions were usually only met with at either end of the sailing season, March and April or October to December. Most of the time we sailed about perfectly safe and dry. But Captain Shaw seemed to like nothing better than to pit himself and his ship against a bit of bad weather if there was any to be had.

We voyaged from the Baltic to the Bay of Biscay and all around the British Isles as far north as the Shetlands. It was a fantastic experience but it was quite trying after a while. Thirty-nine young people arrived aboard every fortnight, and for the first few days they would be a danger to both themselves and the ship. Then, just as they were starting to learn the ropes and become a bit useful, their fortnight would end and after a hectic weekend turn around, we would begin all over again. And apart from six weeks home leave a year, I had no life other than the ship.

I finally signed off the *Malcolm Miller* in 1973 and came home again to Looe and the fishing. By then things had changed out of all recognition. It was fast becoming a young man's world, fishing families were buying their own homes, driving cars and going on holiday. New boats were under construction at the local yards, while many of the older ones had been refitted and re-engined. The winter mackerel fishery had by now expanded into a huge county-wide industry employing over 300 boats, anything from 18-foot cove boats, to 60-foot Newlyn long-liners. After years of near stagnation, coves and quays, ports and harbours throughout the county had come back to life. Ashore, teams of people were employed each evening packing the fish into boxes, weighing and then loading them into the refrigerated lorries that took this fresh Cornish produce all over Europe.

Either side of the mackerel fishery, methods of fishing new to Cornwall were being tried out such as scallop dredging, tangle netting and trawling. It was all upbeat and go-ahead, so very different from 10 years before. In Looe, Moogie in his new boat *Ganesha* was top skipper, still working hours that few could stick in weather that most men were happy to ride out under the lee of a pub bar. There were one or two skippers like him in every port. They were the leaders (some called them greedy bastards), and they dragged the others along in their wake. Many is the poor weather day that the fleet landed a good catch, but initially no one would have ventured out if the top men hadn't cast off and lead the way.

17

A New Role

By the mid-1970s the old men and their luggers had all but faded from the scene, retiring with honour and dignity. They had kept the spark of a once great industry alive through many bleak years; now it was the turn of the young men joining this new, up-and-coming industry to restore the fortunes of the Cornish fishing ports, and they have done so magnificently.

Around the Cornish coast a handful of the better luggers did carry on working, but not in their old trade. They were refitted to go trawling, mackerel fishing, crabbing and wreck netting. Some remained working into the 1980s, two or three even survived into the 1990s. By then, in amongst the modern fishing boats now mainly constructed from either glass fibre or steel, they looked like something that had escaped from a maritime museum. But everyone loved to see those gallant old survivors still earning a living from the sea. One of the very last luggers fishing commercially was the *Happy Return*, built at Porthleven in 1906 and later renamed *Britannia*. She worked out of Weymouth as a crabber, landing her final catch in the spring of 1998.

That could well have been the end of the story. Four hundred years of service now encapsulated in the past, preserved only in museum models, pictures and old photographs. Happily that was not the way things turned out. If the last luggers had been withdrawn from service in the 1950s, I doubt any would be around today. But as with vintage cars or antique furniture, the secret of survival is to get past the stage of being considered as nothing more than old fashioned, worn out and fit only for scrapping. But the stark fact was, after so many years of hard usage and frugal maintenance, these boats were not in any way fit for further service.

A lugger at the end of her working days would usually be making a fair amount of water through the hull. Her deck would also be leaking and probably sagging in reverse camber, with depressions worn in it over the years by the boots of the crew standing at their work stations. Bulwarks so shaky that a boy could have knocked them asunder with a 2lbs pound hammer. Gribble worm in the keel, and most of the iron bolts and fastenings in the hull rusted to danger point and beyond, and that was only for starters. A detailed survey would usually show that she was so far gone as to be well beyond economic repair.

But a new generation of leisure sailors had come into being who weren't interested in the latest super-efficient, sleek, factory-built sailing machines in shining-white fibreglass. No, these 'classic boat' enthusiasts had an eye to history and wanted vessels from the age of working sail. The words 'beyond economic repair' held no terrors for such people. They spent, and still do spend, thousands of pounds and hours to match, rebuilding a boat from the keel up, if that's what it takes to get an historic craft back to sea once more. They come from all walks of life, from every trade and profession, and it is thanks to them that so many of Britain and Europe's traditional sailing vessels have been brought back to life.

So, for the surviving luggers, salvation was at hand; their good looks, fine lines and legendary sailing qualities had not escaped the notice of these people. Because they are now scattered world wide, it is very difficult to say exactly how many Cornish luggers are still in existence today, but I estimate it to be 60 plus and, of them, probably 30 or more are in sea-going order. The oldest is the *Barnabas* of St Ives, built in 1881; the youngest of the originals is the motor lugger *Lindy Lou*, built at Looe in 1947. But the tally is always on the increase, as news from somewhere in the British Isles, Europe or even America comes in of some long-forgotten craft, putting yet another name back on to the list. Typically, she is either somebody's well maintained pride and joy or a sorry old bundle of sticks that some brave soul has every prospect of breaking both their heart and bank balance in rebuilding. But without these people there would be very few traditional boats on the water.

An example of this is the crabber from Weymouth, the old *Britannia*. After 92-years' service she was shattered and, to save her from the chainsaw,

a group of friends in Penzance formed the Mount's Bay Lugger Association
to raise the many thousands of pounds necessary to finance her rebuild.
Now back under her original name and dipping lug rig, the *Happy Return*
sails the seas once more and is (we hope) good for another 100 years.
Another is the *Ripple*, a St Ives lugger built in 1896 and owned by John
Lambourne of Newlyn. Having established a temporary yard on Newlyn
quay, he and his shipwrights are now undertaking her restoration. Two
new luggers have been launched in recent years: in 1993 Norman Laity and
friends built the *Dolly Pentreath* of St Ives, 34 feet long with dipping lug
rig. Skippered by Norman's son Mike, she takes summer visitors on trips
around the bay and occasionally takes part in sailing regattas. In August
2004, Jane Hayman and Marcus Rowden launched the 32-foot *Veracity* at
Dartmouth that they had built her themselves with help and advice from
local shipwright Brian Pomeroy. An exact replica of the original lugger of
the same name, she carries a dipping lug rig and has no engine, therefore
joining the elite company of the *Guide Me, Reliance, Pet* and the *Vilona
May*, the pure sailers of the fleet.

Technically a sailing vessel is known by its rig, and among the luggers
there are a number sporting a gaff rig as well as those with dipping and
standing lug rigs. But it is what they were, and the family of boats that they
belong to, that ensures they are still classed as luggers. Every summer they
can be seen racing at the classic boat regattas around the coast of the West
Country and over in Brittany, and they remain some of the fastest pieces
of wood on the water. Many a smartly-attired yachtsman has been amazed
(not to say well choked-off) by having his expensive piece of polished plastic
overhauled by an ancient lugger, crewed by a hairy-arsed bunch in tatty
smocks. These vessels are not just confined to jaunting around the coast on
fine summer days. Some very serious voyages have been undertaken in a few
of them, and doubtlessly there will be more in the future.

The *Vilona May*, 28 feet and built in Looe in 1896 is strongly rumoured
to have made a voyage to Australia in the mid-1950s, although I haven't
seen any solid evidence of it. She has cruised around Europe extensively; rig,
gaff cutter and no engine. Latterly rebuilt and skippered by Chris Rees of
Millbrook, Cornwall. In November 2005 he and his family sailed the Atlantic
to winter in the West Indies before voyaging up to Boston. Chris was then

joined by Graham Butler and together they headed up to Greenland before Chris undertook the three week voyage back to Cornwall single-handed; the only mishap occurred in fog at night when the bowsprit struck an iceberg.

The *Lily*, 28 feet and built in Looe in 1898 was renamed *Moonraker* during the 1950s when Dr Peter Pye and his wife Anne crossed the Atlantic in her on a number of occasions and also cruised the Pacific. They sailed extensively for many years, wrote of their adventures and the books are now sailing classics. Now owned by Andy Pritchard of Woodbridge, Suffolk, she is presently undergoing a rebuild. These two boats are technically classed as Polperro gaffers, but they are always included with the luggers.

The *Guide Me* (FY 233), 40 feet and built in Looe in 1911, was bought by Jono and Judy Brickhill and family who rebuilt her in the 1970s. They have since covered many thousands of sea miles, visiting South Africa, South America and the West Indies. A very well known boat in the sailing fraternity. Rig, dipping lug, no engine.

Guiding Star (FY 363), 40 feet and built in Looe in 1907, crossed the Atlantic to Panama in the 1950s. From 1960 to 1990 she was owned by Brigadier Jack Glennie and his wife Marguerite who regularly cruised from the Baltic to Spain. She was later purchased by Barry Jobson and Jackie Gallespie who, after a major rebuild, took her on her second Atlantic crossing to the West Indies. Rig: dandy ketch.

The *White Heather* (FH 34), 38 feet and built in Looe in 1926, was refitted in 2002 for an Atlantic crossing and explored the coast of Brazil and the West Indies. Rig: dandy ketch plus square foresail; skipper Mike Mckay- Lewis.

Rosalind, 45ft and built in St Ives in 1898, cruised the Mediterranean and eastern seaboard of the USA. Rig: gaff ketch; skipper Richard Griffeths.

Du Kerins (FY 290), ex-*Dos Amigos*, ex-*Our Francis*, 38 feet and built in St Ives in 1920; owners Sue and Mike Darlington took a winter off to cruise in the Mediterranean, leaving and returning to their home port of Looe. Rig: dandy ketch.

Swift (FY 405), 45 feet and built in Looe in 1920, became a research vessel based at the Galapagos Islands in the Pacific and was renamed *Beagle* after the brig that Charles Darwin sailed on. Sadly, she was wrecked on a reef sometime in the late 1960s. Rig: gaff ketch.

There are several others known to be voyaging about, among them are two Looe luggers, the *Janie* (FY 227) and the *Seagull* (FY 408), plus another St Ives' boat called *Gratitude*.

The luggers of Cornwall have existed in various forms for at least 400 years, fulfilling the roles of smuggler, privateer and fishing vessel. Now they are evolving again to play a new and very different role, this time as classic yachts. They are swift, sea kindly and very good-looking, causing a stir of admiration wherever they go. In particular, the harbours that the engineless ones are leaving or entering echo to the cheers and applause of onlookers as their crews bend to the sweeps. In the sailing days, regattas were held at all the major fishing ports: St Ives, Newlyn, Mevagissey and Looe. These events were well attended, not only by the home port's fleet, but by the 'flyers' from other harbours. There was great prestige for your boat and town if you scooped the silverware at another port's regatta, as with the *Little Charlie* at Mevagissey. When engines became more reliable and powerful enough, the sailing rigs were cut right back and eventually abandoned altogether. So were the regattas, nobody saw much skill or challenge in motoring around a course, although in recent times the trawler race has become an important event at some of the bigger harbours.

The massive upsurge of interest in historic and classic sail in the latter quarter of the last century led to some of us at Looe doing some research and coming to the conclusion that there were just enough of the old boats back under sail to reinstate the regatta under the banner of the Cornish Lugger Association. So, in June 1989, a sight was seen in Looe bay that was then only remembered by some of the oldest residents: sailing luggers racing for silver cups. After a break of 78 years, they were back.

Our first event was attended by about five actual luggers, so to pack out the numbers and make it a bit more of a spectacle we invited various other classic boats from around the coast to attend as well, which they very kindly did. That weekend was hailed as a great success and, with the publicity it enjoyed, the foundations were laid for much greater things. Our regatta is now held biannually and is usually attended by 20-plus class 'A' luggers, the 30- to 45-foot fully decked type, and as many class 'B' vessels, 18 to 25 feet, open or part-decked boats, pretty little craft that originally gained their living on the inshore fishery working crab pots, hand lines and drift nets. The nickname for these boats was 'two men on a plank'.

The biggest section of that class is made up by the Beer luggers, chunky, tough, clinker-built open boats of around 20 feet in length, once used in the sprat and crab fishery working off the open beach. Today they can still be seen hauled up to the top of that Devon beach, but now they are sailed for pleasure by a crowd of enthusiasts under the heading of the Beer Lugger Club. A lovely gang, who attend our regatta with a dozen or so boats, and by the time family and friends join in, their party alone numbers about 50 people. Our event would not be the same without them.

Vessels from Brittany voyage over to join in, adding a huge helping of laughter, music and song to the proceedings. One of them is the *Grande Lejon*, a St Brieuc lugger that has attended all our events since she was launched in 1992. Her crew are a real fun crowd and they have made many friends in Looe over the years.

The sailing gigs also create a lot of interest. These lean, brightly painted craft knife around the bay at a great rate, looking like large wind-assisted pencils. You have to be bright-eyed and bushy-tailed to sail one of them in a fresh breeze.

At Looe we try to maintain the spirit of the old regattas. It is, first and foremost, an event for the boats and their crews, although the weekend does boost the economy of the town a fair bit as hundreds of people come to watch the racing. Hotels, guesthouses and holiday cottages do well as vacations are booked to coincide with our event, and this has a spin off for the shops, pubs and restaurants, which is all to the good as many of our sponsors run such businesses. But unlike some festivals, the boats are not kept alongside the quay for the weekend to act as harbour dressing to attract the maximum number of visitors. After about ten o'clock, the harbour is empty and all the boats are in the bay hoisting sail in readiness for the racing; the atmosphere is electric.

Race days mean an early start for Leo Bowdler and his son Brian. For many years they have volunteered their trawler *Maret* as the committee boat, and to this end they are out in the bay long before most have even stirred out of their bunks. So, by the time the luggers leave the quay, Leo and Brian have gauged the weather, laid out the course then come to anchor to form the start line. For the rest of us, the day begins just after breakfast. By then crowds of locals and visitors are strolling the quays watching the crews as they make their boats ready for sea and head out into the bay to set sail and jockey for a good position on the starting line.

Once the starting cannon is fired on the committee boat, the luggers storm over the line heeling to the breeze with every stitch of canvas set, the skippers clinging to the tillers while the crews trim the sails to get every last ounce of speed out of them. On the press boats, the television cameras roll and photographers from the local papers snap away as if there was a prize for the one taking the most pictures. All the while a flotilla of pleasure boats weaves around the racing fleet trying to gain the best view. Ashore, hundreds of people gather on the cliffs overlooking the bay to watch this wonderful sight, binoculars and cameras at the ready. If the sun is shining and the breeze is just right, everyone seems to be brimming with happiness and the atmosphere in the town over that weekend is unique.

On the Saturday night a dance is held under the fish market with a band and bar, and once the alcohol has worked its magic, it's not just the young ones that are up strutting their stuff. Dance styles that were honed to perfection in discos many years ago are once more in evidence as fine demonstrations of wedding reception style 'Dad' dancing break out. I have even seen a few old ravers up flicking a dusty hoof with walking sticks in hand, bless 'em all.

Sunday night is prize-giving night, an event that has become rather predictable in the class 'A' section; the winners from way back are still the winners today, and do what they may, the other boats just can't touch them. First place has always been taken by the *Guide Me* (FY 233) while second and third places are shared between the 1903 Mevagissey lugger *Reliance* (FY 59) and the 1898 Porthleven-built *George Glasson* (FH 173). The sailing performance of these very ancient craft is nothing short of astounding; they cut through the rest of the fleet like a knife through butter and will very often lap them. To the more competitive crews left in their wake, they are a benchmark to try and come up to: new and bigger sails are cut, new sheet leads are tried and a multitude of modifications take place, but so far the flyers seem to be virtually untouchable. But not to worry, the Olympic games maxim, as corny as it may sound, rings very true at the Looe regatta: 'It's not the winning but the taking part that counts', but I know several skippers who would say. "Bollocks, you wait until the next time!" In truth though, it's both those attitudes that make a good classic boat regatta, and long may it be so.

Postscript

The five luggers working out of Looe when I first went to sea are all still in service. The *Guide Me* was rebuilt and re-rigged by Jono and Judy Brickhill, bringing up four children aboard while she was their home for many years. They have cruised her extensively, winning the Antigua classics in the West Indies and today she is the flyer of the fleet.

The *Our Daddy* fished from Looe until the early 1980s. She was then bought by a Plymouth businessman who had her extensively rebuilt and converted into a no-expense spared luxury classic yacht, which rather gives her the air of a grand old duchess. Now owned by Looe businessman Mike Cotton in partnership with her skipper Mike Darlington, they do charter work and day sailing from Looe.

After many years in limbo, the *Eileen* is now back in good order, thanks to the hard work put in by her owner and skipper Lorain Harris of Penryn. She is a dipping lug rig and can be seen every summer taking part in the local regattas.

The *Our Boys* is splendidly refitted as a charter yacht, sporting a massive standing lug rig. She is now working out of Cowes in the Isle of Wight under skipper Richard Parr.

Last, but not least, is my old ship the *Iris*. When her fishing days ended in the early 1970s she eventually became a houseboat. Later a local shipwright, Andy Scantlebury, made her into a gaff ketch yacht. Based at Falmouth, he and his family lived on her for several years. Sold on, she suffered a couple of very indifferent owners and by 2000 was in a sorry state. She is now owned by trawler skipper and marine artist Toni Knights of Brixham and is undergoing massive restoration work from the keel up. The 'Old Black Dragon' will rise again.

I visited the *Iris* at the boatyard at Galmpton, up the river from Dartmouth. Craned out high and dry her new decks and hull planking looked fine, while down below she was stripped out from end to end awaiting her new fit out. I looked aft to where the old cabin used to be and in my mind's eye I could still see the sou'westers and mufflers swinging gently from their nails beside each bunk, the old Lister engine clattering away while the coal range puffed smoke from its open door. In his usual corner Harry sat rolling fags from a tin of dog-ends, while up top the decks were once more crowded with baskets of line, and there was Tiddler, Clarence, Moogie and Jack.

For a brief flash of time it was like watching a piece of film that I had somehow stepped into and become part of. I could see, hear and smell it all again. Then someone spoke and the spell was broken; I was no longer 16 years old and out lining in the Channel, I was nearer 60 and standing in a boatyard in Devon.

The lugger Iris *in the early 1920s, Looe, rigged for sail.*

(L-R) Bruce 'Tiddler' Sammels, Clarence Libby, Roy Pengelly, Frank 'Moogie' Pengelly on the Iris *c. 1955.*

The One Accord *in the 1950s: (L-R) Tommy Jolliff; Lando Puckey; Edmund Curtis; Jack Jolliff.*

Hauling nets aboard the Iris *at night: 'Moogie', Harry Stevens and Clarence Libby.*

Shaking out the nets at Looe quay, 1965.

Net cart, c. 1910 (same one used in the 1960s). Charles Clausen holding the shafts, with James Toms, ? Prynn and Richard Pearce.

Albert 'the Belgie' Daems, the Iris's 'scruffer'.

The Undaunted, *first lugger in Looe to be fitted with an engine.*

Iris *coming into Looe.*

The first motorised sailing luggers in Looe, still carrying full sailing rig.

The crew of
the Looe lugger
Iris, 1966. (L-R)
Alfred 'Tiddler'
Sammels; Harry
'Slender' Stevens;
Paul Greenwood;
Michael Pengelly;
Frank 'Moogie'
Pengelly;
Jack Harris
(foreground).

Iris, April 1965.
End of the
Channel lining
season, the
pilchards have
arrived. Hauling
the big summer
fleet aboard.

April 1965, at the end of the longline season. Hauling the main fleet aboard the Iris *to start the summer pilchard fishing.*

Guide Me *entering Looe harbour with passengers.*

Luggers putting to sea in the days of sail.

The Iris *during a 'paint-up' in 1965. (L-R) Jack Moore; Harry Stevens; Paul Greenwood; Alfred 'Tiddler' Sammels; Michael Pengelly; Frank 'Moogie' Pengelly.*

The Iris *during her last working days in the early 1970s.* Eileen *and* Our Daddy *in the background.*

The author aboard the Our Boys *with his wife, Maggie.*

The author (left) with 326-lb Mako shark caught aboard the Guiding Star *in 1970.*

The Iris *in 1965 ('Skips' Ransome right, on quay).*

Our Boys *hand lining for mackerel, 1967.*

*Brothers Harold 'Nibblo'
Butters (left) and Lewis
'Bonzo' Butters.*

Cousin Jack *of Penzance.*

End of a day's trawling on Ibis, *1984.*

The author (right) with crewman Chris Rees, landing fish from Ibis *in Looe 1984.*

Looe fish market, 1980s.

Ibis *racing under full sail in Looe Bay, 1993.*

The author (left) with Chris Rees, landing fish from Ibis *in Looe, 1984.*

Ibis *entering Looe, 1980s.*

Scots' purse seiner landing catch.

The Ibis *bringing a Scots trawler to a halt off the Dodman.*

Crew of the Ibis *in 1981: Chris Rees (left), 'Nezzer' and the author (right).*

Mackerel boats in Looe, 1980s.

The author landing trawl fish from Ibis *in Looe.*

Graham Jolliff on Polperro mackerel *boat, hand line with a hydraulic gurdey.*

The author at the wheel of Ibis.

Mackerel catch using handline.

MORE TALES FROM
A CORNISH LUGGER

Introduction

Cornwall, a county officially classed as the poorest in England, especially in the winter time, with high unemployment and a very low average wage, generally makes for pretty grim reading. For years now the place has been marketed as a sort of Disneyesque theme park, a land of myth and legend, of smugglers and pirates, mining and fishing, most of it now safely locked into the past.

The industries that once earned so many people in this county a living have slipped, or are slipping, away. The mines, unable to compete with foreign competition but still rich in tin, copper, lead and silver now lie silent and overgrown, and the men who once worked them relocated to hard rock mines all over the globe. While today, farmers take part time jobs to keep the wolf from the door and many have converted their barns into holiday accommodation.

Global competition has led to massive job cuts in the once mighty china clay industry, while European government policy ensures that the fishing fleet continues to shrink. All but a handful of the boatyards have closed down, their now oh-so desirable waterside locations cleared to make way for luxury flats that will overlook yet another marina; their skilled workforce scattered to make a living elsewhere as car park attendants or building site chippies. The only traditional industry still thriving, though I doubt the Cornish play much of a part in it nowadays, is smuggling: cheap booze and tobacco is not hard to come by, while in the quiet coves and bays, cargoes of illegal drugs must be coming ashore by the ton.

It would seem that just to survive in their own county, many Cornish people have few options but to attend to the tourists and be thankful for their little low-paid seasonal jobs. Meanwhile every quaint cottage becomes a holiday home, snapped up at prices that no local could possibly afford. Many villages now have no communities other than a transient population of Home Counties 4x4 drivers, plump and pink and resplendent in their smart seaside casuals.

And if funding can be secured, once the last of the smelly fishing boats have gone, many harbours have plans for marinas, complete with posh restaurants and art galleries.

Cornwall always was the poor relation of England, but what little it did have was at least real. Today it is still the poor relative but now, with the way industry is evaporating, the county will soon be trying to earn a living with little more to purvey than myths and legends and the beauty of its scenery. This seems to be the fate of Cornwall, and maybe we should be thankful that at least the place has the tourism when all else is failing. And if, by chance, a wealthy entrepreneur was to appear on the scene with a master plan that would create 3,000 jobs on the south Cornish coast throughout the winter months; one that didn't involve millions of pounds of funding, retraining, or despoiling the entire area, then that man would be hailed as a genius, a hero. But in the late 1960s and early 1970s, that's exactly what did happen, though without the aid of a wealthy businessman or massive grants, and in wintertime, created and run entirely on private enterprise. It was the great Cornish mackerel fishery. From a very doubtful beginning it grew and flourished beyond all expectations, and then it was allowed to fade away. I witnessed at first hand its inception and its demise, and it makes me feel at best, sad; at worst very angry at what was allowed to happen. We who were in that industry had it swept from under our feet, and we stood by helpless and unhelped as our hard-won enterprise was left to die.

I wrote my first book, *Once Aboard A Cornish Lugger*, to record the way of life in the last years that those pilchard fishing boats were operating. But after 45 years working out of the port of Looe as a fisherman, boatman and charter skipper, I now look back and realise that so much else has changed in that time, perhaps I should try and tell that story as well. Because the way of life as I knew it has gone and will never return. In the winter time we went commercial fishing, and there was usually plenty of fish to catch and the freedom to do so. Come the spring time, we painted up our sea-worn wooden boats to take the summer visitors out on pleasure trips. The seasons came and went, and I believe we thought that it would go on forever.

1

Mackerel & Pilchards

On a winter's afternoon early in 1966 the Looe lugger *Iris* entered port from an exploratory day's fishing with about 100 stone of prime mackerel on her deck. Big beautiful fish like miniature tuna, and on Plymouth fish market the next morning they made the excellent price of £1 per stone. For the five crew members this meant the best part of a week's wage had been put together in one go, a very good day's work indeed. I remember this incident well because I was one of the crew and, like all the other drifter liners, we had been scratching about trying to earn a living with the nets and lines, and believe you me in the winter time it was usually an awful lot of hard labour for a very meagre reward.

There was rarely a profit to be made, it was purely an exercise to try and keep the wolf from the door, and he was clawing at the paintwork for most of the time. But a chance remark had given our skipper the idea that there might be a few mackerel about off Plymouth Sound. Why, we had no idea. They had never been there before, but as there was nothing to lose, a hand line consisting of 40 fathoms of cod line ending with a dozen feathered hooks and a pound lead was made up for each man, and early one morning we slipped away on the tide to investigate this rumour. 100 stone of fish at £1 a stone was excellent money, and if we could do something like that three or four days a week, not only would the wolf be kept from the door, you wouldn't be able to catch a glimpse of him with a pair of powerful binoculars. But who knows with fishing, there may not be a fish to be caught on the next trip out.

The weather held fine for the next few days and on each of those days we found the mackerel and landed a catch, the price staying steady at a

£1 a stone on Plymouth market. Of course the other skippers had kept a close eye on what the *Iris* was doing, and when our bit of success looked to be more than a one off, the other four drifters in the port got their hand lines made up ready to have a go themselves. So now there were five boats out hunting about: joining the *Iris* were the *Our Boys*, *Our Daddy*, *Guide Me* and the *Endeavour*, each at the end of the day landing good-quality fish, and what was more, the buyers continued to pay good money for it. And so we fished on like this until March when the shoals faded away and eventually there were none to be found. But what an unexpected bonus we had earned. For the first time in years the crews on the boats had earned a decent living wage in the winter months. Would the mackerel return again the following year? We sincerely hoped so.

The following March the pilchard shoals returned to the Cornish coast once more. Not, at first, in any huge numbers but enough to make a bait up for the long lines. So once again we were doing 24- to 30-hour trips out deep in the Channel shooting and hauling seven thousand hooks on 7 miles of line, to catch ray, conger, ling etc. That was a nasty shock to the system after weeks of tiddling around up and down the shore with a twelve hook hand line.

By the month of May the pilchard shoals became much more prolific; the long lines could now be put ashore and in their place we hauled aboard the full summer fleet of 22 drift nets, being 11 fathoms deep and nearly 2 miles long. Night after night we shot and hauled them to supply fish to the cannery at Newlyn. It was all done by sheer muscle power. A big catch could mean 8 or 10 hours work non stop. That was what it took just to get the fleet of nets back aboard the boat, never mind steaming home, boxing up and landing. In the summer season we also took visitors out shark fishing, a daytime job to go with the night time one we already had. The money was good but sometimes you thought you were going to die on your feet from lack of sleep.

And so October came when once again the pilchard shoals thinned away from the coast and the nets were hauled ashore, dried and stowed back up in the net loft for another winter. Of course the big question then was whether the mackerel shoals would be around again or would we have to spend yet another winter working out of Brixham, living aboard the boat while trying to scratch a living with the herring nets and long lines. We hoped for the former for the latter was a rather grim prospect. So before the herring nets were made ready the hand lines were put aboard to give them a try first, and we weren't disappointed. Up off Plymouth Sound, there they were again, lines full of great big fat mackerel, as bold as brass and as lively as dolphins. Another decent winter season looked to be in prospect.

This sort of work was a real novelty to us because, when a good week's wage was made working the nets and long lines, we were utterly shattered from the sheer physical louster involved, working both by night and day. Rest was something that was taken when the weather turned poor or when we were all on the verge of collapse. And yet there we were, working up and down the shore jigging a little hand line around for the day, home to bed every night and money at the end of the week. It was almost too good to be true.

The boats that first went fishing for mackerel were the ageing survivors from the once mighty Cornish drifter fleet. The oldest were motorised vessels from the days of sail such as the *Guide Me* and the *Our Boys*; others like the *Iris*, *Our Daddy* and the *Eileen* had been auxiliaries, built with both motor and sail for the boom times after the First World War. These boats were 38 to 45 feet long and fully decked, fine sea-kindly old craft. I say sea-kindly rather than seaworthy because at the time most of these boats were well on towards the end of their working life. They were safe enough because they were well handled by men who knew them, but after years of hard times and frugal maintenance I dread to think what a surveyor might have had to say about some of them.

The other class of boats then on the coast were what was known as quatters, mainly built for the boom in the fishing after the Second World War. They were 30 feet to 38 feet in length, with a long foredeck and a full width open-backed wheel house. The working area was a hatch board deck set about waist high down from the rail. They could be fitted out for whatever fishing was good at the time or worked by one man for the pleasure boating in the summertime. Very versatile and economical craft to work, their big disadvantage was that because they were open, every drop of water that came aboard had to be pumped out, by hand of course. And because of the way things were at the time most of these boats were used only in the summer months for pleasure angling; during the winter the skippers got a job ashore, labouring for a builder, painting and decorating or whatever would bring in a week's wage.

But not this winter. Hand lines were made up and boats that hadn't been to sea in the winter time for many years, were out joining in the bonanza. Roles were really being reversed. To make up the crews, painters and decorators, masons, chippies and shipwrights were going to sea for the winter instead of the fishermen coming ashore. The word was out: something new was happening, and coves and quays that had lain dormant for years were coming back to life as shoals of mackerel came in to winter all along the south Cornish coast. Here was a brand new fishery; from catching to marketing there was much to learn and develop, and many new ideas to try out. One of the first things that had to be improved was the hand line itself.

Hauling by hand all day long led to the twine of the back line cutting into your hands, and when shaking the fish off, the hooks nipped into your hands. It was as bad as drift netting, hands raw and sore with pus-swollen fingers. And of course the line itself was difficult to keep running clear, coiled down onto the deck or into a fish box; the wind could and did blow it about, or a fish would land in it, flapping madly, reducing a carefully flaked down line to a birds nest tangle. The leads on the end of the line weren't really heavy enough either and if you jigged the line for just a bit too long the mackerel on the hooks would swim about with it, so when it was lifted aboard instead of a nice string of fish there was something that resembled a big bunch of bananas, the line and hooks all wound up in one tight ball. All this of course had to be cleared before the line could be dropped again. After this had happened to someone three or four times on the run, it would reduce them to a teeth-gnashing fury, ready to bite lumps out of the mast with sheer frustration. A few neatly worded jibes could prove most entertaining.

Various ideas were tried out to improve the working of the lines, but the first real break-through was made by Tommy Paul, a Londoner who along with his merry crew worked an old Thames Bawley out of Looe called the *Onward*. They appeared at sea one Sunday morning with the peddle crank section of a bicycle frame married to a car wheel. Each man had one of these contraptions clamped to the rail of the boat; the line was wrapped around the wheel and when paid out it was retrieved again by turning the peddle. Of course everyone had a damn good snigger at the *Onward*'s crew as they suffered back turns, over ride, and as many tangles as anyone working a hand line.

Tommy and his gang weren't rated very highly as fishermen and this performance only proved what a gang of cowboys they really were. That was until they ironed out the teething problems and started to work two to one against a hand line. Then it was a different story entirely. All of a sudden there was a rush to copy, or improve on Tommy's invention. Many variations were tried out and most of them worked, until by about 1969 the final form of the 'gurdy' came into being. This was a simple device, a wooden wheel made of half jointed 2x2, 18 inches in diameter with deep Vs cut into the end of each of the four arms onto which the line could be wound. A central axle bolt held it to an angle iron stanchion that was clamped to the boat's rail. The wheel was turned by a handle mounted on one of the wheel arms and a fairlead guided the line into place. No more wind blowing the line about and no more fish dancing amongst it. The business end of the line went from a dozen feathered hooks on light gut to double that number with coloured plastic lures all mounted on heavy-duty nylon, terminating in a 3-pound lead, and in those days there were mackerel around big enough to actually swallow these leads.

The fish were still hauled aboard and shaken off by hand, and by that I don't mean that we caught hold of the shank of each hook and tiddled at it until the fish fell off. No, an arm span of line was lifted up and brought down with a whop, jerking six or eight fish off at a go. But by now we protected our hands with heavy industrial plastic gloves, which didn't stop all injuries but certainly prevented about 90 per cent. Hooks pricking into the hands were still an all-day occurrence, but suffering the agony of having to rip a hook out that had gone in past the barb was greatly reduced. And to keep the line flowing free over the boat, lengths of 4- and 6-inch plastic drain pipe were split back and sprung onto the rails, while other lengths were hung over the side between rail and waterline. All this ensured that foul ups were kept to a minimum. We now had the right gear for the job, and catch rates shot up from 100 stone a boat to 100 stone plus per man, in many cases very much more than that.

When the big mackerel were shoaling high in the water, a catch of more than 1,000 stone was not unusual for a smart four-handed crew. Often, with the 30-foot open class of boat, the boat of choice for many of the mackerel men, it was not a question of how much you could catch, but how much you dared haul aboard and remain seaworthy in the weather conditions prevailing on the day. I can't recall a mackerel boat ever foundering, but on fine weather days I have seen them loaded to the point where a good steep wash from a passing merchant ship would have given them serious problems. And to avoid being swamped in poor weather when steaming home, boxes of fish would sometimes have to be dumped overboard to lighten her up a bit and enable the boat to lift more readily to the seas.

Given the amount of fish available to be caught and the size of the boats used to catch them, the catching capacity was as good as it could be. Any better and I think a boat or two would have ended up paying a visit to Neptune.

2

Hand-lining

By the early 1970s the Cornish handline mackerel fishery was expanding at a fantastic rate; it was proving to be very lucrative and very easy to get in on. In those days fishermen had the freedom of the seas. You could buy a boat, any boat, register it and the rest was up to you; the rules, regulations and restrictions were very few indeed.

So, wherever boats were for sale, fishermen from Cornwall were snapping them up. Scotland and Brittany were two good sources of second-hand craft, while here in Cornwall just about anything that floated was pressed into service: summer pleasure steamers and ferry boats, wartime motor launches, motor yachts and retired lifeboats. As a rule of thumb, the more motley the boat then the more motley were the men that crewed them. Farm workers, dock-yardies, hippies, barmen and waiters from the hotels, everyone was out there having a go. And why not; it was much better than the dole and it cost very little to fit out a boat for the job. As you can imagine, many of these types dropped out as quickly as they dropped in, but others persevered and many of them went on to become good fishermen. We laughed at a lot of these people, but in a fishery boom you can't suddenly find hundreds of skilled fishermen; the extra manpower has to come from somewhere as boat numbers had gone from twenty or so at the start to over four hundred in a very short space of time.

It was not only second-hand boats that were in demand. This boom had given the local boatyards full order books because many of the top fishermen invested in powerful new boats. One or two of these new craft were made of fibre glass, but at the time very little was known about that medium so most skippers stayed with wood. Plus, of course, all around the Cornish coast there were still plenty of boatyards building in wood to a very high standard. On bad weather days there were always car-loads of fishermen jaunting off to have a look at some one's new boat then under construction.

All these new boats had to be adaptable to work the different seasons. In Looe they were nearly all of the forward wheelhouse hatch board deck design, able to carry a small hydraulic winch for the stopgap trawling season between the end of the mackerel fishing and the start of summer pleasure angling. In other ports they preferred an aft wheelhouse and a laid deck because they went crabbing, netting or long lining in the summer. And these new boats were a very good investment. There were loans and grants available to help defray the cost, and at the time it was reckoned that a new boat could be paid off within 3 years.

The mackerel boats of the 1970s, and the trawlers and netters that were launched in the 1980s, were to be the last hurrah for the wooden boat, however. Of course the marketing side of things was expanding rapidly to match the landings of this ever increasing fleet, for what had once been a purely local affair had, by the early 1970s, become very big business. In mackerel landing ports such as Newlyn, Falmouth, Mevagissey and Looe, teams of packers stood by each evening ready to box and ice the day's catch before loading up the waiting refrigeration lorries that carried this fresh Cornish produce to the fish markets of all the major cities in the UK as well as to France, Spain, Italy and Greece. When the weather was fine and the fishing heavy, these packing teams would be working right through the night. Many is the time they would still be boxing and icing the previous day's catch when we were going to sea the following morning.

The catch rate for mackerel had increased tenfold, and it was also hard physical work. Depending on where the fish were to be found it could involve some very long hours. But no fisherman worries about a 15- or 18-hour working day if there are fish to be caught. You can have a rest when the winter storms roll in and it's double ropes out to hold the boats to the quay.

Compared with fishermen of today we led a life of great freedom. There was no one telling you what you could or could not fish for; the boat that you went to sea in and the engine that powered it was entirely your business. Each skipper worked the different seasons of the year as he saw fit, old men, young men, old boats and new. But they have all gone now, the boats, the men and the seasons that they worked. These were my main working years and I witnessed it all from the decks of the various boats that I worked on, fair weather and foul, good times and bad, shipwreck and tragedy. It's a tale that any fisherman from my era could tell, but I doubt that they will, so I shall try to put the story together as I saw it while working from the port of Looe.

3

'Doodle Bugs'

In 1973 I returned home to Looe after 2 ½ years away working as bo'sun on the sailing schooner *Malcolm Miller*. It had been a wonderful experience, but it was all sea time and boozing when ashore, which was fun while it lasted but I didn't want to make a career out of it. Returning home, I bought a 30-foot converted ship's lifeboat and with that I worked in the summer months taking visitors on day trips to Fowey and Polperro, combined with inshore angling trips and evening conger fishing. She was a handy little boat for the summer trade, but just wasn't stout enough for winter work out on the mackerel. So, smartly painted up and all in good working order, I put her up for sale, and as luck would have it I soon found a buyer.

After life on the schooner, sailing all around Europe, I felt restless back in Looe. By the spring of 1974 I had money in the bank but no boat to earn a living with and was casting about wondering what I was going to do. I was very tempted to go back sailing on the schooners, but thankfully I managed to talk myself out of it. The question of what to do next however was answered by the sad and untimely death of Theo Matthews, one of the local boatmen. Theo and his son Collin each had a fleet of six, of what in Looe were known as 'doodle bugs', 14-foot clinker-built boats powered by a small inboard engine, hired out to the summer visitors at an hourly rate on a self-drive basis. This form of boating was very popular and a very good earner, so when Theo's widow put his boats up for sale I jumped at the opportunity to buy them. But this was a branch of boating I knew nothing about. At a first glance it looked a very leisurely way to make a living, sitting in a deck chair on the quayside sunning yourself while taking money from people having an hour's spin around the bay or up the river in one of your boats. But it wasn't quite like that. Fortunately Collin was there to show me the basics of the business, such as how to maintain and keep the little two stroke engines running, how to raft up the boats to get them on and off their moorings, in fact there were a thousand and one things to learn that I had never come across before. And yes, there was good money to be earned with them, but on a busy day you just never stopped running about.

A typical day on the 'doodle bugs' would start at about eight o'clock in the morning when the boats would be rafted up and brought from their mid-river moorings to the quayside steps that you worked from. The first job was to go from boat to boat with an old brass hand pump and pump them all dry. Next they had to be fuelled up and the engines checked over, sumps drained out, spark plugs cleaned etc. Then the bottom boards and fore decks were scrubbed and the seats wiped down, by which time the boats were ready for the day's work. On the quay we had an old van in which we kept petrol cans, engine spares, fishing lines and tools, a sort of ready-made store for all the things needed to keep the boats running. It was also where my grub tin and flask of tea were kept plus a deckchair I had pinched from the beach, so with everything ready to go there was just time for a slurp of tea and a sit down before the rush began.

Over the school summer holidays, the really busy times, each boatman employed a boy to help out. They were paid about £1 a day, and it was a fine job for a lad, out in the sunshine all day playing on boats. My first helper was Richard Newman. He was about 10 or 11 years old and a good little worker. But he was the same as all the other lads; if the day was a bit slack they would get bored and then they would all gang up together and get stroppy and very cheeky. The answer to that problem was to await your moment and grab one of them and hurl him overboard. This treatment served to remind them for a while of where they really stood in the pecking order of things and, if it never actually cured them for long, we gained great satisfaction and amusement at the Doppler effect of the howl they uttered as their little bodies carved an arc through the air before hitting the water with a mighty splash.

Around ten o'clock the first holiday makers would start strolling down the quay and the touting would begin: "Boat Sir, self-drive, a lovely day for a trip up the river or out in the bay," was the usual sort of blag. And if all went well young Richard would be rushing down the quay wall ladder to start a boat and bring it in to the steps. I would see the people aboard, give them a few instructions on the engine and how to steer, take the money (then it was £1 a hour) and away they would go. The boats could carry up to six people so it was pretty good value for money.

On a fine sunny summer's morning all the boats could be away one after another and the pattern for the day would be set: a boat would return, Richard would be there to see it in and help the people off as I would be waiting on the quay with another family, money paid and ready to go.

When the tide turned, ebbing away from the quay, the boats would be anchored off in the stream of the river and we would work from the shingle bank getting the people on and off the boats via a couple of wooden boxes to keep their feet dry. And when the tide crept back in again we would work our way back to the steps once more. Around five o'clock trade would almost come to a halt as everyone went home for their tea, and often that was the time to call a halt to the day ourselves. But if the weather looked set fair, it was often worthwhile to stay for the evening trade, working on until dusk descended around half nine or ten o'clock.

It wasn't always plain sailing though. Some days were utter chaos from one end to the other, with boats stuck on the mud up the river, or stranded on rocks out in the bay. There were times when you would be rushing about trying to do so many things at once you would all but disappear up your own backside. But by mid-September the holiday season was all but over, the tourists had returned home and the town was quiet once more. Even the hurdy-gurdy man returned to his winter quarters in Penzance. I can't recall his name, but for many years he tramped the length and breadth of the county pushing a two-wheeled cart, the hurdy-gurdy mounted on top and his camping gear slung underneath. He would always spend a day or so in Looe, stopping in likely spots around the town, his giant musical box producing a near forgotten fairground sound, loud and mechanical, playing songs from the Gilbert & Sullivan operettas and the music halls. He cranked the handle, busking for whatever money people threw into his box. He and a gypsy that toured about in a green horse-drawn caravan must have been among the very last of the itinerants.

Then it was time to put our hard-worked and somewhat battered little motor boats back in their shed for the winter months, elsewhere in Looe shops and cafés would be putting up their shutters. Most of the small pleasure boats were craned ashore and sheeted over, while the bigger craft, those from about 25 feet and upwards would be making ready for the winter mackerel fishery. Most of the men who worked the 'doodle bugs' and small pleasure boats went to sea on the mackerel boats in the wintertime, and there would be many shore workers getting ready to join the boats as crewmen with this profitable, and ever-increasing fleet.

4

'Nibblo' & 'Bonzo'

In the winter of 1974 I had shipped on the *Prosperity*, a fine craft that had been built in Scotland some 20 years before and was about 40 feet long. She was fully decked and had a cruiser stern, an aft wheelhouse and was powered by a 70 HP Gardner engine, owned and skippered by 'Bonzo' Butters. Also sailing with Bonzo was his brother 'Nibblo' who in the summer time was a speedboat driver. Bonzo and Nibblo, whose real names were Lewis and Harold, were both in their middle to late forties and came from an old Looe family, all their forefathers having been fishermen and sailors. In height, neither one of them topped the 5 feet mark, though by the thickness of a fag paper Nibblo claimed he was the taller of the two. In build they were both pretty stocky, and personality wise, well, lurking beneath a very spiky and defensive exterior they were as good as gold, but fight and argue!! I had never seen the likes of it until I shipped up with them. It was like going to sea with a pair of human Jack Russell terriers.

Summer being over we were now eager to get the *Prosperity* ready for the winter fishery. Off the boat and into the store went the summer paraphernalia: the shark chair, the fishing rods and bench seats followed by the sharpie mizzen and the chemical toilet.

And out from the store we dragged, and then shipped up, the heavy pound boards. These were about a foot deep and were fitted both across the beam of the boat and fore and aft so as to divide the deck up into small areas or pounds, thus preventing the catch from sliding about as the boat rolled and plunged at sea. Next, the gaff mizzen was bent on to its spars. This sail, when hoisted and working in conjunction with the engine, would keep the boat riding comfortably head to wind in even the worst of weather, vital when we were working on deck. Where each crewman worked his line, a 10-foot length of plastic drainpipe that had been sawn down its length was sprung into the rail. At sea, a corresponding length was slung over the side on ropes between the rail and waterline to stop the hooks from fouling on the hull when the line were being worked. The gurdies had been wire-brushed and oiled up, all free running and ready for action, while plenty of spare sets of feathers and leads had been stowed in the wheelhouse lockers. Oilskins, aprons and sea boots were hung in the engine room where they would keep warm and dry. Last of all we hauled several stacks of fish boxes down from the fish market and stowed them in the deck pounds. Nibblo shopped for a few stores as Bonzo and I topped up the fuel tanks, and that was it. The good ship *Prosperity* along with her gallant crew stood ready to do battle.

"What time in the morning, Bonz?" asks Nibblo.

"I don't know, what do you reckon?" says his brother.

"Well there's been a few fish out the back of the radar buoy, I suppose we could start there and see what happens," comes the reply.

"Yes, that sounds okay, better make it five o'clock then. That alright with you, Captain?" says Bonzo.

In the 3 years that I sailed on the *Prosperity* I don't think I was ever called by my name. It was 'Captain' from Bonzo, and 'Ned', a nickname I had had for many years, from Nibblo.

"That will do," I reply.

"Right then, five o'clock it is, and don't be late," says Bonzo.

"Huh, who do you think you're talking to, you look out for your own clock, I'll be there," snaps Nibblo.

"'Ark to that little fucker," says Bonzo, addressing me. "I have seen you late plenty of times Nibblo."

"No you fucking haven't."

"Yes I fucking have."

"Ahh, bollocks to you Bonzo, you can poke the *Prosperity* up your arse if you are going to carry on like that."

Things are starting to get out of hand so I chime in: "For fuck's sake cut it out you pair, five o'clock will do us, and I'll see you then."

With that the situation is defused. "Okay, Captain, and don't be late" says Bonzo, looking at me sideways with a devilish twinkle in his eye. One thing about working on the *Prosperity* was that whatever we did, or whatever decisions had to be made, there was always a full crew debate on it before a conclusion was drawn.

Come the morning we are all aboard on time, thank God, and along with the rest of the Looe fleet we steer out SSW for a couple of hours to bring us out south of the radar buoy. What this buoy has to do with radar and why it is there no one seems to know. It marks nothing and is in deep water, but it had become a handy reference point.

Bonzo eases the engine down now with one eye on the echo sounder and one ear cocked to the VHF. The hunt was on. The mizzen is hoisted and the gurdies are clamped onto the rail, with leads and feathers bent on ready to go. All we need now is a 'scry', a big mark on the sounder, or a shout on the VHF that someone is into fish, but so far nothing much is happening. There are little bits of marks every now and then on the sounder, but when you give them a try there is nothing worth having, just a few small and medium mackerel and not many of them.

"Fucking good start to the season," says Bonzo.

"Don't you worry," says Nibblo. "We shall have them in a minute, I can feel it in my water."

"Well, all I hope is that your water can do better than this echo sounder," Bonzo replies. "Anyway, let's have another cup of tea."

"Another cup of tea! I've made three on the way out already. Any more and you'll piss yourself," comes the retort.

"Nibblo, if I want a cup of tea I'll have one."

"Well, you had better go down forward and make the bastard thing yourself. What do you think I am aboard of this boat, your servant?"

"Servant? You little twat, you aren't smart enough for that."

Oh look out, I think to myself, here they go again.

"Right, I am going down to put the kettle on," I shout. "You don't want a cup then, Nibblo?"

"Of course I do, Ned, I just wasn't going to be seen running around after that short-arsed little fucker in the wheelhouse there."

But arguing about it was as near as we got to that brew of tea, for as we spoke the prop was suddenly thrashing astern and Bonzo was winding up the throttle to bring the boat to halt, shouting "Down lines, a big mark here on the meter."

Nibblo and I paid our hooks over the side and let the lead carry them down into the depths, the arms of our gurdies rotating around like miniature windmills.

"Look out boys, here they are, this feels like the right stuff," shouts Nibblo as both our lines hit into the fish that were shoaling ten fathoms or so beneath our keel. A quick jig on the line to make sure it was full, and the upward wind begins. Twenty-five large and lively mackerel, weighing about two pounds each or more can put up quite a fight especially if they happen to try and dive together, but come up they must, and we were soon lifting strings of these beautiful fish aboard.

An arm span of fish is lifted chest high then brought down with a 'whap' and the catch flies off, blood and slime splattering everywhere, while the tails of gasping fish rap out a tattoo on the deck. Three goes like that and the line is clear, released, and the lead takes it down for more. With a kick ahead now and then on the engine, the old boat rides comfortably on her mizzen, head up to the light westerly breeze. What a start to the season. This is excellent fishing, and to make the best of it the three of us toil away as if being urged on by the Devil himself. The chatter on the VHF has at last ceased, and scattered all around us, boats from Looe, Polperro and Mevagissey are also hauling aboard string after string of big glittering mackerel.

When the fishing was like that, time had no meaning. You stop briefly to clear a tangle in the line, or to pull a fouled hook out of your glove or oilskin and then on you go. It is not until the mackerel are lying on the deck so thick that you are no longer able to shuffle up and down the few feet of deck needed to work the line that a brief halt has to be called. This might be the time for the man nearest the cabin hatch to slip down and put the kettle on, while the fish are hosed down and scooped into boxes or pounds to clear the working area. If a line needs changing or several hooks and lures are missing, now is the time to cut it off and bend on a new set. A quick sandwich and a mug of tea and on we go again, total stop time fifteen minutes, maybe less. That is a luxury. On some boats they only stop to scoop the fish. All afternoon we haul aboard line after line of jumbo mackerel. The boxes are stacked up brim full, and the deck pounds are topped off level with the rail, our backs are aching, our hands are sore and everything not covered in mackerel is cascading with a thick layer of bloody slime and scales including our oilskins and faces.

There is one minor diversion during the afternoon when Nibblo suddenly shouts out: "I've got the bastard, look out here he goes." He has caught a shark and his line was now paying out at a terrific rate.

I have seen plenty of sharks played on a gurdy, but I have never ever seen one brought to the gaff despite some very skilled attempts to do so. And it was no different this time. After a minute of two, it parts away and a new set of gear has to be bent on.

By now the light is going out of the water and the mackerel are starting to go off the feed.

"Well, personally, I think we have had a very good day," says our skipper. "What say you we head for home to mother?"

"Fucking good idea," comes from me and Nibblo.

"Okay then, slack the mizzen and I'll bring her around."

I clamber aft, balancing along the tops of the pound boards to get to the sheets. Bonzo goes into the wheelhouse and jams the engine into gear and winds up the throttle. The old engine belches out a huge cloud of black smoke to clear its throat after a day on tick-over before settling down clean and clear, rumbling away at a steady 900 RPM. Nibblo nips down into the cabin to put the kettle on, and there we are, tired out and homeward bound with a good catch of fish. There is no better feeling.

We approach the Banjo pier at Looe and Bonzo winds back on the throttle to enter the harbour at a respectable speed. Then, slowing down to tick over and finally knocking her out of gear, we nudge alongside the quay to get our fish ashore, but what a clamour. Thirty boats all wanting to land at once; everyone wants to get home and it is utter mayhem. On the decks of deeply laden craft, men are working flat out, hoses and buckets in action, to wash the catch. Fish are being hurriedly sorted and scooped into 5-stone boxes, then flung up onto the quay and stacked up onto wooden pallets. Boats that have landed are manoeuvring to let another alongside the quayside. From one end to the other the quay is twinkling with working and navigation lights, there's plenty of shouting and banter, and all to the background thrum of the diesel engine. But eventually, out of this chaos comes order, and within a couple of hours or so, all is tranquil once more and the boats are snubbing quietly at their moorings A few terns are shrieking on the river, and the only human sounds now are of the muffled voices and laughter of the packing gang (twenty or so men) inside the fish market, working long into the night to get the day's catch boxed, iced and loaded onto the lorries.

5

Prosperity

Shoals of mackerel, trillions strong, were arriving to winter off the Cornish coast. While we were making big catches in the Radar Buoy area, the Newlyn boats were loading off at the back of St Michael's Mount. But this handy to home fishing was not to last for very long, because the over-wintering area of choice for these huge shoals seemed to lay somewhere between the Western Blackhead and Dodman Point, with the biggest concentrations usually in the Falmouth Bay area. It was here that the shoals sometimes packed in so densely boats could steam over them for miles on end with their echo sounders blacked out from top to bottom. Even the most experienced skippers had never witnessed anything quite like it before.

As the shoal that we had started to fish on moved west, the one in Mount's Bay came east. Both made their way to Falmouth, followed closely by the boats that had been hunting them. So effectively the whole of the Cornish mackerel fleet were focusing their efforts in the one area, all working on one immense concentration of fish.

In those days, it took the boats an average of 4 hours to open up St Anthony's light in Falmouth Bay from Looe, bashing away against the wind that always seemed to be blowing fresh and gusty from somewhere in the westerly quarter. Rare was the morning we weren't in for a bumpy ride with plenty of flying spray, but thankfully this also gave us a fair run home which is definitely the right way around when making passage in a heavily laden boat. Having such a long steam to the fishing grounds each morning meant, tides permitting, we had a very early start to the day. By four o'clock in the morning, Looe harbour would be a rumble of activity, the muffled chat and laughter as crewmen dragged tiers of boxes from under the fish market to be stacked aboard for the coming day's fishing; the clattering mechanical roar followed by clouds of choking grey smoke as yet another well-worn engine erupted into life. Much chit chat as legs and fenders are unshipped, the sharp tinkling noise made by the quayside mooring rings when the ropes are slipped. And when the last boat burbles its way out to sea, peace and tranquillity descend again, harbour lights reflecting into glassy calm water, the only sounds the mewing of a few terns and gulls. The occupants of the cottages close to the harbour side roll over in bed and try and snatch a little more sleep; bottles rattle intermittently in their crate as a milkman does his round, door to door.

Out in Looe Bay and while still in the shelter of the island, the boats stop for a few minutes to hoist their mizzen sails. Tightly sheeted home, this sail will act like a shock absorber, easing out much of the plunge, roll and jump when steaming head to sea.

Aboard the *Prosperity* we quickly set our mizzen and then nip smartly for the shelter of the wheelhouse, closing the door behind us. It's not in the least bit inviting out there, cold, dark, wet and windy. Bonzo winds the engine into gear and proceeds to pick a way down the shallow rocky channel that runs between Looe Island and the mainland. Scrabbling at the wheelhouse door, Nibblo bursts in, pot of tea in hand, his donkey jacket and hat sparkling with beads of water. He has just run the gauntlet from the cabin hatch on the fore deck, and for his trouble he has been lashed with a cat's paw of spray.

"Well done, that's just the job," we greet him.

"All I can say is, I hope you pair appreciate the things I do for you," comes the reply.

"You're a wonderful little chap, of that there is no doubt," I parry.

"Bollocks," he retorts. "Put the light on a minute Bonz so I can see to pour the tea."

There's a click, and a begrudging yellow glow seeps around the wheelhouse, three mucky chipped mugs are pulled out from wherever they had been wedged, a slop of tea tipped into one is swilled from mug to mug and then jettisoned out of the lee window. Thus, suitably washed out, the ready-milked and sugared tea is poured into them and from the same pot through the course of a long day may well come coffee, soup or cocoa. The light is quickly switched off – the man steering must not lose his night vision. Braced against the roll and pitch of the boat we enjoy a breakfast of tea and biscuits. Nibblo hangs off the end of the first of his forty Woodbines, the smoke from which thickens up the cold damp air of the wheelhouse.

In the pitch darkness, the loom of the land can be made out on the starboard hand, black against a dark grey sky. Clearing the island channel, Bonzo puts on a bit of port wheel to clear Oarstone Point and then gives the engine full throttle; SW by W will take us clear of the Dodman Point and on down to Falmouth Bay. Polperro light is winking away on the cliffs abeam of us while over the luff of the starboard bow the distant lights of Gorran Haven and Mevagissey appear to dance in between the vicious winter squalls whirling out of Par Bay. All around us the red and green navigation lights of our fleet bob and curtsy, while their white masthead lights slice madly about in the blackness above them.

In the *Prosperity*'s wheelhouse Bonzo is perched up on the steering chair while Nibblo and I are on the bench seat aft. The only illumination is the low glimmer of the master clock on the old Mark V Decca Navigator clicking endlessly around, red, green, purple, red, green, purple, the colours in deep hypnotic shades. A tiny yellow diode glowing on the front panel of the VHF radio indicates that it is switched on, but of that we are very well aware as the air is now full of gossip from the other boats; channel eight is red hot with news of how the local pool and darts teams are fairing, an update on the health of someone's wife or mother who had recently been poorly, or just general leg-pulling and joke telling, all vital stuff. We are now starting to pick up the SW ground swell, a long lazy surge under running the messy top wash caused by the fresh nor'westerly wind now blowing. And so we plunge along, our old engine burbling away comfortably in the engine room beneath our feet. The faster boats such as the *Tethra*, *Ella* and *Ganesha* have now opened up a lead over the rest of us. These three are among the newest in the fleet and have the power to touch nine knots, while most of the others are lucky to average seven or maybe eight if you really strangle the last bit of power out of the engines, something very few skippers like to do. But those three greyhounds have not got it all their own way because the old lugger *Our Boys*, now under the ownership of two keen young fishermen, Tony and Robert Chapman, has recently had a massive refit and sports two powerful modern engines. And what a gallant sight the old girl makes, stern tucked down in the water, stem sloping back like a First World War destroyer, cutting through the fleet at a good nine knots, not bad for a craft that started life under sail and oar back in 1904.

Pencarrow Point comes abeam and we open up Lantic Bay before the lights of Fowey come clear of Punchy Cross and Gribben Head marks the start of Par Bay, a horrible stretch of water when a fresh north west wind is blowing. Waves, steep and angry, can build up over a 10-mile fetch and smash against the side of the boat sending sheets of spray flying across the deck. Every now and then the boat will synchronise her rolling with the waves, and then it's hang on tight as she wallows rail to rail, the sudden and violent motion giving everything in the wheelhouse a good excuse to jump from its place and roll madly around the floor.

Leads and feathers, cups and spanners have all escaped and are going crazy. Bonzo is clinging to the wheel while Nibblo and I are trying to catch and stow the gear that has made a bid for freedom, giving the *Prosperity* a round and thorough cursing at the same time.

"Don't talk to my boat like that," says Bonzo.

"Fuck her," says Nibblo. "Look what the old cow has just done."

With order restored we plough on, the lashing spray and energy-sapping motion starting to ease a bit as we battle across the bay, the lights of Mevagissey fading down behind Chapel Point and thankfully we start to gain more of a lee. Dodman Point now looms high on the starboard hand, marking the halfway point of our voyage. The fleet ploughs on at a steady six or seven knots, gaining in number as boats from the fishing villages we pass along the way join us on the dark and windy trek westward. Landmarks are mentally ticked off in a vain attempt to get away from the Dodman that seems to linger close astern forever. Verryan Bay, Gull Rock and Gerrans Bay crawl past us in the darkness, and then St Anthony's Head, the eastern sentinel of our goal, Falmouth Bay, is abeam. Not only that, after a false dawn lasting so long you think it is never going to happen, daylight arrives, filtered meanly through low scudding winter clouds. It lifts your mood, driving away the lonely isolated feeling that darkness always gives. The towns of Mylor, St Mawes, Flushing, Penryn and Falmouth play host during the mackerel season to the boats from Padstow, Newquay, St Ives, Penberth Cove, Newlyn, Penzance, Porthlevan and Cadgwith, and what a cross section of craft there are. 20-foot open boats from the coves of Penberth and Cadgwith, French trawlers, Scots ring netters, Devon crabbers, Cornish luggers, Thames bawlies, Newlyn long liners and every class of fishing vessel ever built in Cornwall. These boats are now pouring out past Black Rock and into the bay, and it's not long before the skippers of the lead boats are on the radio blaring out the news of solid markings on the echo sounder and jumbo mackerel up in the water. Aboard the *Prosperity* we pull on our sea boots and oilskins, Nibblo and I go out on deck to ship up the gurdies and make ready. Nothing more can be done until we join the fleet, now becoming visible as a forest of masts and black smoke on the western skyline.

6

Pilot Whales

A mile away from the main fleet the echo sounder is switched on and instantly the graph paper is blacking out from top to bottom. It hasn't suddenly developed a fault, this is solid fish and whales as well. Hundreds of pilot whales have gathered in the bay, not to hunt mackerel as they don't seem the least bit interested in them, but the squid that lie under the mackerel shoals.

Bonzo passes the wheel over to me and goes forward to his line. Nibblo fishes amidships and I work aft by the wheel house door. How I became skipper when we worked the lines I have no idea. Nothing was ever said, it just happened. Getting very close to the fleet I eased the engine back, just nudging along to get through the whales.

"Give her a try here," says Bonzo.

"Hang on a minute," I reply, "I just want to get her up by the Castle Wray, they've got them solid".

In truth every one 'had them solid' but in a fleet of boats numbering hundreds you have to start somewhere. I stop her up a couple of boat lengths astern of the St Ives long liner *Castle Wray* and away go the lines, but not very far. The top hooks are only just under the water when the downward plummet of the 3-pound lead is arrested, by the sheer mass of fish fighting to get on the hooks. These fish are so big and lively that you nearly need two hands to wind your gurdy up, but come up they must. An arm span at a time, the line is lifted aboard as you move backward along your working space, here and there dropping bights of line into a fish box or over a pound board to try and prevent tangles. The last fish aboard leaves the lead on its long strop hanging over the rail then, a span at a time, the fish are whacked off the line with a sharp jerk, and when all is clear down you go for more. And so we carried on, lineful after lineful, only stopping to clear the odd tangle or to scoop the working area clear when you could no longer move your feet. With the mizzen set, a dab ahead on the engine every couple of minutes keeps the boat up head to wind, a nice steady working platform whatever the weather.

We fish on like this until around midday, by which time the deck is like a slaughter house with blood, slime and scales thickly lagged onto everything, your hat, face, oilskin and every part of the boat. The sets of gear are worn out, and we can hardly stem our boots through the fish that lay calf deep in the working area. And hunger and thirst are overtaking us. It is high time for a clear up and a bite to eat.

Nibblo grabs the deck hose to clean off his boots and oilskin before going down forward to put the kettle on while Bonzo and I proceed to scoop the fish into boxes and deck pounds to clear the working areas. The hose is then slashed about to try and clean things up a bit, by which time Nibblo is filling the mugs with steaming hot tea. Labour now ceases for ten minutes or so while we attend to the loudly protesting inner man. Standing on deck with a mug of tea in one hand and a sandwich in the other allows time to look about, and what a scene presents itself. One that I will never forget. Hundreds of boats working a shoal of fish several miles wide, while the space between every boat is filled with pilot whales, diving and swimming or just laying on the surface looking at us. The air and sea full of birds, gulls fighting and squawking, gannets quacking loudly as they plunge after fish, skuers robbing the gulls, and guillemots in little groups quietly going about their business. It was a scene that was nothing short of spectacular, and I doubt I shall witness its like again.

When the tea mugs are drained, we cut off the old feather sets and bend on new, but on the first drop we find a much smaller grade of fish. We have drifted too far to lee, so have to steam back up to the main fleet to find the big jumbos again. The only snag is that the whales are lying around us so tightly we daren't move the boat. Nibblo goes to the bow shouting and bawling at them and banging the hull with a broom but that does no good.

"Alright," says Bonzo, "we will have a bit more of a sort out until they shift enough for us to move."

There is nothing more we can do, so for a few minutes we wash the fish and scoop them into boxes, picking out the odd small one as we go. But at last there is a gap in the whales and we are able to move ahead.

"Aye, aye Captain," says Bonzo. "Put her in gear, but for Christ's sake don't hit one, he'd sink us."

At no more than three knots I con the *Prosperity* back to the fleet and we resume our fishing. The lines are released, back line playing through the right hand, the fingers of the left tap tapping on the arms of the spinning gurdy to prevent override, the lead plunging away down through millions of voracious fish darting like missiles at the lured hooks dragged behind it. A quick jig on the line to make sure all the hooks are taken, and then up they come. As the top swivel of the line breaks clear of the water, frenzied mackerel swim the line to the surface in a desperate fight to regain their liberty. As the afternoon wears on, all the pounds and boxes are brimming with mackerel and we are each struggling to work with so many fish laying on the deck. It can't be very far away from home time, and as if to corroborate this thought, billows of black smoke are to be seen here and there around the fleet indicating some of the boats are already underway.

"Here, Ned," says Nibblo, observing this. "What's the time by the wheelhouse clock?"

I glance in the door: "Three o'clock," I reply.

"Bonze," he says. "It's going to be late enough time we steam home and land this lot."

Bonzo looks up from his line. "It's not often I agree with you Nibblo, but this time I do. Up lines, it's time to head for the hills."

Up come the lines and the last fish of the day are shaken off and the worn out sets of gear are cut from the swivel. Gurdies are unclamped from the rail to be stowed down in the fish room. Next we hose each other down with the deck wash and broom to remove the thick coating of slime, blood and scales clinging heavily to our boots and oilskins. That done, the skipper comes aft to steer, down goes the wheel and the engine throws up a huge plume of smoke as he winds on the throttle.

"Sheet away the mizzen," he shouts, and we are soon around on course for home.

By now nearly all the boats are under way; those from Falmouth will be in and landing within an hour, but the Looe boats have furthest of all to go. It will be eight o'clock or more before we can take our oilskins off.

Apart from a ten minute break at lunch time we had been hard at it since just after dawn, and now the thing we all need is a sit down, a mug of tea and a bite to eat. Nibblo appears with a pot of tea and for twenty minutes or so we enjoy a well-earned break. But all too soon, Nibblo tosses his fag end out of the open door of the wheelhouse and stands up.

"Come on then, Ned." he says. "We've got a lot of work to do before we can land this lot."

Bonzo turns around from his steering. "How many do you reckon we've got?" he asks.

Between the three of us we tally over the pounds and boxes and agree that it must be around 600 stone, a very good day's work. Mind you, if we have got six hundred then some of the hard driving four-handed boats will probably have well over a 1,000 stone. Daylight is fading so the deck lights are switched on as Nibblo and I hobble stiffly out on deck to start washing and grading the fish. Mackerel are put into three grades, large, medium and small, but because this catch is basically all large, the grading won't take too long. It's a big catch so we have no spare boxes. Instead a box is emptied on to the deck and hosed out clean, then another box of fish is hosed and tipped into the first one, picking out the odd medium or small as we go, and so on. When the boxes are all sorted and stacked, we start on the pounds. First a pound is cleared of its fish and hosed out, then it's refilled, a scoopful at a time, picking and sorting as we go, the deck wash playing on them meanwhile. By the time the last pound is sorted we are abeam of Polperro; half an hour to go to Looe, and just time for a final pot of tea.

Steaming into harbour, the usual mayhem awaits us. A hundred tired and hungry men just wanting to put their catch ashore, moor the boat up and get home for dinner and some kip. The noise: engines revving and thrumming, the metallic quaking of VHF radios, the shouting, laughter and banter of voices, mooring chains tinkling, the scraping sound of boxes being dragged along the quay, a sharp crack as a pallet is dropped in place and the rumble of heavily laden pallet trucks as a packers pull the swaying load up to the market. And of course the gulls! Shitting, squawking, fighting and robbing fish wherever and whenever an opportunity presents itself. We join this chaos, slamming the pallets, dragging the boxes and swearing at the gulls and by half past eight the three of us are stood on the quay ready to go home, the catch put ashore, the boat moored up snugly and all scrubbed down.

"Fuck it," says Nibblo. "I think I've had enough for one day." And so say all of us.

7

Heavy Weather

High pressure dominated the weather system over the south-west for the next few days, giving the fleet the blessing of some calm clear days and enabling it to work some very long hours hauling deck loads of jumbo mackerel aboard off Falmouth. Make the most of it, we said to ourselves, conditions like this won't hold for long in winter time and, of course, they didn't.

On our third day out the weather was forecast to change. A massive low pressure system was working its way in from the Atlantic and radio broadcasts had been interrupted to issue gale warnings for Portland, Plymouth, Lundy, Fastnet and Irish Sea: south-west, force five to seven, perhaps gale eight later. But as a light breeze was still blowing off the land and as the tide would be ebbing for most of the day, we were fairly confidant of coming home with yet another good catch before it hit us. That's if it did. Among fishermen, weather forecasters are not held in very high regard. Skippers will bear a forecast in mind, but make their own decisions about the weather conditions, with many of the harder men working hours into a rising gale to win a day's pay. They were not reckless in their actions, never running to lee to look for fish on a poor forecast, always to weather when, if it did come on to blow, they would have a fair run home.

And so, in the darkness of a calm winter's morning, the Looe boats ploughed their watery furrows down to Falmouth bay, joined en route by others from Polperro, Fowey and Mevagissey. We met the rest of the Cornish fleet halfway between St Anthony's Head and the Manacles reef where they lay with their echo sounders blacked out quietly awaiting the dawn while drifting over a massive shoal of fish. And when at last daylight did creep down into the tarry black depths we released our lines, to be rewarded instantly with a magnificent jumbo mackerel on every hook, fighting and glittering, green, blue and silver as we toiled hour after hour to haul seemingly endless strings of them over the rail, to expire on the deck, a mass of blood, scales and machine gun bursts of beating tails.

As we fished, an oily ground swell started to work its way into the bay from the south-west and the sun, shining like a disc of cheap lacquered brass, climbed up into a powder blue sky. By late morning the coming bad weather was starting to show its hand, the boats now with their bows pointing to the south-west from where irritable little draughts of wind began to ruffle the surface of the sea. The western sky brooded and sulked, as angry looking clouds billowed and rolled, while low along the southern horizon 'post boys', puffy little white clouds, broadcast their warning as did the tiny chunk of rainbow alongside the sun, aptly called a sun dog. Nature was writing its storm warnings up in the sky, loud and clear. At midday we stopped for our usual quick bite to eat and to clear the deck up a bit. This also gave us a chance to look around.

Bonzo glanced to the west, to the south and up at the sun, then carried on scooping fish into boxes. Nibblo carried the pot of tea aft to the wheelhouse and we trooped in after him.

"Have you pair seen that lot up in the sky?" he said.

"I know what our father would say if he was here now," replied Bonzo.

"Yes," said Nibblo. "Fuck off a bit quick."

But to drive fishermen off good fishing takes more than the threat of bad weather, so the last bite of sandwich was swallowed down with a mouthful of tea and back to the lines we went. On and on we worked, hardly looking left or right, brains in neutral. I dabbed the engine in and out of gear to keep the lines up and down in the water to prevent us from driving back out of the shoal of the fish and lessen the chances of fouling the lines up. But by now the breeze was increasing and the engine was in gear more often as the bow heaved up and down in the oncoming swell. We were all aware that this would probably be the last chance to earn any money for several days. The fish were of the right sort, big ravenous and easy to catch, right up in the water, so all the boats fished on. By now some of the smaller open boats were starting to look well down in the water, but still they rode to the seas and carried on fishing. Eventually the 20-foot cove boats peeled away from the fleet and got underway for home, heavily laden as they surfed in towards Falmouth, rail deep in foam. Two men on a plank, we called them, tiller steered and open to all the weather, the only bit of comfort aboard was a flask of tea. Theirs was the toughest call of all.

By now it was not looking very good at all. The wind was a good force five and signs in the sky were telling us the bellows would soon be blowing much harder. Everyone had got a good day's work aboard, but still most were tempted to stay on just that bit longer; none of the bigger boats wanted to be seen getting underway at the same time as the little cove boats. The engine was hardly out of gear now, the old gearbox grinding away as we stemmed into the cresting and breaking seas, the gurdies whirling around like little windmills as ever more fish were pulled aboard. The VHF radio came to life as a few of the boats got underway.

"We've just had a beauty sea smash aboard, washed everything around, the crew are digging out on the pump. I am going to take that as a sign to get underway," said one skipper.

"Aye aye, skipper, we are in along with you. We're loaded deep enough for this weather, that's for sure," came his mate's reply. And so the day's fishing began to draw to a close as boat after boat peeled away from the main fleet and headed for home. The wind was now a good force six/seven and the seas were steep and building, cresting and breaking. It promised to be a lively ride back up the coast.

Aboard the *Prosperity* I gave a wave to the Looe boat *Paula* as she surfed past us heading up towards the Dodman.

"Here, do you pair think we've got enough aboard, or what?" I ask.

"What's up with you, Ned, got the water in or something?" shouts Nibblo as he thrashes another lineful of mackerel down on the deck.

"Water in be fucked," I reply. "If we don't get underway soon we'll be lucky if we don't get half the fish swept off the deck as we bring her around."

"My line is about fucked and I'm not going to bend on a new one this time of day," chips in Bonzo.

"Look here," retorts Nibblo. "The *Our Daddy* is still fishing, and I am buggered if we are going to get underway before her."

So nothing more is said and we fish on. By now the engine is continually in gear; in fact I have put the throttle on a bit to keep her driving up into the weather.

After another ten minutes or so Bonzo looks up: "It's high time we got underway. If you want to stay on, Nibblo, I'll launch the life raft and you can float around for the night in that."

"'Ark to that little bastard," says Nibblo to me, a look of wounded pride on his face. "Trying to make the best of the day, and that's all the thanks I get."

"It's fuck all to do with that," retorts Bonzo. "All you're worried about was the *Our Daddy*. Anyway she's just coming around now, so if you really don't mind we'll do the same."

"Do what you like, you miserable little fucker," Nibblo glares back. "I'm going down to put the kettle on." And with that, he hoses off his oilskin and flounces off down the cabin.

"Whatever can you do with a little twat like that?" says Bonzo to me.

"It looks like you've upset him again," I reply, trying to stay as neutral as possible. He and I hose the muck off our own oilskins and boots

"Righto, Captain," says Bonzo. "Stand by the mizzen sheets. I'll pick the moment to bring her around."

We ride head to for a minute or so and then, rearing up over a great lump of a sea, we swoop down the other side. Our moment has arrived, down goes the wheel and on goes the throttle.

"Slack away the sheet," yells my little ginger captain and so, to a fanfare of engine roar and a plume of black smoke, the *Prosperity* comes about, putting her stern to the weather as clean as you like, no waves breaking over us and nothing rolling off the deck. Now we are running before the weather and it feels like a different world, the sting goes out of the wind and the seas don't seem half as menacing. Although we are surfing along on some real monsters at times, with a good boat under our feet and a good man at the helm the trip was, in an odd way, a pleasure and not a danger.

Nibblo bursts into the wheelhouse, pot of tea in hand, looking like he had just come around Cape Horn with it.

"Fucking glad I'm not on one of the open boats," he exclaims. "It's fairly piping out there now."

"It won't be much fun on one of them right now," I join in.

Bonzo turns from the wheel to take his mug of tea: "Did you see the state of the *Ella* and *Ganesha*?" he exclaims. "Loaded right down in weather like this, and the greedy bastards were still fishing when we left... Look out boys, here's a big one!"

The old boat is now tearing along on the crest of a huge breaking sea, the deck awash in foam and the engine governor going crazy because the boat is going faster than the engine can rev. The sea then overtakes us and we slide down its back into the trough behind, only to be picked up by another one not much smaller than the first.

"We shall be home in record time tonight," I say, listening to the governor trying to control the engine. Voices crackle over the VHF, telling us that all the boats are now heading homeward. Some of the heavily laden open boats are shipping a drop of water, and there is a fair bit of pumping going on to keep them free, but providing none of their pumps choke up they will be okay. Let's hope that God has got them all under his wing tonight.

After a bite to eat, Nibblo and I go out on deck on hands and knees to try and sort out some of the pounds of fish. This we partially succeed in doing, but it is dreadfully hard work in such conditions, and eventually we say fuck it and crawl back into the wheelhouse to finish the job later, back in harbour.

To enter the peace and safety of the harbour from the boiling breaking seas of a winter's gale is a truly wonderful feeling. On the *Prosperity*, a 40-foot, fully decked boat, we were in no real danger unless something went badly wrong, but many of the working fleet at that time were 25- to 38-feet length of hull with an open hatch board deck in the working area, and any seas breaking aboard had to be pumped out. A few were of recent construction, packing plenty of power for their day, with both hand and engine operated bilge pumps. But many of the fleet were getting on in years, most of them very under powered and possibly with only one hand pump to keep them free. Plus some pretty ancient luggers were still in commission, fine old sea boats with a track record second to none, but when it came to a real good hammering the crew could be as busy on the pump as the men on the open boats. Being caught out in a breeze was something that had to be accepted if you went commercial fishing for a living, although in a well found craft the dangers were not great providing everything does what it is supposed to do. It's when the unexpected happens, like a pump choking up, or the engine stopping, whatever it may be. In fine weather it's not hard to clear the pump or find out what is wrong with the engine. But in bad weather everything is ten times harder to achieve, and if a tow home is needed, then there can be some very big problems for all concerned. In a gale of wind you can go from all's well to a potentially life threatening situation in the blink of an eye. Upon arriving safely in harbour after such an event the first thing you want to know is who has yet to make it in. And nobody will rest until the last boat is safely home.

One by one, the heavily laden boats make it back into port, many of them still pumping as they steam in, with both men and boats looking battered and weary, well reflecting what they have just been through. When such a gale blows you arrive home feeling exhausted, but the likelihood of conditions being fit to go to sea the next day are minimal, so there is usually the chance of a good night's kip to recover. A few jobs would need to be done on the boat the next morning, tip diesel, scrub down and do the usual running repairs that keep a wooden boat seaworthy. After that, a pint in the pub before lunch where, around the fire, tales of the previous day's heroics would be recounted while smocks and overalls turn white as the salt in them dries out, causing fish scales to shed onto the floor and tables like a miniature snowstorm. The favourite pub was the Salutation in East Looe, and when the place was full of fishermen the scale problem was so great that the landlord, George Rider, would detail a barmaid to go around with a dustpan and brush sweeping up. The bar, the floor and all the tables would be smothered in mackerel scales. I remember apologising once for the mess, to which George replied that it would be a very poor time for all concerned when there were no scales to sweep up. How very prophetic that statement proved to be.

8

Searching

A winter gale might be over and gone in 24 hours. There again, it might last a week, or a really bad spell of weather could set in making it impossible to go to sea for a month. You never knew; life as a fisherman is a complete lottery. There are good times when you think you will never be poor again, and times when the boats are double roped and fendered alongside the quay as the storms run up through the Channel one after the other. Meanwhile, the bit of money that you managed to put by in the good times is draining fast away, while at the same time bills, for the moment totally un-payable, pile up on the mantelpiece. It is then that you seriously doubt the wisdom of the life, but when the sun shines again and you can once more enjoy the freedom to range the Channel hunting the mackerel shoals, then bad times are soon forgotten and you wouldn't swap your way of life with anyone.

Leaving port in the darkness of a fine morning after the gales have passed, I watch the sun rising in the south-east and claw its way low into the sky, there to blind you all day long as it carves an arc just above the southern horizon. Both sea and sky are pale indigo in colour, while the boats rise and fall on the ground swell running on an otherwise calm sea.

Where the shoals of mackerel might be found nobody could tell. After a period of very turbulent weather the fish will seek sanctuary in deep water. But the search for them will be conducted from Bigbury Bay, east of Plymouth, to the Runnelstone buoy down near Lands End. Three hundred boats will be combing the Channel with their echo sounders, so someone will find them sooner or later. But until the big shoals settle back in Falmouth Bay or wherever, and everyone knows once again where to head for, we are all playing a guessing game. The boats that found the fish would load off, and those within a reasonable steaming distance would make a day's work. But others too far away would go home empty and content themselves with the knowledge that they know in which direction to head the next day.

There was a sly method of avoiding the big search and this was practised by a few crafty skippers, enabling them to land a modest catch, burn very little diesel and then benefit the next day from those who had been out looking. There is an area off Whitsand Bay known as the 'mud', and here a small stock of jumbo mackerel lived. The same sort of thing could be found off Plymouth Sound, tiny marks on the sounder would render a couple of lines-full and with patience 100 stone or so of quality fish could be landed at the end of the day. There was nothing wrong with that, except that these sly characters would be the first away the next day, once they knew where the big shoals had been located. Take all and risk nothing was their motto.

A week of storms eventually passed up through the Channel before the boats were able to get back to sea. On the first day out, the *Prosperity* was headed out to the SSW, a course that took us out to the Radar Buoy ground, a fairly fishy area, but it was also middle ground and gave us a fighting chance both east and west if a scry went up.

All was made ready for action, the gurdies were clamped on the rail, each one sporting a brand new set of feathers; channel eight on the VHF was jammed with traffic but it was all the usual old bollocks: pool, darts, news and gossip. By dawn light we were out at the Radar Buoy, the echo sounder was switched on and the hunt commenced. And it was all eyes about, for there was much to look out for, such as gannets diving, other boats suddenly coming around, marks on the echo sounder or a shout on the VHF. Everyone was wound up like a clock spring hoping that when the scry went up it was us that found it, or at least whoever did was within reasonable steaming distance of us. But this particular day that had started with high hopes led on to frustration and finally, as the fruitless hours rolled on, boredom and indifference. It was a syndrome known as 'Red hot meter and empty tanks'. Hundreds of boats steaming hundreds of miles and nothing worthwhile was found, just a few small marks on the meter resulting in a few lines full of immature fish. The winter storms had driven the mackerel shoals well off the coast and we just had to be patient and wait until they reappeared. So we arrived back in harbour late in the afternoon with a few boxes of small stuff that wouldn't pay for the tea bags we had used, let alone the diesel that had been burnt. Fishermen live all their lives with the great uncertainty; it would all come good another day, but today was not to be that day.

And come good again it did. Over the winter season we chased the mackerel shoals from Bigbury Bay to the Lizard for big catches and small on days when the sea sparkled calm in the sunshine and other days so horrible you wouldn't wish the misery of it on condemned prisoners.

By early March the hand line season was all but over. The fish were migrating from the coast, leaving just a few harum-scarum shoals here and there, and they were hardly worth the effort of hunting down. Everyone who had taken part in the hand line fishery had earned good wages, and now many of the boats would simply mark time until the paint up in May and the commencement of the summer pleasure angling. By the time the older wooden boats had finished a winter's fishing there was no denying they were in very desperate need of some TLC. Many would be showing their plank seams from stem to stern through hard driving while heavily laden in poor weather, or when the Atlantic ground swells were running high they had motored to the top of a big sea only to find the next one missing, the crew, wide eyed and white knuckled, brace themselves as the boat plummets with a tooth shattering crash down into a deep watery pit. For a split second the air in the cabin and wheelhouse is full of flying objects as leads and spanners, tea mugs and sets of feathers are propelled from their stowage, while on deck pound boards unship, letting boxes of fish capsize. The boat has gone from order to utter crashing rolling mayhem in about two seconds. The fight is on to get back up head to wind and regain control because the next wave may well break foaming over her and as a boat can't float on foam she gets buried in it, to be left wallowing like a half tide rock. It's then 'pump, boys, pump' because one more like that and it's goodnight Vienna. It was really not surprising that the poor old boats looked a bit forlorn come spring. The deck wash and broom, the fish scoop, boxes, fish and lines all conspired to strip the boats back to bare wood. Add to this a leak or two in the hull and there's the full picture of how a mackerel boat may well look at the closing of the winter season. Not a pretty sight, but nothing that a good paint up and refit couldn't cure.

9

Trawling

To bridge the gap between the end of the mackerel season and the spring paint up, the *Prosperity*'s crew would wind on the trawling gear. Two boats, the *Tethera*, skipper Ivan Chaston, and the *Anne Louise* (formerly *One Accord*), skipper Charlie Jaycock, trawled full time, while two or three others like the *Prosperity* used it as a useful stopgap between seasons. Today Looe has been a trawling port for many years, but back then it was a new trade and there was much to learn. Bonzo did fit the boat out with good trawling equipment later on, but at the time I am writing about it was all a bit of a lash up.

The gantry that took the hanging blocks and trawl doors was fabricated out of scaffold poles, the hydraulic winch had come off a much smaller boat and was never man enough for the job. We had to jump up and down on the bridles to get it to haul the last few fathoms aboard; that's if it didn't blow a hydraulic pipe, a not uncommon occurrence when hauling with a big swell running. Below decks, rolling and slipping around in spilled hydraulic oil, brandishing a well worn pair of Stilsons, trying to change pipes was not a lot of fun. Another thing we had to be a bit wary of was the warps jumping out of their lead blocks. These Bonzo had utilised from open-sided guide wheels from her seining days in Scotland. A shackle catching in them at the wrong angle would result in them jumping out and flying across the deck in fine style. It's a wonder nobody was fired over board or had their head cut off.

All the paraphernalia of mackerel fishing was carried ashore and stored away, to be replaced by all the gear for trawling. A new set of wire warps was stretched down the quay to be measured and marked, then wound on to the winch, while combination spans and bridles were fathomed out and spliced up. The otter boards were slung on their chains on either side of the gantry and the starboard waterways became a net pound in which we stowed two trawls: one a wing trawl, to catch whiting, squid, monk etc, and a ground trawl for flat fish, such as lemon sole and plaice.

For our first day out with the trawl, Bonzo decided to stick to a safe bit of inshore ground known as the 'Edges', which ran up and down the shore just to seaward of the coastal rocks between Whitsand Bay and Fowey, a handy place to trial everything out. Having toiled long and hard to get the boat ready we now had to mark time for a couple of days to let a spell of blowy weather pass over, and pass it did. On the third day the weather was perfect. Bonzo laid the *Prosperity* broadside to a chilly NW wind just as dawn was clawing its way up over the eastern horizon. Nibblo and I shot the trawl away, first the thick braided net of the cod end, then one each side on the seam ropes. We paid away the much lighter net of the lengthener, then the back and belly net and finally the foot rope, wound in its chain, and the head rope with its orange plastic floats. This was all pulled out clear from the side of the boat as she drifted on the wind. Going ahead on the engine, the trawl and spans were then towed out taught astern of us from the hanging blocks in the gantry. With everything clear and looking good, the brakes on the winch were slackened off and away went the bridles, thirty fathoms of thirty mil combination. Next came the flat shackles. I am aft and clip on the doors then unchain them from the gantry. Going ahead on the engine, the starboard brake on the winch is released and the door hits the water with a splash; warp is paid out to the ten fathom mark, and the brake is wound on again. The door takes up its position and pulls down and out to starboard. All is well. Bonzo at the wheel gives a nod to Nibblo on the winch, who drops away the port door to the same effect. A plume of smoke now erupts from the funnel as the engine is wound up to a furious 750 RPM. Nibblo releases the winch brakes and with just enough tension on them to keep the gear taught, the rest of the warps are shot away out to the towing marks just shy of the bitter end. These are formed from coloured twine wound in to the lay of the warp to a length of 6 inches or so. At these marks the chain stoppers are wound on and the heavy rope towing bridles hooked in; the winch brakes are gently slacked away to let the bridles, made fast to the mizzen mast 6 foot off the deck, take the strain. Towing from a central point makes it much easier to steer. With the warps over the stern well spread and level, things are looking OK so unless a door falls over, or we come fast on a hitch, we shall tow along to give the trawl 3 hours fishing time before winching it back in to find out how well it has been performing. It might take a several drags to get everything adjusted and working properly, but this is where we begin.

Bonzo takes the first watch, tracking our progress on the Decca navigator as we wander down over the ground. With the tide up our arse, we are making about two knots. The time is passed drinking tea and yarning until we are ready to engage the the clutches on the winch, the engine is eased down and the warps are wound back on to the drums. The doors break surface and are chained to the gantry before being unclipped to allow the bridles to be hauled. The poor old winch grunts and complains by the time the wing ends of the trawl reach the rail. The rest of the operation is done by hand; the foot rope is pulled aboard followed by the head rope, then as we lay broadside to weather, the trawl is hauled aboard hand over hand on the seam ropes. Hang on tight as she rolls back on a sea, and haul in the slack as she drops back again. The net narrows back like a funnel until the cod end is reached, the very last section where the fish will be. To get this aboard, a stout rope strop is wound around the net and a lifting tackle hanging from a derrick, known as a gilson, is hooked in. The tail of this is led through a lead block in the deck to the whipping drum on the winch, and the catch is hoisted aboard and lowered to just above the deck. One man reaches under the bulging net and pulls the slip knot on the cod end rope, releasing a small avalanche of trapped fish out on to the deck.

The trawl had been working well. In fact, for a first drag it was very good, five or six boxes of fine big Channel whiting, several nice monkfish, some plaice, a few cod, hake and squid. With two more drags to go, we should make a decent day's pay if the buyers don't rob us on tomorrow's market. While I retied the cod end, Bonzo has a quick look at the steel shoeing on the bottom of the doors to make sure the shine on them shows that they were down on the sea bed evenly, then the gear is quickly shot away again. Nothing builds enthusiasm like a bit of success. With the warps once more out, taut and fair under our stern, we get down on hands and knees to sort out the catch, all the different species boxed up, one from the other. All the rubbish, weed, shell, crabs and small fish etc. are shovelled overboard; the gutting knives are sharpened up and then, in the company of a million screaming squawking gulls, the catch is gutted, washed and graded. An hour sees the job done and everything washed down clean and neat; then a break for a pot of tea and a bite to eat before it's time to haul again. The trawl looks to be working well, putting us all in a good mood, so just maybe Bonzo and Nibblo won't start arguing, but it's something that you would never put money on; the slightest thing can set them off. And sure enough, in conversation Bonzo can't resist the temptation to needle his brother, and Nibblo has no more sense than to bite on the bait and away they go, hammer and tongs, shouting, swearing, turning purple and leaping up and down in absolute fury. Nibblo ends it by storming out of the wheelhouse and going down the cabin.

"There," says Bonzo, turning to me. "What do you make of that little fucker?"

"Well," I reply. "You know he bites, and you just can't resist winding him up."

"I know," responds Bonzo with a chuckle. "He makes such good sport, and I always reckon it helps to keep the blood circulating."

"While Nibblo is peaceable," I said, "you should leave him alone. It's cruel to upset someone for the sport of it."

Bonzo grins down from the wheelhouse chair, blue eyes sparkling, ginger hair bristling from under his hat. "Right then, captain," he says. "We had better see if we can sweeten him up again. Go down forward and make another pot of tea to coax him out of his bunk, and I will make sure I don't upset him."

Here I go, peace-making between the little pair again. In the cabin I fill the kettle and put it on the stove to boil. Right up in the bow, Nibblo is in his bunk, buried in blankets, only his nose is visible. I swill the teapot out and throw in a few tea bags, then sit down on the cabin locker to await the water to boil, braced against that easy roll a trawler develops in fine weather, ears cocked the while to the reassuring background rumble of the old Gardner engine as it tirelessly thrashes the prop around. After a few moments silence I hear the expected lines from the injured party.

"What do think about that little short-arsed ginger bastard? There was no need for him to carry on like that."

"I know," I reply, "I told him I thought he was a bit out of order. Anyway I am making a nice pot of tea. Are you coming up for one before we haul again?"

"Yes, alright Ned, I'll be up in a minute," he answers.

A screeching noise erupts from the kettle. Switching off the gas, I tip its bubbling contents into the pot, milk and sugar are stirred in and aft to the wheelhouse I go. As I fill up the mugs Nibblo joins us, flouncing in and not saying a word. Bonzo offers an olive branch.

"You alright now, Nibblo?" he enquires.

"Alright be fucked," comes the retort. "I was speaking to Ned down the cabin just now and he reckons you're a little c**t as well!"

Jesus wept, I think, now we are all going to be fighting. "Nibblo, I said no such thing, and you know it," I bellow. "Now, for fuck's sake, pack it in the pair of you. That's enough shouting and bawling for one day."

It does the trick. Our tea is drank in sulky silence. Bonzo glances up at the clock. "It's time to haul again," he grunts.

Thankfully, by the time we nose our way into the harbour to land our catch that evening, all the day's fighting has been forgotten. Peace on the *Prosperity* was always a fragile thing; many is the time after we had landed our catch Nibblo would tie his oilskin and sea boots up in a neat bundle and step ashore with them, swearing that he would never go to sea with his brother again. But nevertheless he was always there on time the next morning, and nothing more was said. They were two of the feistiest little buggers that I ever went to sea with. When we were mackerel fishing, many were the times we were hauling strings of big fish aboard and an argument kicked off, resulting in them both belaying up their lines to stand foursquare to one another, nose to nose, shouting loudly, with steam blowing out of their ears, fearlessly brandishing the waggly finger. But, for as much as they fought each other, they were intensely loyal and would have stood shoulder to shoulder to fight off the whole world if they considered that family or friends were in need of their help.

10

The Edges

The ground we called 'Edges' was always good for a day's work with the trawl. A good mix of fish could nearly always be caught there, but greater rewards were very often to be had by venturing further off.

Around the end of February the lemon-soles would appear, first up off Plymouth Sound on a big area of trawling ground known as 'Sleepy Valley' and then, after a week or so, they would work down and out into the Channel and by May they would be gone. This was clean, easy fishing and the soles could make good money on the market, so a close eye was always kept on the Plymouth boats who spent much of their time up that way. And when word filtered through that they were catching a few stone of lemons, it was time for us to shackle on the ground trawl and get up there and have a go. Working the Plymouth ground was fine, easy trawling. Apart from two well-charted wrecks, there was nothing to come fast on or do any damage to the gear, hence its name. The only danger was the chance of fouling the gear of another boat because in the morning the Plymouth boats would be at the eastern end of the ground towing west, while the Looe boats would be at the western end towing east and we would all meet in the middle. This daily fleet manoeuvre called for much skilful judgment and cooperation via the VHF. Usually we all got away with it, but now and again there were a few memorable, not to say monumental, cock ups. Trawl doors dragged through a trawl, cutting it to ribbons; two lots of gear locked together and everything cable-laid. It could be enough sometimes to make you want to sell the boat and buy a farm.

Looe is an unhandy port to work from over the neap tides. You often can't get in harbour until late at night, and you have to be away again in the very early hours so, rather than go through all that rigmarole, several of the Looe boats would work out of Plymouth until the tides eased a bit.

It was pleasant easy work. You could enter and leave Sutton Pool at whatever time suited you, there was no tide to have to consider, plus, to me it always seemed like a little holiday to work from another port for a few days. We would nudge into the landing steps at the Barbican quay each evening to get our catch ashore, and when it was weighed, tallied and stowed into the fridge, the boat would be moored up for the night alongside one of the Plymouth trawlers. The next move was to get spruced up for a bit of a run ashore; oilskins and sea boots were taken off (that was a relief in itself), then to try and make ourselves a little more presentable, a bowl of hot water was shared at the galley sink to scrub the bulk of the slime, scales and general blackness off hands and faces. Overalls and smocks were removed and a comb pulled through the hair (mind you, we could never quite get rid of that just-removed-the-hat look). And now the evening was ours: first a meal would be enjoyed in one of the little cafes or restaurants around the Barbican, apologising for the smell of fish and diesel that always entered with us (thankfully nobody seemed to mind, or if they did they were very polite about it). After a good dinner had been stowed under our belts it was time to consider a nightcap; for this the Dolphin was always favourite, a fine old pub that was situated right opposite the fish market.

Sitting around the fire with a decent pint to round off a very long day was always a great pleasure, as was the company. Old fishermen recalling the times they spent on the sailing smacks, steam trawlers and drifters; the landlady might be playing her accordion for a bit of singing and dancing, gangs of matlots or students out on the razzle would wander in, as might one or two ladies of the night, in their outrageous outfits and trowelled-on make-up.

After a couple of drinks our bunks would be calling, so after saying good night to the landlady and the old men we had been yarning with, the three of us would make our way back aboard the *Prosperity*. A quick last-minute piddle over the rail, then to slip below into the warmth of the cabin, kick off our shoes and climb in our bunks, snug warm and comfortable, we would be asleep within minutes. And as the old saying goes: "You wouldn't call the King your uncle."

But no sooner had your head hit the pillow than the alarm was ringing. It's five o'clock and another day lay ahead of us. Bleary-eyed and tousle-haired, we scramble out of the bunks, pulling on overalls, smocks and sea boots. The first one togged up would put the kettle on for a pot of tea. Nibblo would then nip up to the baker's somewhere up Southside Street to get some pies and cakes as grub for the day.

Bonzo would disappear down into the engine room to check everything over before firing up the engine. When cold, the old L3 Gardner could wipe out Sutton Pool in smoke; in fact, on a still morning if two or three trawlers fired up at the same time you couldn't see a boat's length anywhere. I would check over the cod end of the trawl, and then shorten up the ropes ready to cast off.

In the cold darkness of a winter's morning the boats would pass Mount Batten Pier, then head south-west to pick up the western end of the breakwater and after that, due south out to the trawling grounds, passing Picklecombe Fort, Cawsand and Penlee Point marking the end of the sheltered water. After that, if there was a fresh wind blowing the boat would start to plunge about and throw back the spray.

As the light of a winter's day was being dragged grey and unwilling up over the eastern horizon, we lay broadside to a freshening westerly wind and shot the trawl away. The doors splashed, the winch and guide blocks whirled and squealed as the boat bashed ahead on full throttle to drag out the warps and keep everything tight. Drenching cat's paws of spray lash across deck, we were all humped up like hunchbacks in our oilskins, hoods pulled down low, trying to keep warm and dry. Another day of the glorious uncertainty that is fishing had begun.

"Fuck me, it's cold and wet out there," says Nibblo as he bursts in through the wheelhouse door bearing our second pot of tea for the morning. Bonzo is perched up on the wheelhouse seat steering along a tow, the navigator clicking and flashing up its lights: red, green and purple.

"What have you bought us to eat today?" he enquires.

"Well, there is a big fruit cake, a bag of doughnuts and steak and kidney pies," his brother replies.

"We shan't starve today," says Bonzo as a large slice of cake is served as breakfast, and we chat, laugh and spin a few yarns to pass the three hours of the first watch. Then it's out on deck in the wet and the cold, braced against the relentless rolling and pitching to haul and shoot the trawl, and later gut and clean the catch. If all goes to plan we will do three drags for the day and be back in harbour and landed by about eight o'clock in the evening. We were working around 15 hours a day and that, in commercial fishing, is not hard going.

11

Summer Season

Through the remaining winter and into early spring we earned a living with the trawl. When the weather was reasonable the boats worked what, for those days, was out deep, chasing the lemon-soles down-Channel into ever rougher and more dangerous ground for the trawls and engine power that we had in those days. And if the weather was only just workable we stayed in 'Edges' after whiting, monk and plaice.

The month of May marked the end of winter. Spring had arrived and it was now time to get ready for the summer season. The *Prosperity* was stripped of all the paraphernalia of the winter fishery and taken over to West Looe for her spring paint up. And did she need it. All those old wooden boats at the end of a hard winter's fishing looked a sorry sight.

The spring paint up was a lovely time of year. If the sun shone, it would take the three of us about a fortnight of easy hours to get the old girl smart and presentable and back into her best frock for the summer visitors. At the same time I would be hauling my little motor boats out of their shed one by one and treating them to paint and varnish before re-launching them to their moorings to staunch up before putting the engines back in.

At the end of May we would all go our separate ways for the summer season: Nibblo to work his speedboat from the steps at the end of the Banjo pier doing thrill trips around the bay and pleasure trips to Fowey and Plymouth; I would be letting out my self-drive boats for trips up the river and around the bay, while Bonzo would take anglers out shark fishing in the *Prosperity*, helped by one of the local lads who wanted a holiday job. I loved the life in those days; we worked three seasons through the year and if one of these was failure for some reason, then the others would sure to be OK. We were never at anything long enough to get bored or fed up, because a new season was always just over the horizon and, what is more, compared with the ugly gnome of bureaucracy that clings parasitically to the back of every one today, we enjoyed great freedom.

I had a feeling that the summer of 1975 was going to be, shall I say, interesting, for one very good reason. Collin Mathews had put his fleet of boats up for sale and they had been purchased by Johnny Bettinson. Now Johnny was one of life's characters, about 30 years old and from an old Looe family. As a boy he had worked with his father on the motor boats before joining up and serving for 10 years in the army, followed by a spell as a painter in the dockyard in Devonport. I had been working my boats for about a week before Johnny arrived on the scene. Down the river he came one morning, his boats all smartly painted and ready to go.

"Morning, Johnny," I say as I take his ropes.

"Morning, Ned," he replies as he scrambles up the ladder on to the quay. "Fuck me! What a struggle I have had to get these bastard boats ready".

"Why, what happened?" I reply.

"Well, you know what it's like leaving everything to the last minute. I was hoping to be down here yesterday but I didn't quite make it".

"What caused the delay then?" I ask.

"Well, me and the missis went out for a drink down the sports club and I made the mistake of getting involved in a round. Anyway, in the end I got that pissed I couldn't stay on my feet to get home. Sue couldn't carry me, and was going to leave me in the hedge, but as it was lashing down with rain she was afraid I would die of exposure, and she would get the blame."

This is a classic Johnny yarn unfolding here.

"Anyway, the only way she could get me to move was to beat me along with her umbrella. So there I was crawling along on me hands and knees in the pissing rain, and every time I stopped, the missis was screaming and shouting and beating the fuck out of me."

I am rolling down with laughter by this time. "How long did it take to get home then?" I enquired.

"I don't know, ages I should think. Anyway when I woke up yesterday morning not only did I have a screaming hangover but my ass and back were bruised black and blue, the knees were out of me best trousers and the toes all scratched off me best shoes, and what's more the missis is moaning because her best umbrella is all bent."

"Good start to the season then, Johnny. Do you reckon it's an omen of how the summer may pan out?" I quip.

"For fuck's sake, I hope the rest of the season doesn't match that experience," he grins.

But this is typical Johnny because only a few minutes later it is happening to him again. A few people were strolling around the quay so we start touting.

"Self-drive motor boats, lovely day for a trip up the river ..." etc. Johnny gets his first let. It's a bloke and his son of about 10 years old.

"Right sir," he says, "You go down the steps and I will bring the boat in to you." And with that he nips down the quay ladder to his raft of boats. He is on the third boat before he gets an engine to start, and by this time he is all worked up in a fluster, going as fast as he can to get the boat alongside and away before that engine failed as well. Clambering onto the foredeck to let a rope go, he trips on the bow cleat, emits a loud squawk and plunges headlong into the river. Now he really is in a panic, but never say die. With water pouring off him, he scrambles back aboard the boat and motors it into the steps, saying not a word to his astonished customers. His trendy bubble perm hairdo is plastered down on his head, his clothes cling to him as if vacuum-packed, and every time he takes a step, little decorative fountains of water play from his brogue pattern platform shoes. He takes their money and gives them the usual spiel about how to work the engine and where they could and couldn't go around the bay and up the river.

What the people thought, I have no idea, but the whole episode was quite surreal, like something from the Goon show or the Muppets.

"Fuck me, Ned, that was my first let for the season, what's the rest of it going to be like?" And with that he squelches up to Mutton and Martin's, the clothes shop, to get a whole new rig of gear, on tick. I worked with him for the next two summers and discovered that there was no such thing as a dull day when Johnny was about. Even his dog was mad, and its name was Crabmeat. To this day I can never work out why.

12

Looe Harbour

We were blessed with plenty of fine sunny days during that summer of 1975 and over the school holidays (the busiest period) our little motor boats were working from morning till night. It was hard work and there was always all manner of chaos going on. People, not understanding the tides, would strand their boat on a sandbank up the river or on a rock out in the bay. Nobody was ever hurt or injured, but the poor old boats took a right bashing and a long day would be extended still further by a late night expedition to retrieve a stranded boat.

The only day of the week likely to be quiet was Saturday, change-over day. People would either be arriving to start their holiday or going home at the end of it. Although we didn't earn much on a day like that, it was a blessing just to rest a bit and sit in our deck chairs drinking tea and yarning. But Charlie and Richard, the boys who worked for us, never seemed to run out of energy and would end up driving us nuts endlessly scrounging for sweets and ice creams, getting more stroppy and cheeky all the while. Eventually Johnny and I would lunge up out of our chairs at them, sending them scampering away for safety into the back streets, there to lurk about for a while keeping out of our way.

On such a day, and getting very bored myself, I was toying with the big copper petrol funnel, thinking to myself that Johnny would never fall for this old chestnut but it must be worth a try.

"Johnny," I said. "Have you ever tried the penny in the funnel trick?"

"Never heard of it," he replied.

I am in with a chance, thought I. This could be a bit of fun. "Well, get up on your hind legs a minute, I'll show you what it's about."

Adopting a very cautious manner, he hauls up out of his chair. "Oh yes, what's this all about then?"

Trying to sound as innocent and as green as possible, I say, "It's nothing, just a daft thing to pass the time, but it is not as easy as it looks."

"All right," says Johnny, "but what the fuck is it?"

"Right, I'll give you a demo. You stuff the funnel down your trousers, like so, and then put your head back and rest a coin on your forehead. Then, with eyes closed, you have to drop the coin into the funnel. It's the best of five goes, adding a coin each time you hit the target."

I could see various thoughts passing across his face as he tried to work out the catch, but in the end saw none.

"Well there's fuck all in that," he chirped.

"Tell you what, it's a lot harder than it looks," I intoned, sounding as oily as an estate agent. "I'll lay you a quid you won't get five in on the run."

Johnny cautiously takes the bait and pokes the funnel down his pants, head back with a ten pence coin on his forehead.

"Careful," I said. "Nod your head, and drop it on target." Clunk, in it goes. "Now two coins, and steady as she goes." Two coins, no problem. "Bloody hell, I'm going to lose my quid here I can see that." Johnny is chuckling and scores a bull's eye with three and four. "You lying bastard, you've done this before," I chide.

"No I haven't, honestly," he protests.

"Well, I've never seen anyone get them all in like that," I snivel. "Last go coming up, and I hope you make a balls of it."

With eyes firmly shut and five coins on his forehead he composes himself for the final drop, at the same instant I slop the funnel full, from a bucket concealed under my chair. The effect was most wonderful to behold. With eyes out on stalks, he blows his fag about fifty yards down the quay, twenty different emotions play over his face all at once as water drenches down his trouser legs onto the tarmac. "You twat, Greenwood, how the fuck did I fall for that," he howled, before convulsing into uncontrollable laughter, eyes streaming, face screwed up tight and turning a brilliant shade of purple. Way beyond being able to talk, he sort of spluttered and choked while flapping one hand around in the air. "What a gag. What a fucking gag," he was eventually able to croak. Once I get hold of a dry pair of jeans there's going to be a few bastards around here caught on that one today."

And so there was. For a couple of hours we chided passers-by who looked gullible enough to take part in the great Cornish penny in the funnel championship. In the end Claude Tamblin, who hired out boats at a set of steps further up the quay, came down to investigate. "What the hell is going on?" he questioned. "I keep hearing howls of laughter from you pair, and then some poor bugger plods up past with his trousers streaming wet."

As the old saying goes, "We hadn't laughed so much since granny caught her tits in the mangle."

* * *

Working from the harbour, the tides were always a big factor in our lives. Neap tides were fine, no big rush of water and the tide in for most of the working day, but spring tides, well, stand by for an action packed day.

The river at flood and ebb would run at about three knots. Our boats with their 1 ½ HP engines did at best about five, so the people would go hurtling up the river in fine style on the flood, but the return journey could take forever. Conversely when a boat was returning to the steps with the tide, we would signal with a big sweeping arm motion to the driver to turn into the currant, and then signal them to slow the engine right down so as to come along side in an ordered manner, and most people did just that. But every now and then a boat would come flying in on the tide, everyone aboard chatting, laughing and looking about, taking no notice what so ever of our ever more frantic signals and shouting. They would go shooting past the steps, engine still going flat out, panic then setting in, as they realise that they should now be doing something, if only they could work out what it was. Ending back out in the river again, after a few shouted instructions a second attempt would usually be more successful.

At low water we would drop the boats out into the bay and work them from a little quay called Pen Rock, at the eastern side of the beach. This always entailed plenty of anchor-work wading around in sea boots, and if there happened to be a ground swell running, you could end up wet to the waist. But it was all part of the job, and I don't think anyone would have swapped it for a job in a factory or an office.

13

Catching a Bomb

In the mid-1970s the coastal towns and villages of Cornwall were enjoying quite prosperous times. In the prime summer months the camp sites, B&Bs, hotels and boarding houses would be full to capacity and this in turn ensured that the shops, pubs, cafés and restaurants also did a very good trade. As for the boating, the most weather dependent of all holiday activities, if the gods smiled on us then you just couldn't fail. There were more people wanting to go out boating and fishing than there were boats to take them.

Coupled with the rapid expansion of the winter mackerel fishery there was plenty of work to be had when the autumn curtains came down on the summer season. Crewing on the boats, working with the packing gangs, making up the waxed cardboard boxes that the fish were packed into, plus the many ancillary jobs and trades that kept the fleet running and, of course, the boat yards going flat out to fulfil orders for new fishing boats. A living wage could now be earned the year round, and for many people in Cornwall that was a huge bonus.

The winter of 1975/76 followed the usual pattern; huge shoals of mackerel wintering off the coast, attended by thousands of seabirds and, on occasions, an escort of scores of pilot whales. Of course, all mixed up with this was the Cornish hand line fleet, hundreds strong. On a fine calm day the fleet would drift away in the winter sunshine, working their lines over the vast shoal of fish, the crews yarning and joking boat to boat, fending off with a broom or a gaff if they got to close. Beautiful days that will never be forgotten.

Conversely there were days when the west or north-west wind was blowing very fresh and every now and then we would be beaten off the deck to seek shelter in the wheelhouse as brief but extremely vicious squalls whirled off the land bearing storm force winds and hail enough to flail the skin off your face. The wind was nearly always in the westerly cant, meaning a lumpy trip down and a fine run home, but up to now none of us had thought of making use of that wind. Until one day we watched as two Mevagissey boats, the *Francis* and the *Lindy Lou*, sprout sails as they made ready for the homeward trek. I had had some sailing experience and straight away thought what a good idea. Sails would steady the boat up a fair bit, making it much easier to work on deck and maybe give us an extra knot of speed. Bonzo and Nibblo had the same thought, so on our next day in harbour we scrumped around for some canvas to fly and in the end we managed to procure two big baggy old jibs, one of which we could fly from the mizzen mast as a stay sail and the other would set from the fore masthead to the stem head. We could hardly wait to give them a try.

And we weren't disappointed for on our next run home from Falmouth Bay, we had a brisk south-west wind. With the mizzen sheeted away, our two extra sails trimmed and drawing well on the starboard tack, the *Prosperity* steadied right up, losing most of her old roll and wallow and, what is more, we gained a good knot in speed. This knocked about half an hour off the travelling time, putting us ahead of many of the other boats, therefore greatly reducing the immediate competition for a landing berth, boxes and pallets, which was certainly a blessing. As for the saving on diesel, well there obviously was one, but in those days it was just pennies a gallon and I can't remember it even being considered.

At one time the big shoal moved much further west and was then to be found off the Western Black Head, making the journey back and forth to Looe very much longer. As we had a good cabin on the *Prosperity* we decided to land our fish at Falmouth, it being a pleasant port to work from and made a nice change, the main attraction of course being that many hours were shorn off the working day. We landed up the river towards Penryn on what was known as Coast Lines Quay. It was one huge mackerel packing and marketing organisation, and an awful lot of boats landed their catches there. At the close of a day's fishing, rows of boats would be ranked off the quayside eight and ten deep, loaded down like half-tide rocks, awaiting a turn to swing their fish ashore. When the fishing was heavy the operation just kept rolling, teams of packers working in shifts twenty four hours a day to clear the backlog. It was all one hell of a pantomime, but many is the time we would be landed and back down at Falmouth, ready to go ashore for a meal and a pint, while on the VHF we could hear the Looe fleet chatting away, still ploughing a furrow for home.

At Customs House Quay we would be moored with boats that hailed from ports all over Cornwall, Newquay, Padstow, St Ives and Newlyn. The bigger boats had to tie up on the outside of the quay, ranked off ten or twelve abreast, while the smaller ones would be crammed like a log jam into the little inner harbour. There were no ladders fitted to the outside wall, so to get ashore we had to scramble up a length of trawl warp that hung at each berth. But as we were all pretty fit, climbing up and down like that didn't present anything of a problem. Even Willie Bishop, a St Ives man who at the time was of pension age, if not older, could shin up the wires like a monkey.

Our evening meal was usually taken in a corner café situated just a few yards up from the quay. Fish and chips, bread and butter and a mug of tea was our favourite fare. And after dinner it was then only a short stroll to the Chain Locker for a night cap. This old pub was famous for the landlord's collection of nauticalia. Beams and walls were festooned with enough gear to fit out a clipper ship and photographs and artefacts told the story of the famous rescue of Captain Carlson and the crew of the *Flying Enterprise*, a ship rumoured to be carrying gold that foundered in the Channel during a terrible winter storm. It was a very pleasant way to bring yet another long day to a close, sat around the fire with a pint, swapping yarns with men from the other boats. Someone might lead off in song, usually the old Cornish favourites, *Little Eyes*, *Camborne Hill*, *Lamorna* etc, three-part harmony on the verse and all hands roaring out the chorus. When the landlord called time, it was out again into the keen night air, all rumped up in our jackets, to yarn our way back to the welcome of the *Prosperity*'s cabin with its little black coal stove keeping it warm and snug for us. After squirting the last of the landlord's good ale over the rail, it was time for some well earned kip. A new day was beckoning, and it wasn't many hours away.

Leaving Falmouth in the morning was like joining a spring tide ebb of boats. They streamed out from everywhere: Penryn, Flushing, Mylor and St Mawes and from moorings all up and down the river, A sharp lookout had to be maintained to keep clear of each other, although in the dark the biggest menace was Black Rock, a single unlit rock at the entrance to Carrick Roads. That thing was always a worry.

Out fishing one day, we had an incident that makes any fisherman's heart sink into his boots. Our steady, reliable old Gardner engine decided to throw a wobbler. It died down to a bare tick over, the boat fell away off the wind and we started to roll away broadside through the fleet. Bonzo immediately dived down into the engine room to find out what was ailing our trusty motor to discover that the diaphragm of the fuel lift pump had split and there wasn't a spare aboard. Here was a problem; nobody would want to stop fishing to tow us back in to Falmouth, although someone would have done just that if we had asked. The answer was to hoist the sails and see what sort of progress we could make with them. When our little bits of canvas were up and drawing, we discovered she would waddle along at about two knots and it was blowing about a five. The engine could just bear turning the prop, so at least we weren't dragging it, and the fair tide was giving us one of our two knots. But never mind, we were safe and heading in the right direction. Bonzo got on the VHF to relay our plight to the other boats, saying that we were okay but if anyone came by us, please give us a tow in. We managed to sail in to abeam of Pendennis Point and were just pondering the optimum moment to sheet home and try to make away up the river, when one of the Falmouth boats hove alongside and took our rope. Bob Harvey George was our saviour in his powerful ex-French trawler; he very soon took us up to Custom House Quay where we thankfully got our ropes ashore, glad our ordeal under sail was over. And for the cost of the petrol, Bonzo managed to organise a lift up to Looe to get the spare parts that we needed. Upon his return, an hour's work on the lift pump soon put everything back to rights.

That winter aboard the *Prosperity*, we chased the mackerel shoals from Bigbury Bay to the Lizard then, as usual, by late February their great exodus began. Where they migrated to we had no idea, but it became very much harder to make a catch. And so, to carry us through to the month of May and the spring paint up, the trawls were hauled aboard to try our luck on the lemon-sole, monk and whiting.

Trawling, if all goes according to plan, isn't usually a very exciting way to earn a living. The skipper decides where he fancies trying his luck, and this is very often based on trying to tease the truth out of the smokescreen of lies and bullshit broadcast by other skippers on the VHF the previous day. A day hauler will do three 'drags' before going in for the night, while a bigger vessel may well stay at sea for a week or more, plodding up and down the ground, day in day out, 24 hours a day, forever adding to her catch. Working on what is called clean ground, trawling can be a steady but a very tedious way to earn a living, but it is when the skipper decides to break open some new ground that things can become much more interesting. To do this might be very rewarding, haul after haul of good prime fish, and that is why the chance is taken. But unlike the old familiar ground you don't know what is lying on the sea bed and it is then that trawling can go from days of utter boredom, to all the excitement you could possibly manage. The boat slows to a stop, the engine starts to labour and the warps come in together, the trawl has snagged on some obstacle on the sea bed, probably a rock or a piece of wreckage. The skipper might have a go at freeing it by easing back on the engine to let the boat fall back over the warps, then to put the engine flat out and charge ahead to try and drag the trawl free. This may well work and you start to move ahead again, the doors pick up and drag the warps apart and all seems okay. But at the back of your mind you are wondering if the 'fastener' has ripped the trawl and that the rest of the drag will be complete waste of time. So you either carry on, agonising in the hope that all is well, or haul to make sure that it is. It's the skipper's choice. When the trawl refuses to budge, the winch has to be engaged and the gear hauled to try and free it. If there is any tide running at the time, this operation can be quite hair-raising to say the very least. The winch grunting under the strain, the boat laying over at a crazy angle, pulled down by the warps and at the same time being swept by the tide, decks awash as she is unable to rise to the passing seas. This is a time of maximum danger; men can and do get killed and injured and trawlers can be pulled under or capsized when caught down in big tides. If the gear really won't budge then the warps are paid out again to ease the strain and the skipper will call up someone with a bigger trawler, and when it arrives the warp ends are passed over to it: then it is 'shit or bust' as the saying goes. Sometimes the trawl can be retrieved having suffered very little damage, while at other times it is hauled aboard looking as if a war party of Zulus have been through it. Occasionally the gear is never seen again, having come hard and fast into a wreck and that is that - goodnight Vienna. The warps or the combination part away and it's back to harbour for a new set of gear.

The other scenario is a weight in the trawl. The boat slows down but doesn't actually stop, the warps close in together and the engine starts to bark and black smoke with the extra strain. Once again the winch is engaged and the haul begins. The warps are wound onto the drums and the doors are chained to the gantry and unclipped. If there is something serious caught in the trawl the band will really start to play as you try to wind on the combination. The winch will be grunting and straining as it fights to bring the trawl up, inch by inch. The boat lies sluggish in the water unwilling to rise to the swell, guide and hanging blocks screech with the stress on them. At last the wing ends of the trawl appear, the brakes on the winch are wound on and you then try to get some idea of what it is that is causing all this aggro. The trawl is now hanging vertically in the water, stretched so tight that it could be made out of fencing wire. The cause could one of any number of things: fathoms of heavy steel cable abandoned by a merchant ship or a tug wrapped around the wing end, all sharp spikes and rust. A ship's anchor caught by its fluke on the foot rope, a granite boulder that has lain in wait since the last ice age lodged back in the cod end. Whatever it is, it has to be dealt with. The heaviest lifting tackle is rigged, and inch by inch the obstacle is brought to view and then is either cut away, to plunge back to the seabed, or stropped up, lifted aboard the trawler and lashed down, to be disposed of later in the trip.

By far the most unnerving of items to bring up in a trawl are old explosive devices such as bombs, depth charges, mines and torpedoes. Thousands of these things were lost or dumped at sea in the two world wars and trawlers, when exploring new grounds, would sometimes catch them. Up in the net they would come, all battered and rusty, maybe sprouting horns or fins. Some would fizz in the most alarming manner, others spewing horrible liquids and explosives from their broken casings. Even the smallest of them, if activated, was more than capable of blowing a small wooden fishing boat to kingdom come, and probably a bit further than that. Every trawlerman can recall times spent struggling with these horrifying devices, crewmen refusing to help, hiding down in the cabin or right up the bow, white with fear when they realise just what sort of a gift Neptune had sent them. The skipper has to stay cool as he works out the best way to deal with the several-hundred pounds of potentially instant death now in their midst. Mind you, cool as he may look, if someone were to burst a paper bag behind him he would probably jump right over the mast.

We once caught a huge bomb on the *Prosperity*. It was about 8 feet long by 18 inches wide and it was lodged right back in the cod end, so it had to be lifted aboard. The only consoling thought was that if it did detonate we wouldn't know a thing about it. We clapped a tackle on it and hauled it out of the way to spend the afternoon lashed down on the foredeck with the hose playing on it until it could be dumped over some rocky ground, and very glad we were to see it go.

There is an amusing tale of a skipper who, upon hauling a mine up in his net, got on the radio to a fellow skipper to seek his advice. Having heard the sorry tale, the advice was that there was only one course of action: "Repeat after me. Our Father which art in heaven …"

When the casings of these things rust through the explosive in them spills out and ends up rolling around the sea bed. Phosphorous will ignite when exposed to the air and water won't put it out; a dreadful substance to have aboard a boat. Other forms of high explosive may look harmless enough, but by the time the fishermen catch them they are old and likely to be very unstable. One skipper hauled up what he thought were chunks of marble and rather liking the look of it he collected it up and took it home, thinking it would make a nice decorative addition to his rockery. By all accounts it looked very well and all who saw it admired his handy work and the pretty white 'marble' glinting in amongst the alpines. Then one day a friend (who happened to be a bomb disposal expert) dropped by and when he caught sight of this rockery, he nearly had a blue fit. For there, before his disbelieving eyes, were several hundred pounds of very tastefully arranged high explosive. How it hadn't gone up taking everything with it he just couldn't begin to guess. Needless to say the whole area had to be evacuated and, with all due precaution, it was removed and disposed of.

At one time, scallopers working in Falmouth Bay were bringing up in their dredges what looked like clay. One skipper calling to another on the VHF enquired if he too had caught any of this 'cheesy stuff'.

"Yes," he said, "the lads are making model boats with it."

"So were my crew," came the reply. "But every time they dried out in the sun they exploded."

"Bugger me," chimed in a third, "I thought it was fire clay. I've got a lump of it home in the shed that I was going to do the Rayburn with."

But catching these things was never a joke. A scalloper working in Falmouth Bay once activated a device with his dredges and, although the resulting explosion was two hundred yards or so astern of him, it collapsed his wheelhouse and shook the caulking out of the hull. No life was lost and the boat was saved, but the dredges that were on the end of his warps had vanished. But you don't always get away with it when you tangle with these things. The owners of the Brixham trawler *Twilight Waters* were becoming somewhat concerned when they couldn't contact her on the radio, so they began shouting around to other trawlers to try and get some sort of a report on her, but all to no avail. They knew the area she was working in, but none of the boats in that area could report a sighting of her. The search was then widened in case the skipper had steamed off in the night to some secret trawling ground and was maintaining radio silence because he didn't want other boats getting in on his good fishing. An 'all ships' alert was put out, but still there was no sight nor sign of the *Twilight Waters*. Where had she gone? None could say but it was starting to look very serious.

Eventually one skipper reported hearing a distant explosion during the night in the area she was known to have been in. And upon further investigation, that proved to be the clue to her fate. The verdict on the *Twilight Waters* was that she and her crew had been blown from the face of the earth when a mine or a bomb caught in the trawl had detonated as they were trying to deal with it. Nothing more than a battered lifebelt was ever found to bear witness to her tragic end.

Statistically speaking, commercial fishing has always been a very hazardous occupation, but add in bombs and mines and it must go right off the scale. Thankfully most of these things have long since been cleared off the main trawling grounds, but it's the men who worked there, 30 and 50 years ago, we have to thank for that.

All other mariners use their vessels to get from A to B, preferably as swiftly as possible. But not the fishermen; the sea is where they live and work, handling their boats and gear with great skill and daring, working 18 to 20 hours a day in all weathers and conditions. And yet fishing is classed as unskilled labour. Surely, in truth, fishermen must be some of the toughest and most skilled mariners out on the water today.

14

Hot Work

It seems to me that every 20 years or so the gods that rule the elements decide that they will bless us with some really nice summer weather. This, I consider, must be as a consolation prize for all the many wet to mediocre ones that we in Britain optimistically plod through. And for the summer of 1976 they certainly pulled out all the stops.

Day after day the sun arced across a clear and cloudless sky; the wind, if it blew at all, was only in gentle zephyrs, while the sea remained like a sheet of deep blue glass. You lot want a good summer? Then try some of this. Neptune and his buddies really socked it to us that year. Johnny and I were working our boats as usual, and the pace was relentless. The weather was just so hot that people who wouldn't normally go boating ventured out just to enjoy the cooler air of the bay. Our little boats were running flat out from about ten in the morning, when people first strolled down to the quayside after their breakfast, until dusk when we called the last ones in from out of the gathering darkness. We had seven boats each, and at the slipway to seaward of us, Derrick Toms with Harry Pengelly worked a like number. While at the steps fifty yards to the north of us Claude Tamblin and brothers Stan and Darrel Hoskin operated their fleets. Freddie Lewis and Malcolm Solt worked from the steps one hundred yards north again. At Pearns boatyard above the bridge twenty five more were for hire. Collectively, about ninety 'doodle bugs' were plying from Looe, turning the harbour into what resembled a water-borne game of bumper cars The sound of summer was the massed pluttering of their Stewart Turner engines. Ninety boats for hire and people were queuing at the steps for them; we had never ever been so consistently busy, or ever sweated so much, running around in that heat. Seven days a week, week after week, we worked until one day I ended up with such a red-raw sweat rash down between the cheeks of my behind. I was in agony and walking as if I had a nasty accident in the trouser area and I just had to have a day off to recuperate a little.

Charlie Butters was the boy working with me that year. I gave him his day's money and asked him to put the boats back on their moorings then, with a bandy legged gait, I hobbled back home. A day's rest did square me up a fair bit and the following morning as I was readying my boats, Johnny came over and passed me a bundle of money.

"What's this for," I enquired.

"Well," he said. "Yesterday we were so busy we were soon out of boats, so I sent the boy up after yours and we worked them as well."

I couldn't believe it, a man and a boy working fourteen boats, they must have been jumping around like meerkats on speed. But what a kind and thoughtful gesture. As the summer wore on, the heat baked the once-green fields and gardens into shades of dull yellow and brown; tar melted in the roads and drinking water was rationed. Out on the cliffs the bracken and gorse first dried to tinder, then with a blaze it went afire, sending towers of black and grey smoke drifting up into the still air. It burned and smouldered for weeks the whole coast around, leaving behind acres of blackened land. And on a post high above the town, the fire siren wailed by day and night, calling to action the exhausted volunteer brigade time and again. Builders were starting work at five in the morning to avoid having to work through the punishing heat of the afternoons. Holiday makers and locals alike flocked for relief to the beaches, spending the day in and out of the sea trying to keep cool, the water feeling like a warm bath; careless sunbathers had the skin seared off of them, to peel away later in ragged pennants.

By night, the heat of the sun retained in the walls and roofs of many of the houses made sleep all but impossible, driving people to move outdoors to sleep on camp beds made up in backyards and on sheltered lawns. Brewers, lemonade factories and ice cream makers just couldn't keep pace with the demand. It must have been the weather they had all been collectively praying for, for generations.

And still the temperatures climbed ever upward, peaking finally at 110 Fahrenheit, at least that was the highest reading we experienced working on the quay. Then one day in late September this record-breaking summer came to an end that was as dramatic as it had been hot.

A rain storm of tropical intensity was unleashed across the county, ending both the drought and the long hot summer. For one village, tucked tightly in its cliffside valley, this was going to be a night of horrors. A wall of flood water, backing up 8 feet and 10 feet deep in places, tore through Polperro. Many of the houses and cottages were devastated, flooded through from floor to ceiling, doors and windows ripped away and they, with the contents of the rooms, were to be found floating in the harbour the next morning, along with smashed up sheds, and battered cars, plus one body - that of an elderly gentleman swept to his death by the torrent that raged through his front room, carried from the hands of his daughter as she tried to guide him to safety.

It was a stark and shocking finish to a record-breaking summer.

15

Scottish Invaders

I doubt there was ever a fishery that suited the Cornish fisherman as well as the hand line mackerel fishery. Any small fishing boat could be fitted out for it, and for a very modest outlay. Running expenses were low, and the returns (as in all branches of the fishing industry) matched the amount of hard work you were prepared to put into it. Those who worked the worst weather and the longest hours made the most money, and there were some very good wages to be earned. It was a selective fishery or, in the buzz word of today, very 'green'. If you stopped on a shoal of fish and tried your line only to find that they were immature, you moved on until a shoal of mature ones was found. And there is no way that a fleet of hand liners, no matter how many there might be, could ever endanger a stock of fish. As with Cornwall's two other great fisheries, drift netting and long lining, their very method of operation guaranteed a healthy stock of fish for the next generation to earn a living with.

Simply because passive fishing methods, practised in small boats, ensured that both the fish and their habitats were not destroyed, men earned a living, not a fortune, and still left Mother Nature with the upper hand. But by the second half of the twentieth century all these methods were rapidly becoming obsolete. Modern fishing technology and development had now given man, for the very first time, the upper hand over nature, and for the marine environment that has proved to be very bad news indeed.

The story of the decline of the Cornish hand line fishery must begin in Norway, for it is here that they pioneered the research and development of the purse seine as an efficient way to catch herring. Its success was astounding, and it soon proved to be the ultimate way to catch any pelagic fish. The final development of the purse seiner was a highly specialised vessel that was as big as a coastal merchant ship that could encircle huge shoals of fish with a curtain of net in excess of a mile in circumference and as deep as any of the waters around the continental shelf.

With the aid of loans and grants from the Highlands and Islands development board, many of Scotland's leading fishermen invested in these purse seiners; one hell of an investment made by some very smart men. And indeed their forward thinking and hard work paid dividends, for an assault on the herring shoals could now be mounted like none that had ever been mounted before. Operated by skilled and dedicated fishermen, these vessels proved to be all too effective because by the early 1970s, the marine biologists published a report announcing that as far as they could calculate, the North Sea herring stocks had been so reduced as to be on the point of collapse and recommended an immediate ban on further catching to give the much-depleted shoals a chance to regenerate. Accepting the scientists' findings, the government placed a 3-year ban on fishing for North Sea herring.

This ban, as necessary as it must have been, caused huge problems, because here were these massively expensive, highly specialised vessels (they could not turn to another method of fishing) tied up with nothing to do. It was not just the fishermen who would go bankrupt, the government (who had encouraged their construction), would also lose the many millions of pounds invested in them in the form of loans and grants. And so, to keep their boats running the Scotsmen came south, working out of Plymouth and Falmouth to try their luck on the mackerel shoals off the Cornish coast.

Against the Scots' fishing capability, the Cornish hand line fleet looked pathetic, a cottage industry. One Scots purser could catch more in a night than the whole Cornish fleet could land in a week. We had no chance, and neither were we given one. When news reached us that they were coming to Cornwall, there was uproar in the Cornish fishing fraternity; protest meetings were held and our MPs were lobbied. But there was precious little they could do. The Scots were British registered fishing vessels and as the law then stood, provided they stayed outside of the three mile limit, they were perfectly entitled to fish where and when they liked. We were assured that they wouldn't interfere with our operation as the market for their fish was very different from ours and they would be operating way out in the Channel. So we were told, we had nothing to fear and really they were quite friendly and fluffy and would do us no harm whatsoever. Our collective answer to that was 'bollocks'. They had destroyed their own herring fishery up north, so given time why would they not destroy our mackerel fishery here in the south? And all the oily, platitude-peddling, lying bastards who were in authority at the time assured us that it would not go that way, and we in return told them exactly what we thought and so it proved.

The first of the Scots vessels to arrive probably couldn't believe their luck. From a few of miles off the coast to hard into the bays, the place was teaming with prime mackerel and night after night these huge seiners were loaded down to near sinking point. Of course, as word of their success spread, more and more of them came down to join in this bonanza. And it was not just purse seiners, every boat powerful enough to tow a mid-water trawl turned up, including a number of monster stern trawlers from Hull and Grimsby. These were the vessels that had done so much damage to the Arctic cod stocks that a war had been fought by Iceland to get them off of their fishing grounds. And here they all were, operating just a few miles off our coastline; vessels that, because of their size and power, had all but succeeded in wiping out the fishery that they had been built to prosecute.

The relentless slaughter of the mackerel shoals now gathered apace as day in, day out, fair weather or foul, thousands of tons of prime fish were brailed and pumped ashore from the holds of these mighty industrial fishers. Much of it was traded to a fleet of Russian factory ships (converted whalers) riding to their anchors in the Carrick Roads at Falmouth. While in Plymouth's Millbay Docks and at other wharfs around the Sound, refrigerated lorries lined up to load boxes of prime quality fish destined for the UK and continental markets, while the subprime stuff was convoyed away like so much manure, bound for the fish meal factories. In every area that these vessels operated in, the sea bed would be thickly carpeted with dead mackerel that they had somehow slipped or lost. Local trawlers hauled their nets to find them full to bursting point with stinking fish, hanging rotten from out of their skins, while the deaths of dolphins and pilot whales was also often in evidence.

The Cornish fishermen protested long and often, and to throw us a sop, half-baked limits, checks and balances were put into place to be enforced by the local fishery patrol boats and a mine sweeper from the Royal Navy's fishery protection squadron. This proved to be about as effective as having a dead bulldog guarding a pile of money up a dark alley; they had rings run around them. Here was some very big business indeed, with money to match, and money talks. Fish merchants and hauliers had probably never had it so good. And while these big boys were leading the dance, our little boats in their harbours, making their irregular little catches, would have to take their chance. Because of the huge bulk of fish these industrial boats landed, they could afford to market their catches at bulk prices and still make a lot of money. But the hand liners needed a fair price for their fish, simply to make a decent average wage, because the winter gales could blow for days at a time when nothing could be earned. But business is business, and a merchant isn't going to pay a pound a stone for an uncertain supply of prime mackerel from the hand liners when a regular supply can be obtained from the pursers at fifty pence.

And so our prices tumbled, fifty pence for large fish down to five and ten pence for small, and of course our markets became less certain. Limits of 120 stone per boat a day started to creep in, or we could land as much as we liked provided it was all large fish, and as we were now fishing on very mixed shoals, that was a nonsense. In the early days of the mackerel fishing the shoals were all in their year class, a shoal was either all small or medium or large and you would rarely catch mixed fish. But I think that probably because of the continual driving, harassing and slaughter of the fish, breaking up the big year class shoals, the survivors joined together for mutual self help. And no longer did they winter in the bays up and down the shore but instead they were often to be found well out to sea, flighty and always on the move. With their echo sounders going, the hand line fleet would put to sea in search of them, and it very often took many hours steaming about to locate a decent shoal, and then working like demons to try and load the boat down, because 100 stone was no good now, the prices were much too low.

To add insult to injury we now acted as markers for the big boys, for when they slipped away from Plymouth or Falmouth, they only had to listen to their VHFs or switch on their radar to find the Cornish fleet sat over the fish they too were looking for. Our efforts must have saved them hours of searching because by late in the afternoon they would often be steaming around us sounding out the shoals we were on. Then they would just lay and wait for us to pack up for the day before wiping it out with a purse seine or smashing through it with a mid-water trawl. Sometimes they become impatient and would blow their fog horns, the skipper waving out of the wheelhouse window for us to clear off. Either way there would be nothing left for us to fish on the next day, meaning hours of searching to find yet another shoal for them to come out and decimate.

One morning the Cornish fleet was working a shoal of fish out off the Dodman when along came a Scots pair team on the hunt. They circled around the hand liners and then went out to seaward and shot their trawl, steering right at the shoal that we were working. This would have finished off our day's work because there would have been nothing left to fish on once they had been through it. Furious at their actions, I got on the VHF to one of the Falmouth boats, the skipper of which was a bit of a hot head, and suggested that for once we ought to fight back and not let these bastards have it all their own way. He agreed with me, and the upshot was that about twenty or so hand liners ceased fishing and steamed out to meet the pair trawlers. The Scots boats were big powerful craft, steel built and about 70 feet long. Our only chance to annoy them was to get ahead of them and slow right down to try and bring them to a halt. This in turn would make their gear sink to the bottom and they would have to haul it or risk fouling it on the rocks. But if the skippers held their nerve and carried on towing we would have to put the throttle on a bit quick to get out from under their bow before they sank us.

Tucked under the bow of a vessel like that is not a comfortable place to be but a couple of us went right in under the flare of each boat while the rest ranged alongside of them shouting and harassing like the angry men that they were. For a moment the Scotsmen looked astounded; they had never experienced this sort of treatment before. A man was up on each of their whalebacks shouting and waving back to the skipper in the wheelhouse as we slowed down and got ever closer to their great steel bows. It was a battle of nerves, but the Scotsmen's nerve went first and they slowed down and down until they stopped and had to haul their gear. The men in the surrounding boats had by now worked themselves up to a pitch of absolute fury and were threatening the Scots with everything from being flung overboard to murder if they ever caught them ashore. The Scots skippers could now be heard on channel sixteen shouting for the help of the fishery protection boat and reporting the incident ashore to the coastguards. Once their gear was hauled, they buggered off as hard as they could go and we, having won a small victory, went back to our day's fishing.

What we didn't expect was the publicity that that incident attracted. It was reported on the television news and in many of the national papers the next day. And by the dramatic way it was reported you would imagine the sea to be littered with dead bodies and wreckage. A sea battle had taken place between the Scots and the Cornish fishermen off the notorious Dodman Point etc, etc. In reality we had gained a few hours fishing that we wouldn't have had; the Scots had been rattled a bit, but doubtless they came back and slaughtered that shoal once we had left it. We, the Cornish hand liners, had vented our frustration and fury at what was happening to us, but in the end it made no difference.

Our markets were going, the fish were becoming much harder to find, and when we did find them it was mainly for the benefit of the opposition. By the middle of the 1980s the Cornish hand line industry was very fragmented; every harbour still had a fleet, but it shrank each successive season as men gave up and went ashore or looked elsewhere to earn a living, such as trawling or netting. The jobs that provided those vital winter wages were slipping away as boats' crews and fish packing gangs were no longer needed. But the Scotsmen were still out there earning big money, smashing up the shoals, carpeting the seabed with dead fish and sending thousands of tons of good fish to be made into fertiliser. That is progress, so it's okay then. No it wasn't, it was shameful crime that nobody in authority saw fit to stop.

16

The *Eileen*

In the spring of 1977 I sold my motor boats to buy the 44-foot lugger *Eileen*. Ernie Toms, her owner, had sadly passed on and his son Edward wanted rid of her to buy a smaller boat. She had been built in Looe in 1920 and packed two 30 HP Lister engines and, typical of the old drifters, both props came out of the port quarter. For the asking price of £2,000 she came complete with her summer sharking gear, mackerel gurdies for the winter fishing and plenty of assorted engine spares. The deal was done, and after giving the old vessel a good refit and paint up, crewman Don Lang and I spent a pleasant summer taking visitors out shark angling. We suffered a couple of minor breakdowns: a cylinder head cracked on one of the engines and another time the voltage regulator failed nearly setting the engine room afire, but it was all put to rights with very little loss of sea time. By mid-September the holiday season was drawing to a close so Don and I made ready for the winter fishing, but with a boat of the *Eileen*'s size I needed at least two more crewmen. I put the word about and pretty soon had some results in the form of Mother's Lamb and Killer Combes.

Now Killer had a tidy reputation for thuggery, burgling, boozing and bullshit and for some of his more outrageous efforts he had enjoyed a few long holidays paid for by Her Majesty. Probably not long back from one of his holidays, he appeared on the quay one day.

"Morning Ned," he bellowed.

"Hello Mike, how are you doing?" I replied.

"Okay. I hear you are looking for crew. I'll come with you for the winter if you like."

To be honest I didn't like, not really, but what do you say to somebody like that. "If that's the case you had better come down aboard and give me and Don a hand to get the boat ready," I said with much more conviction than I really felt. And that was it, deal done. Mike Combes, 'Killer' to his friends and enemies (and he had plenty of both), shipped aboard for the winter.

I recruited the last hand at a party that weekend. Howard Bowden, the youngest son of a local well-to-do family fancied a go at the fishing, so I said I would give him a try. I think he was about eighteen at the time; he had a rather foppish air about him and spoke with a very posh Cornish accent. His mother, concerned for the well-being of her youngest son, once said to me, "I hope you will look after my Howard, because he is mother's lamb, you know." And that was it. He was 'Mother's Lamb' from then on.

I don't think I have ever been to sea with a more diverse set of characters than that winter on the *Eileen*. Don Lang, small and wiry of build, was in his late thirties, a pipe smoking mad inventor type, who could repair and maintain anything from a valve radio to a diesel engine. Mike Combes, in his early thirties, built like a brick chicken house and with a few pints down his neck he could be hell on wheels, but sober and at sea, he was a good worker. And last but not least, Howard Bowden, Mother's Lamb. On bad weather days at sea he would be back aft buried up in his oilskins, winding away on his gurdy, cold, wet and miserable. I would look aft and say, "All right, my Laaamb?" and he would glance from under his hood and go "Baaa" with all the pathos that sound could be made to carry.

With the *Eileen*'s cabin painted out clean and smart, and a coal stove installed to make it warm and cosy, we lived aboard for much of the winter, following the shoals of fish. We ranged the coast, landing our catches in Falmouth and Penzance. That was the only time I ever worked out of that port, in fact a small fleet of us operated from there, because Newlyn was full right up and just couldn't handle any more boats.

One morning, while in the usual process of hauling aboard endless lines full of fish, there came an anguished howl from the foredeck area. This was the mighty Killer announcing that he had a hook buried right in his hand. For a man who had made an art of being macho, he suddenly wasn't looking quite so tough. When a hook goes in past the barb you daren't think twice about it, it has to be ripped out there and then or you'll never do it and will spend the rest of the sorry day sat down in the cabin waiting to get ashore to see the doctor. Glancing up at Killer, who at that moment didn't quite know what he was going to do, I yelled at him, "For fuck's sake, we have just got into some good fishing and you have got a hook in your hand. Rip the bloody thing out and get on with it."

If looks could kill I should have been dead, but he ripped it out and carried on fishing with blood running out of his glove. The following day the same thing happened to me, but out it had to come, with no hesitation; I daren't after the way I had shouted at Mike. It wasn't the first or the last time I ever had to do that, but the pain of it fairly makes your eyes boggle. When the day's work was done and we were safely moored up for the night, we would sit around the cabin fire for our evening meal of pasties, pies or fish and chips, all washed down with a mug of tea, to be followed by an easy stroll ashore for a nightcap in the nearest pub. Don, with a pint of real ale, would commandeer a comfy chair and smoke his pipe, talking cars or engines to somebody. I would be chatting to other fishermen about the day's events, while Killer would be at the bar, bigging it up as only he knew how. As for Mother's Lamb, he rarely if ever had a run ashore; a day at sea and he was totally knackered, stripped down to his leopard skin underpants, he would crawl into his sleeping bag soon after dinner, and that would be it until I roused him out the next morning.

One fog-bound morning in Falmouth, all hope of going to sea abandoned, the *Eileen* was moored on the outside of a rank of boats at Custom House Quay. I was on deck squaring things up when I happened to catch sight of a stoutly built old boy in a dinghy working his way along the foreshore with a long handled hoe. It was low tide, and he was gazing down, picking up oysters in the shallow water. But what grabbed my attention was his little sausage dog companion, who was scampering from thwart to thwart, sticking his head over the side and barking fit to bust. Even at a distance the constant yapping was enough to drive you mad, but the old chap seemed not to notice it, and carried on hoeing up his oysters. As he drifted down past the *Eileen* I wished him a good morning and asked why his dog was so excited.

"He do look for Beaky," came the reply, as if I should know who Beaky was, and he carried on hoeing.

"Well, who is Beaky?" I asked.

"Beaky's a dolphin," he said, looking up from under the peak of his cap, "and lives around here. He do come alongside the boat to take my dog for a ride."

Oh yes, I thought. "And how does he do that then?"

"Well," he said. "He do lay alongside and I puts the dog on his back and Beaky takes him for a little trip out and around, and if the dog's not ready when Beaky arrives he's up over the side of the boat looking for him, barks like hell out on the dolphin as well, he does." With that he drifted off in to the fog.

Now this, I thought, was a yarn too far; a good one for the emmets, so I stowed it to the back of my mind. Maybe I would ask about that ashore later on. Enjoying a pint in the Chain Locker that evening, I got into conversation with one of the hovellers called Snowy, and mentioned this old boy and his dog and the dolphin. Snowy confirmed every word of the story and added many more to it. Beaky the dolphin was evidently very well known in Falmouth; he was an unbridled show off with a wicked sense of humour. That same old boy, Snowy told me, was one day trying to anchor his boat in the river to work an oyster dredge. Three times he flung the anchor away and as many times Beaky retrieved it and tossed it back aboard. At the fourth attempt the dolphin, instead of throwing it back, kept a grip of it and proceeded down the river at high speed towing the boat astern of him. The old chap was sat aft hanging on for grim death while his dog, right up on the stem, ears flapping in the breeze, barked his head off. They paraded down the river in this manner for a good half-mile, looking like something out of Greek mythology, until Beaky, deciding that the joke was over, dropped the anchor and swam off.

This dolphin was known to have waited outside of Customs House Quay when the mackerel boats were slipping away to sea in the dark of an early morning, going from boat to boat pushing them about. Some of the men were very nearly in need of clean trousers, momentarily convinced that something supernatural was happening to their boat. RNLI bigwigs and local dignitaries had gathered one day for the launching of a new high speed inshore lifeboat. The Mayor quacked at the crowd and champagne was poured. The gallant crew in full regalia then thundered off around the bay to showcase their new piece of kit. But it was Beaky who did the showing off; he stole their thunder entirely, for it was not 'Oh look at that boat!' but 'Oh look the dolphin!' Beaky was jumping from side to side high over the lifeboat.

He would play with the children swimming at Swan Pool beach and divers in the area lived in dread of him appearing, because he always insisted on rescuing them. The crew of the Irish purse seiner *Quo Vadis* stumbled into the bar of the Chain Locker one evening looking pale and frightened. Coming ashore in their RIB on a pitch-dark night they found themselves being spun around in endless circles. Knowing nothing of Beaky, and being good Catholics, they were nearly ready to renounce all of their worldly goods and become monks if only the good Lord would show them some mercy. "That bloody fish frightened the soul case out of us," said the skipper. A 10-minute run had taken nearly an hour.

Beaky became the talk of Falmouth, but one day he was gone. Where to, nobody knew. His japes had certainly been very amusing, providing of course you were an onlooker and not the one selected to take part in his idea of a fun time.

When the mackerel faded from the coast in late February we returned home to Looe, but it was a long time to try and live from then until June when the first holidaymakers put in an appearance. As a stopgap we had a go at long lining but there were just so many frustrations and uncertainties in that game and we gave it up. The biggest trouble was getting hold of fresh bait; there was a good supply of frozen mackerel available but it wasn't good enough. If we did get the bait, would the weather be fine enough, or would the tide be running too hard? It was a never-ending headache, something different had to be done.

I had worked the *Eileen* for a year and had made quite a decent living with her, but she couldn't be fitted for that vital third season, trawling, leaving a huge between-seasons gap where the money just drained away. And as well as that, after nearly 60 years of hard work, the old boat was getting rather tired. Both her engines were well worn, and she needed plenty of pumping when at sea in any weather. So, in the spring of 1978, I put her up for sale, having first spruced her right up, everything clean neat and freshly painted, with engines and all equipment aboard put into good working order. Of all people, a taxi driver from Plymouth bought her. He was full of what a wonderful fellow he was, and how much money he was going to make. Whether he did or not, I have no idea, but at the time he did have enough money to buy the *Eileen*.

I was now in the market for something of more recent construction that would fit the bill for our yearly three seasons. A little Scots ring-netter or a Devon crabber maybe, but definitely not another ancient Cornish lugger. After a month or more of scanning the boats for sale section in the *Fishing News*, and driving about looking at craft that over the phone sounded just fine, but upon inspection turned out to be little more than a tarted-up bundle of worn out old sticks (much like I had just got rid of), I was beginning to lose faith. My father, a shipwright by trade, kept mentioning the fact that the lugger *Ibis* was up for sale at Porthleven and suggested we go and have a look at her. I kept telling him that I had had enough of worn out old boats and wasn't interested.

This one, he said, was built by Percy Mitchell and anything built by him had got to be worth a look. So more to keep him happy and have a day out, I made arrangements to go and see her. Herbie Uren, the *Ibis*'s owner, met us in the car park at Porthleven, and the three of us strolled down to the harbour in the warm June sunshine. It was low tide, and his boat lay against the quay wall looking ill-kempt and embarrassed. Climbing down a wall ladder we arrived on deck and it was not a very inspiring sight. Herbie was more of a boat killer than a maintainer, so after a few years in his tender care and a long lay-up, the *Ibis*, to put it mildly, was looking far from her best.

She was 42 feet long and had been built in 1930 by the best of the best, and for most of her life she had been well maintained. Her planking was of pitch pine, and each plank ran the full length of the hull and rang like a bell under Dad's little surveying hammer. Also, as with all Cornish boats of her era, she was of tight seam construction, so there were no butts to leak or caulking to fall out. The deck and bulwarks were serviceable, but the wheelhouse was rough and empty of gear; there was no sounder or radio, just a compass and the wheel. While down in the engine room sat a fine old 82 HP Gardner diesel engine, worn but there was life in it yet. So beneath all the muck and neglect it seemed to me that a good boat was waiting to reappear. I was impressed and very surprised.

Herbie had gone back to his cottage while Dad and I did the surveying, so we wandered up to have a yarn with him. I was interested in his boat, but only if the price was right. It turned out that several fishermen had been to look at her but few had shown any real interest, and after many months of this, Herbie was by now desperate to be rid of her. Just the sort of vendor you need for driving home a hard bargain. I forget what his asking price had been, but I knew what I was prepared to pay, £2,500, and on that the deal was struck.

I lodged at Porthleven for a couple of days while I made her fit to steam back to Looe. The poor old thing was full of junk and rubbish, the batteries were flat, the chain steering was ceased, etc, etc. But I managed to get everything working again and got her home without incident. I next laid her up for a few weeks to give her a good overhaul, fitting her out for the three seasons that we then worked. I obtained a fine old belt-driven winch from Scarborough and brought it back to Looe via a relay of fish lorries. My father built and fitted a new wheelhouse and did any shipwright work that was needed, a few new stanchions in the bulwarks, capping rail etc. Pete the weld fabricated the trawling gantry and lead blocks, while Jack Statton the local engineer made up my mackerel gurdies. Next, a good paint up both inside and out really brought the old girl back to life, and as I had kept back all the fishing rods when I had sold the *Eileen*, the *Ibis* was now ready to earn her keep once more.

I shipped up two crewmen, Nezzer and the Goat. Nezzer (his real name being Simon Keane) was 16 years old and had just left school. The Goat (real name Neal Cumston) was in his early thirties, an ex-matlot and ex many other things as well, as crafty as a bag of weasels as his nickname implied, but as tough as hemp. Neither man had ever been fishing before so the winter of 1978/79 was a sort of shake-down training period. Nezzer suffered with seasickness, while nothing whatsoever affected the Goat. After a week or so, both of them had got to grips with the mackerel fishing and were making a pretty good job of it as we chased the shoals from Bigbury Bay to the Lizard.

The *Ibis* proved to be a good boat, sound and seaworthy and, unlike most of the old luggers, she didn't leak in poor weather. I looked after her, and she in return never played me up. Over time I greatly altered the work I did with her, but I earned a living with the *Ibis* for the next 23 years. Come the early spring of 1979 we shipped up the trawl and went after the lemon-soles, working up off Plymouth and then south of the Eddystone and west on the clean trawling ground that lies to seaward of the reefs of rocks known as the Bretons and west again seaward of the Plashets, yet another collection of reefs. From there, we hauled out south a bit to clear the radar buoy and then west again passing the back of two wrecks, first the *Victoria* and then the *Silver Laurel*. By now the Dodman Point was handy and Falmouth Bay was in view; to go on any further required a more powerful boat and heavier gear as the ground became rough and uncertain with a very good chance of coming fast and tearing the trawl or worse still losing the lot. So in the early days of trawling, that was our ground.

17

Tragedy at Sea

A generation ago, the fishermen of Looe always maintained that God had got the port under his wing. This was because, despite of all the dangers in wresting a living from the sea in small boats in summer and winter, tragedies had mercifully been very few. But, as in every fishing port the world over, sooner or later someone's luck is going to run out, and when it does the effect is utterly devastating.

In January of 1979 a mackerel boat, the *Do It Again*, new to the port of Looe, had a small winch and gantry fitted to enable her to do a bit of trawling for those vital weeks at the end of the winter mackerel fishery and before the May month paint up. Being an open boat of only 30 feet long she was never going to be out deep working in any poor weather, but I suppose she might have scratched up a week's work up and down the shore in reasonable conditions.

One Saturday, towards the end of the month, the job was done and everything was aboard ready to go, so on the afternoon tide they slipped away for sea trials. This was to check that the winch was working okay and that the lead blocks were running fair, also to get some idea of what adjustments were needed to both trawl and trawl boards to get the gear working properly. John Haines was the skipper, a keen young chap just 19 years old, while his crew was Charlie Tregenna aged 17, the same lad who worked with us on the motor boats as a schoolboy. They shot the trawl away on the inside trawling ground, just a couple of miles off the shore and proceeded to tow down Channel with the tide. The weather was a bit fresh, SW 4-6, poor enough for her, but they were only going out for a couple hours and would have a fair run home before the sea.

That same afternoon, Jack Jollif, a retired fisherman from Polperro, was out strolling on the cliff path and happened to observe this little boat bashing her way slowly to the westward. Upon looking out again some minutes later he could no longer make her out. He was somewhat perplexed that she had apparently hauled her gear and gone from view in so short a time but continued his walk, although he was far from easy in his mind.

The Polperro boat *Westward*, skipper Bill Cowan and crew John Courtis, were out that day scallop fishing when they received a brief but desperate shout over the VHF radio: "Help, Do It Again." Bill snatched up the phone, broadcasting back: "Do It Again, this is the Westward, do you receive me?" There was only silence. He tried several more times but could not get a reply. He then shouted an open message over the air to try and find out if any other boats had heard that awful shout, but again there was complete silence. Not being familiar with the boat's name, Bill had no idea who she was or where the call might had come from, and as he could make no contact with any other vessels, there was nothing more he could do but carry on with his day's fishing.

Back in Looe, the parents of both boys knew that they were only out on trials and shouldn't be away for very long, but when darkness fell and they still hadn't returned, those dreadful pangs of doubt and worry started to gnaw at them. John's father spoke of his concern to his eldest son David who was a volunteer coastguard. From the coastguards' station, David tried time and again to contact his brother on the VHF but had no luck and, after making a few more checks as to their likely whereabouts and drawing a blank each time, he decided it was time to raise the alarm. Both Fowey and Plymouth lifeboats were launched to search for them, but the big problem was that nobody knew exactly where they had gone for their trials, east or west, on the inside or outside trawling grounds. Jack Joliff was the only witness to the *Do It Again*'s whereabouts but he was totally unaware of what was happening.

Knowing nothing of this unfolding drama, the Looe trawler *La Quete* nudged alongside the quay that evening. It had been a long and tiring day at sea and skipper Mike Soady and his crewman Leo Bowdler were glad to get their catch landed and go their separate ways home. Mike had just sat down to dinner when he received a call from the coastguards explaining the situation with the *Do It Again*. He then phoned Leo to tell him what he had learnt. Both men then knew that, as weary as they were, they had to head back out to sea again and join in the search. There was no time to rouse others; if they didn't haste away immediately their boat would be aground on the tide.

At that time there would have still been the hope that maybe they had wrapped the trawl in the propeller and needed a tow in, or that they had come hard and fast and were awaiting the turn of the tide to get the trawl free, but why hadn't they answered the radio calls? Or called others to let them know what they were doing? Things were not adding up. Early the next morning the quay was abuzz with the dreadful news, and as we made our boats ready for sea, everyone knew that a very grim day indeed lay ahead of us all. The two lifeboats and the *La Quete* had been searching through night and had found nothing. It was all so sad. By daybreak word had spread as boats from Polperro, Fowey and Mevagissey joined us, line abreast, doing a sweep search up and down the coast, hour after hour, looking for any sign at all of the missing *Do It Again* and the boys that were on her. We knew by then that she had gone, but it was the how and the why and the where that needed answering, and most urgent of all, to try and locate the bodies of her poor drowned crew. For the sake of their grieving families it was paramount that they be found but secretly, for the sake of your own nightmares you wished that honour on others and not yourself.

And then a shout went up on the VHF. It was Bill Wadling, skipper of the *Our Daddy* announcing that he had located a body floating close to his starboard bow and was going to try and retrieve it. One of the lifeboats told him to hold fast, they would come over and lift the body as they had the gear to do so. Praises be! One found, one to go. The fleet searched on, up and down, in and out with no further result, neither could we locate the wreck on our echo sounders, for the thought was that maybe the other man, Charlie (for it was John, the skipper's body that had been found), might be trapped in the cabin.

By sundown we had abandoned the search and returned to harbour, the end of a sad, sad day. Mike Soady on the *La Quete* decided to see the week out searching for Charlie and the wreck while the rest of the fleet returned to the fishing. Inadvertently, any boats working the inside trawling ground were also helping with the search as well, as there are few things better than a trawl to bring up anything laying on the sea bed. And so it was that a few days later, Ivan Chaston and Eric Brown on the *Tethera* were towing their trawl when, on a previously clear piece of ground, they came fast. As they winched back to retrieve the gear. Mike Soady came over in the *La Quete* and marked the obstruction on his sounder. There it was as plain as a pike staff; it had to be the wreck of the *Do It Again*. Ivan danned off his gear while Mike contacted the Navy in Plymouth.

The next day a team of divers from the bomb disposal squad went down to take a look, and when they surfaced they confirmed that the wreck had been found. First they cleared Ivan's trawl away and then attached some surface marker buoys. The divers then cradled the hull with two lifting strops so that the wreck could now be raised.

The following day, as the weather still held fine, Polperro skipper Kevin Curtis manoeuvred his powerful ex-French trawler the *Veronique* over the wreck site and sent down two heavy nylon warps. The divers waiting below on the wreck then shackled them to the lifting strops, checked and checked again that all was ready, then sent a signal to the surface for the lift to begin. Aboard the *Veronique* the winch was engaged, first to take up the slack and then, after a final check with the divers below that all was well, the lift commenced. The engine slowed a few revolutions, working hard to power the winch, its drive belt joining links, clack-clacking as they hit the jockey wheel. The warps hissed water, singing like harp strings as they passed through the gantry hanging blocks, the old trawler now under considerable strain, cluckied down a couple of planks lower in the water as the wreck rose up to meet her. Kevin lifted the *Do It Again* as tight up under his boat as he could and then at high tide the *La Quete* towed him into Talland Bay. There, in shallow water, the wreck was lowered to the bottom to allow the divers to attach lifting bags and draw her into where she would be exposed at low tide. When this had been achieved, the surveyors inspected her to try and come to a verdict as to why she had sunk. First of all there was no body in the cabin, and secondly, after endless debate and deliberation, no really hard and fast evidence was ever found or conclusion drawn as to what had caused the fateful sinking. It remained an open verdict.

One theory amongst the fishermen at the time was that her gantry looked proportionally high for a small boat and that maybe she had capsized, but tests carried out proved that it was not so. And again, if John had enough time to broadcast a brief distress call then strip off his clothes to swim, why were the life jackets and life raft left untouched. But exactly how do you react when suddenly traumatised and facing the prospect of death? Not always logically I suspect. There are many questions that were, and now always will remain unanswered.

The tragic loss of those two young Looe fishermen plunged the whole community into mourning, and when skipper John Haines was laid to rest it was standing room only in the church, while the sorrow and utter heartbreaking grief of that occasion I just cannot begin to convey in words. When the body of young John was brought in from the sea, at least the Haines family could hold a funeral, enabling them to draw something of a line under the tragedy, although it could do nothing to ease the grief of their loss. But for the Tregenna family there was no such solace; their son Christopher (Charlie had been his nickname) was still missing at sea. For months they lived in fear and expectation of a phone call informing them that somewhere, somehow, his remains had been discovered.

It was six months before the sea gave up its dead. Remains that were later identified as that of Christopher were found washed up on a beach in Whitsand Bay.

18

Mounts Bay

The winter of 1981/82 was a very tough time in many ways. The mackerel season had failed in the Looe and Falmouth areas and the only 'scry' we knew of was in Mounts Bay. So, after weeks of scratching about earning very little, most of the Looe fleet steamed westward around the Lizard to work out of Newlyn, a rugged old port to work from in the winter time. The Atlantic ground swell can run like an endless procession of undulating hills with an angry top wash overlaying it, created by whatever wind was venting its anger at the time. Two boats, one each in a trough either side of a sea, would be out of sight of one another, maybe even the mast heads hidden from view. But if the choice was to stay at home and go into debt, or work out of Newlyn there's no choice. Newlyn it was.

The harbour in those days was jam-packed with boats. There was a fleet of beamers, stern draggers, side-winders, long liners and netters, and in addition it was also playing host to a couple of hundred mackerel boats from all around Cornwall. I have heard the old men talk of the herring fishing days when harbours were so busy you could walk across them from boat to boat. Well, that was Newlyn that winter. Boats were moored in tiers twelve or sixteen deep off the quay and scrambling across from boat to boat to get ropes ashore was a nightmare after a hard day at sea. And on the occasions that a gale raged in from the south-east, ropes and fenders had to be continually attended to as these huge tiers of boats slewed about in the wind, while waves and spray bursting over the harbour wall put the smaller open boats in danger of being sunk.

The crews of most of the visiting craft lived within reasonable commuting distance of Newlyn and would rattle back and forth daily in a shaky assortment of cars and vans. Unfortunately, Looe was just too far away to do that, so we all had to stay in Newlyn for the week, going home for the weekend late on Friday afternoon and returning again early on Sunday morning. In some of the vehicles we had in those days, journeying from Looe to Newlyn could be an event, not quite the sort of trip you packed a blanket, a flask of tea and sandwiches, but not far off.

The men on the larger deck boats such as my *Ibis*, the *Maret*, *Prosperity* and the *Gratitude* lived aboard, as we all had decent cabins with comfortable bunks and a coal fire to keep things warm and dry. Certainly it was rough and ready living, and a world away from the word luxury, but we were all used to that way of life and didn't consider it to be a hardship one bit. While the crews of the smaller Looe boats, such as the *Ganesha*, *Claire*, *Seabird*, *Paula* etc. only had tiny fore peak cuddies that were usually shared with the engine. They were okay to sit in and have your grub, or as somewhere to get in out of the weather for a bit and warm up, but they were such that I rather suspect a skipper would have been up on a charge of cruelty if he tried to keep a rat in there for the winter, let alone his crew. To solve the problem, two or three crews would band together to rent a flat or a cottage; an extra expense but at least they had somewhere decent to live.

When working out of a harbour as busy as Newlyn, landing your catch at the end of the day could take ages. Boat after boat would be ranked off the quay, loaded down with mackerel, the crews all busy grading, washing and boxing up. Perilously loaded fish lorries would be trundling back and forth to the packing sheds, all to a background noise of boats' engines, VHF radios and the laughter and back chat of the men. Eventually your turn would come to get your fish ashore, loaded on to the lorry and all tallied up. 'Thank God for that' was the usual sort of utterance as you manoeuvred away from the hustle and chaos of the landing berths, to go and moor up for the night.

Once the ropes and fenders were out and the old boat was safe, it was off with smock and overalls, a swill off in the deck bucket and then ashore for a meal and a pint. Food-wise there were two choices: fish and chips or a Chinese take-away, so we used to go day about, bearing our greasy paper-wrapped meal into the fishermen's mission where we could buy a mug of tea to wash it down with. Once dinner was over there were a couple of choices as to how the rest of the evening could be spent. A stroll about the quayside to let your dinner go down and then back aboard the boat for an early night was one option, not a very attractive prospect when you are a young man, or a pint or two at the Star Inn. Now that sounded much more like it. And many a good night we spent in there, yarning of the day's events with other fishermen, singing the old songs, dancing to the juke box or playing darts and cards, while the drinking often carried on long after closing time. Then, glowing from both the drink and the events of the evening, we would stagger out into the cold night air and down to the harbour side where the first problem for a beer-befuddled brain was to try and remember which particular rank of boats yours was tied up in. When that was sorted, the task of getting aboard began, up down, over and across all different shapes and sizes of craft, trying to avoid dodgy deck boards, unshipped hatches, pound boards, gurdies and boxes. Half cut and in the dark, this could be quite a challenge. The ultimate piss off was to reach the outside boat not having found your own, for the simple reason you were in the wrong tier. Now that really could cause a sense of humour failure.

After 12 or 14 hours hard labour and a gut full of beer, sleep came just minutes after you scrambled into the bunk. It was the alarm clock jangling away at five o'clock in the morning that was the problem: oh the thick head and the aching limbs. The crew emerge from their bunks, bleary-eyed, scratching and farting, to pull on damp and dirty overalls, smocks and hats, followed by their sea boots, then to clamber up on deck to take a look at the day. It was usually dark, wet and cold with a fresh wind blowing from somewhere in the westerly cant. Surrounded by the noise of engines grinding and roaring into life, fogging up the harbour with billows of thick oily exhaust, navigation lights glowing, deck lights twinkling, there is banter and chatter as ropes are cast off. Boats are steering for the pier head gaps and away out to sea. It's time to go; the gurdies are passed up from the fish room and clamped onto the rail, then oilskins are chucked up from the engine room. These were full length things made of canvas backed PVC, perpetually cold wet and slimy, and to don them you always had to fight your way in, hands punching into the sleeves, head nodding and shaking to get up into and through the neck; they stank inside of diesel and stale fish and felt like armour to wear. And there we would be, ready for action. With mooring ropes and fenders stowed, we would join the procession of craft making for the harbour entrance.

In the dark of the wheelhouse I keep a sharp lookout as we steer up across the bay, the boat lifting to the ground swell and throwing back cat's paws of spray from the wind-blown top wash. Nezzer is perched on the seat behind me, while down in the cabin, the Goat is hunched over the fire, smoking a fag and reading a girlie mag as he waits for the kettle to boil. The forecast is far from good, in fact it's fucking awful, but if we can work away head to wind in some steady fishing the weather won't be too much of a problem. Daylight begins to creep into the sky and that makes things feel much better; on the VHF a few skippers are talking of decent marks on the sounder up off Porthlevan, so it's hoist the mizzen and bend on a new set of feathers. The day's labour will soon begin.

The white trace paper of the echo sounder slowly winds across the illuminated screen, the stylus on its rubber belt faithfully recording the depth of water and shoals of fish as it blurs around with a scratch, scratch, scratch sound. A few peppery marks, known as fly shit, show up, then some nice big swipes, top to bottom of the paper, and a bit further on the screen is blacked out with solid fish. The first boats away are already riding head to wind above this lot, as are the gannets; both men and birds are awaiting the daylight to penetrate down into the water. As light chases dark over the western horizon the birds take to the air, we drop our lines, still too early yet; we foul hook one or two but can feel mackerel in their hundreds hitting on the lines. We breakfast on tea and pork pies, glancing to weather; a teasy wind kicks up sea bobs while the sky, heavy with great billowing clouds, backs the forecasters' predictions, south west six to gale eight. A boat nearby pulls a line full of big mackerel aboard. Daylight is at last in the water and the gannets are going berserk.

Two hundred boats, from 50 feet to 20 feet long, lie head to wind, bows rising and falling on the sea, mizzens hauled up as tight as drum skins ripple in the freshening breeze. Their crews toil ceaselessly to get as many fish aboard as they can before the worsening weather conditions drive them back to port. By early afternoon the wind-blown top wash starts to heap up the ground sea. It's all looking very ugly. If the forecasters are right we shall be confined to harbour for several days while the storm lashes its way up-Channel, so as much as possible has to be squeezed out of this day.

Good steady fishing on decent quality fish tempted us all to work for much too long into a rising gale, and by the time we did get under way daylight was often rapidly fading and conditions were wild to say the least. Keeping a watch three waves ahead gave you time to pick out the seas that were going to give you trouble: the high, wall-fronted combers that were just about to break or that were already breaking, they were the ones. So it's ease down the engine and wind down the wheel to take them fine on the luff of the bow. Up she rises, bow pointing skyward, spray lashing the wheelhouse like a power hose, swooping down into the trough on the other side, it's just green water all around and the sky above, and up again on the next one and now it's big rollers all about you and okay to get back on course once more. In such conditions it is patience, tenacity and good seamanship that get you back to harbour safe and sound.

But however good the boat handling and however sharp the lookout, every now and then a sea so steep, big and horrible that you know you can do nothing with it, will roll your way.

"Hang on tight boys!" is a typical shout as something that could well be your doom breaks over the boat. Stopped dead in its tracks and buried under tons of boiling angry sea, the boat is now fighting for her life. Wallowing and rolling, she climbs up out of it awash to the gunnels, shaking like a gundog emerging from a river, the scuppers streaming like waterfalls. Fight it, girl, fight it, you say to encourage the boat, because if another sea like that drops on us before she frees herself we will all have had it. But, thank God, that doesn't happen. Everything is working and everything is still intact, so you plough on again.

Such a sea caught us that night. Enough water went down the cabin chimney to wash the fire clean out of the stove, leaving the sole a crunching, gritty mass of wet coal and ash. In fact the whole cabin was awash, even the clothes and bedding in the bunks were wet and soggy. One or two of the small open boats were very fortunate to get back to port at all that night. The Looe boat *Sandy D*, just 24 feet long, got caught broadside in the tube of a large breaking sea, just like a surfer. Mike Darlington, the skipper, thought for a moment that they had had it, but they shot out the other end of the tube, intact and unscathed - a minor miracle. Broadside to weather, two hundred heavily laden boats fought their way home in the dark across a storm-lashed Mounts Bay, and for some it was a very close call. But battered and weary, they all made it back to land their catches.

Working from Newlyn that winter, there were a few fine days' fishing making it a pleasure to be out on the water, but as I remember it the living was mainly very hard won.

Just before Christmas there was the terrible tragedy of the lifeboat *Solomon Brown*, lost with all hands. Wreckage from her was brought ashore and laid out on the quayside, while the crippled coaster the *Union Star*, whose crew they had gone to rescue, was smashed against the cliff, hull up, and they too had perished. All of Newlyn and Mousehole went into mourning and at the same time, they had to try and deal with the huge media circus that it attracted; everyone wanted a piece of that disaster. Like a snapshot in my memory, I shall always recall the two old men I observed hunched over a table in the Newlyn fishermen's mission, talking closely and quietly together, their weather beaten faces, drawn and gaunt, as if on the point of tears. The ritual of rolling, lighting and smoking cigarettes provided a vital prop for both time and dignity. Several years previously one of them had lost a son at sea from a trawler, and he was now trying to comfort his friend who had just lost a son on the *Solomon Brown*.

Fine, brave old men, battling a mountain of heartbreak as so many other people were doing in Newlyn and Mousehole.

19

Loss of the *Claire*

We fished from Newlyn until the mackerel shoals thinned out late in January of the new year, then all the visiting boats headed back to their home ports. It was a lovely day when the *Ibis* at last departed and as we were turning in the harbour, a shout from the quay caught our attention. It was Ernie George who was crew on one of the other Looe boats, the *Seabird*. For some reason he had not gone home on her, and now jumped aboard us for a lift up to Looe. Catching the first of a young spring flood, we fairly romped up the coast and on rounding the Lizard we had none of the usual jump and bash that the headland is so famous for. Instead we glided around in comfort, mugs of tea in hand, enjoying the afternoon sunshine. Ernie's family had originated from the Lizard area and he spun us many a tale of the cliffs, farms and houses there as we sped around.

The run up to Looe that day took 6 ½ hours, a very smart run for those times. It was good to be back in our home port again. Back with the family for a home-cooked meal and an evening by the fireside instead of fish and chips and the Star Inn, to sleep in your own warm comfortable bed rather than in your bunk, lying fully clothed under a damp blanket. Luxury indeed after weeks of fishing away.

But a living still had to be earned, and it was now our trawling season. All the mackerel fishing equipment, mizzen, gurdies etc were put back into the store and we greased up the winch to wind on the warps and combination, chain the doors up to the gantry and stowed a couple of trawls aboard. We would now be hunting whiting, plaice, monk and lemon-sole instead of the mackerel; a different trade, a different season.

We soon got into the swing of the trawling, and there were plenty of fish to be caught on the home grounds just half-an-hour's steaming from port. A 4-hour tow would result in a mixed bag of fish: whiting, squid, monk, plaice and hake plus a few odds and sods such as conger, spur dogs and ray. Sometimes we would only just get the catch gutted, washed and graded in time for the next haul and then start all over again. Big catches gave a good feeling, but when you are up to your arse in fish so are all the other boats, and it is then that the prices paid by the buyers on the market take a dive.

When trawling, the best wages were always earned with a modest catch of quality fish landed two or three times a week, between the winter gales. The buyers always paid the best money when they were in a state of hair-tearing desperation and fully prepared to cut each other's throats to get enough fish to fulfil their customers' orders. Happy complacent fish merchants are no good to fisherman whatsoever.

A new method of fishing using monofilament netting was finding favour. We had seen boats at Newlyn using it to catch spur dogs, but nearly any species of fish could be caught with the right size mesh. Mike Faulkner of the *Claire*, among others, thought it held some good prospects and had rigged up several fleets of it to catch ling, pollack and cod that were to be found on and around the rocks and rough ground where the trawlers couldn't work. For the maiden shoot, Mike and his crewman Roger Davis had picked a nice fine day. We on the trawlers were at sea, still fishing the inside ground. While the *Claire* was steaming out to the reefs just to seaward of where we were working, I heard the skipper chatting on the VHF saying that he wouldn't be out for long as they were only going to shoot a few fleets away over the rocks to try the gear, and then they would be going back to harbour. And that was it, he was never heard again.

The trawler *Tethera* was the nearest boat to the *Claire* and could see her going from reef to reef shooting away her gear, and then she stopped and just drifted broadside to the light easterly breeze. For a short while there was nothing particularly odd about that. They might have had a bit of trouble with an engine or a pump and had let the boat blow away while they sorted it out. Aboard of the *Tethera*, Ivan Chaston and his crewman Eric Brown kept an eye on the *Claire*, but after an hour they began to suspect all was not well and tried to raise her on the VHF. Again and again they tried. Something was not adding up, so Ivan and Eric hauled their trawl and motored out towards the *Claire* to find out what the trouble might be, trying all the while to raise them on the VHF and still getting no reply. As they approached the boat they could see that her engines were running, but nobody was visible on deck. At first it was assumed that the crew must be in the fore peak sorting something out, but what they couldn't imagine. Ivan put the *Tethera* close alongside and hailed her two or three times to no avail. By now things were not looking good at all. Eric rigged the fenders and Ivan put his boat hard alongside the *Claire* for Eric to jump aboard and investigate. It took but a moment for Eric to realise that the crew was missing. The boat was fine, engine ticking over, echo sounder running - in fact, nothing out of place and no sign of any trouble.

Ivan raised the alarm immediately, calling up Leo Bowdler, the skipper of another Looe trawler, the *Maret*, that Mike's brother Johnny crewed on. I remember that call as if it was yesterday: "Maret, Maret, Tethera. Get up here a bit quick. Tell Johnny that we have just come up to have a look at the Claire and no one's aboard her."

Every boat in the fleet heard that message, and every skipper there and then gave orders to haul the gear. Within ten minutes or so everyone was racing up to the *Tethera*'s position to begin a search. As there was nothing wrong with the *Claire*, Eric had taken her back to port. The first thought was that somehow Mike and Roger had been pulled overboard in an accident while shooting their nets, so skipper John Andrews on another netter, the *Ma Cheri*, proceeded to haul the *Claire*'s gear, but it was all in good order and nothing was fouled in it. Meanwhile a big search had got underway, every fishing boat from all the surrounding ports within a reasonable steaming distance joined in, plus the Plymouth and Fowey lifeboats and a Royal Navy frigate.

As with the loss of the *Do It Again*, everyone formed up line abreast one Decca-tenth apart and proceeded to comb the area, while Mike Soady in his trawler *La Quete* once again acted as the fleet coordinator. When darkness closed about us we still carried on the search, illuminating our way with searchlights and flares, until on a falling tide we had to abandon our quest and return to harbour to land our fish and make ready to resume the search again at first light the next day.

On the following day, word had spread of the loss of the crew of the *Claire* and a huge fleet of craft assembled to join in the hunt for the bodies of Mike Faulkner and Roger Davies. Lifeboats, Royal Navy frigates and fishing boats from Plymouth, Cawsand, Polperro, Fowey and Mevagissey all joined the Looe fleet in its sad and tragic mission. All through the daylight hours we boxed about, in, out, up Channel, down Channel and all to no avail. So many boats had so thoroughly covered such a huge area that we knew that if there was anything to be found someone would have done so. There was now no point in looking further; the bodies of Mike and Roger must have sunk to the bottom. All we could do now was go back to our fishing and maybe eventually, for the sake of the families, someone would bring their remains home.

For the rest of that winter, every time the trawl was hauled we lived in dread of finding a body in the cod end. As with the *Do It Again*, everyone wanted the men to be found but hoped the task would fall to others. And so it was that about six weeks later, John Kitto and his crewman Jim Gowan on the *Bev-An-Dan* hauled their trawl to find an oilskin-clad corpse among the fish in the cod end. As reverently and gently as possible, the trawl was lowered down onto the deck where John took a sharp knife to split the cod end open. The body was carefully eased out from among the fish and laid in the waterways. John was sure it was Mike Faulkner, and it later proved to be. The coastguards were informed of the sad find before the *Bev-An-Dan* headed back for Looe, where they were met by the police and the local undertaker.

The body was later positively identified by a wedding ring as Mike. He left behind his wife Bette and two young children, Tracy and Kevin; and to add to the heartbreak Roger Davies, the missing crewman, was Bette's brother. That poor family had to shoulder a burden of grief that must have been almost too heavy to bear. High up on the Downs overlooking West Looe is a graveyard, and it was there that we said farewell to skipper Mike Faulkner of the *Claire*. As far as I can recall there was no church service, instead hundreds of mourners lined the cemetery for the burial service and to pay their last respects.

Mike and I had crewed together on the old lugger *Iris*, pilchard drifting back in the 1960s, and had shared many a pint and a yarn at the Star Inn at

Newlyn only weeks before when the Looe fleet fished the winter mackerel shoals in Mounts Bay. After the funeral, the *Claire* and all her equipment was sold at an auction held under the fish market and to raise extra money, many of the skippers donated what gear they could spare, nets and trawls etc. Some of it was not much good at all, but every item made very good money.

Of poor Roger Davies, no trace was ever found. He was a single man, a shipwright by trade, with no dependant, but he was part of a large family and is sorely missed to this day. The cause of their loss may never ever be known, but the conclusion that most have drawn is that one man somehow fell overboard and, in trying to rescue him, the other was dragged in as well. There would be no way to get back aboard after that, a scenario to awful to dwell on. A couple of years later the *Claire* also met her end, wrecked on the Rannies, a treacherous reef the eastern side of Looe Island. Fortunately there was no loss of life on that occasion.

20

Shark Fishing

In the days that I write of, there was plenty of fish to catch most of the time and a fisherman's life was free and independent. We chased the mackerel shoals the length of the coast, working from Plymouth to Newlyn, and when they disappeared from the coast in late February we wound on the trawling gear to have a go at the lemon-soles for a few weeks before the spring paint up. After a couple of summer seasons, Nezzer sat his skipper's ticket, so that he and the Goat could take the boat out shark fishing while I stayed on the quay getting customers to keep the *Ibis* running, fully booked, seven days a week.

I wasn't the only one on the quay booking trips. Dave Haines, Louis Portman and Ian Giddings booked their boats for mackerel fishing and evening conger trips. Each skipper had a sign-written board about 4 feet by 18 inches that displayed the boat's name and details of the trips they were plying, plus a little notebook for people to sign for the trip that they fancied. There was also a blackboard that was used to chalk up the forecast and advertise river trips when the weather was too poor to go to sea. Also, for our amusement, completely fictitious events would be neatly written up in eye-catching colours. Visitors were invited to attend the annual display of the Downderry over-eighties nude formation hedgehog-squatting team. A musical evening put on by the Respryn Bridge singing donkeys, performing negro spirituals and songs from the shows. Or maybe a cruise up the river to the wildlife park, there to view mock turtles, clockwork lobsters, unicorns and Cornwall's only colony of ooo-me-goolie birds. There was conger-wrestling, a wrecked pasty ship and underwater fag-rolling, to list just a few of the spoof trips we used to chalk up, and watching people discovering this was always amusing. Reading down the line of boards, they would be offered mackerel fishing, a coastal cruise to Polperro, shark angling, and what's this? Clockwork lobsters? Singing donkeys? Then the penny would drop and it was big laughs and the camera would come out. Staff from the shops would stroll by in their lunch hour for a giggle, and if a trip was up for more than about two days there would be demands for a new one. We were forever racking our brains, but we did come up with some corkers between us, each one dafter than the last.

We even had some serious enquiries, such as, "We hope there was no cruelty involved in teaching those donkeys to sing?" And, "Is it half price for kids at the conger-wrestling?" A sense of humour was vital, especially if somebody pulled what we called a 'stumper' on you. A skipper would bring his boat to the steps to pick up his people and as he was pulling away again someone would shout out to him, "Don't forget your probation officer wants to see you later on," or "Try and keep clear of the killer whales, this time." With good timing and using the right tone of voice, the skipper would be left trying to explain to his somewhat unsettled passengers that it was only a jape. Many is the day there was much more fun going on than work.

That was our year, our three seasons; we earned a good living and enjoyed what we did, but by the mid-1980s things were on the change, and certainly not for the better. Because of the activities of the big Scots industrial fishers, it was becoming ever more difficult to make a regular living from the mackerel seasons so more time had to be spent trawling, a trade that I had only ever enjoyed as a stopgap. The hours spent towing along watching the Decca clocks tick around drove me to distraction and instead of flying by, the day never seemed to end. But like it or loath it, of all the fishing methods, a steady living could always be earned with the trawl. And by now many of the Looe skippers were getting rid of their mackerel boats and buying vessels more suitable for trawling. Some invested in brand new boats, heavily built wooden craft 35 to 40 feet long, many of them launched from Alan Toms' yard at Polruan, or Gerald Pearn's yard at Morval. Others preferred secondhand craft, and a popular choice were the little cruiser-stern Scots built boats like Bonzo's *Prosperity*.

Trawling was a very new trade to most of the Looe fishermen, so there was an awful lot to learn. Charlie Jaycock, Ivan Chaston and Bill Hocking were the only three skippers who knew much about it and their advice was always being sought on how to set the gear up and what type of trawl and trawl doors were best to use. Their experience and advice at this juncture was invaluable. Another man who put a lot of time and effort in to helping out those who were novices at the trade was retired fisherman Jack Soady, known to all as Uncle Jack. On bad weather days Jack would be going from boat to boat all day long, teaching baffled fishermen how to rebuild a badly damaged trawl, knife and needle always at the ready. And when the fleet was at sea he would spend his days in the store making and designing new trawls to order, or repairing nets that had been badly ripped up. For many years he was very much a father figure to the growing Looe trawler fleet, and he carried on working well into his eighties. A kind and jovial man who asked not a penny for all the help he gave, when he made a trawl he charged only pocket money prices.

At this time, all trawl fish landed at Looe was transported by lorry to be auctioned on Plymouth fish market. Looe had once had its own market but that had closed when the long-line fleet declined in the 1950s. But now, once again, tons of prime fish were being landed weekly on Looe quay by a fleet of boats that was expanding rapidly and becoming ever more efficient. These boats were now losing thousands of pounds a year because landing dues had to be paid at both Looe and Plymouth, plus overland fish was always sold last on the market and made the lowest price. And being last to be sold at Plymouth, especially in the summer time, could be disastrous for the quality of the fish at the old Victorian market, open to both sun and wind.

With this in mind, a deputation of the more forward thinking skippers petitioned the Looe harbour commissioners, led by its chairman, skipper Mike Soady, to give serious consideration to the reopening of Looe auction market. This was a bold move. To reopen the auction market didn't just entail scrubbing out the old one and luring a few fish buyers back to Looe. Far from it, this was going to be a huge operation. A brand new market would have to be built with all modern facilities, chill rooms, offices, packing stores etc. The commission was at first a little wary of such a huge commitment but eventually, under the strong leadership of their chairman, they got behind the scheme. Finance, in the form of loans and grants, was sourced from many different organisations, plans were drawn up and scrutinised, hundreds of letters were written and thousands of phone calls were made. Committees and sub-committees held endless meetings, some quiet affairs where things were nodded through, while others became quite heated. But regardless of the differences of opinion, they knew that they dare not fail, as the vast majority of the Looe fishermen were now behind the idea. Eventually, plans were agreed and passed, the finances were in position and stage one, building the new market, could go ahead. But before anything new could go up, a lot of old stuff had to come down; in fact, a huge area of the quay had to be cleared. The old fish market and net lofts, mackerel packing sheds and assorted old tin huts were all levelled by the demolition gang with their iron dinosaurs and monster lorries. And suddenly a huge area of the quay was level and empty, while quite a number of houses and cottages found they now had magnificent uninterrupted harbour views. I hope they enjoyed it.

The construction gang came on site, driving huge piles down through the quays, followed by lorry loads of concrete that cast the foundations. Steel erectors with their crane bolted together a massive skeleton which, when finished, was fleshed out by teams of masons, chippies, roofers, plumbers, electricians and painters. Each in their turn helped to create and complete our brand new fish market.

This brief description glosses over what in reality was months of hard work, and it didn't always go smoothly. There were the usual delays, mistakes, misunderstandings and general balls ups that on occasions led to some truly magnificent displays of frustration. But all came together in time for the grand opening in October 1987. This ceremony was performed by the chairman of the harbour commissioners, Mike Soady, who (looking rather uncomfortable trussed up in suit and tie) made a short speech welcoming guests and dignitaries before unveiling a plaque to commemorate the occasion.

The second stage was the building of the fish packing units and offices, an imposing construction that at the time proved to be rather controversial. Completed by 1990, the guest of honour at the opening ceremony was our local MP, Sir Robert Hicks. Faith in the Looe fleet was not misplaced; the market took off from the word go and at its peak a few years later, 27 trawlers were working from the port, plus a handful of netters and crabbers. Trucks and lorries brought fish to the market overland from Polperro, Mevagissey, Newquay etc. It soon built a reputation for top quality day-caught fish, supplying customers the length of the country, plus a booming export trade to Europe. Much of the market's success was down to the management skills and business acumen of the Blue Sail Fish Company run by Steve Farrah and Hugh Symonds. A market can be built, but someone has got to have the know-how to run it. They were definitely the right men in the right place at the right time.

East Looe Quay was now a hive of activity for virtually 24 hours a day. In the small hours of the morning, long before daylight greys the eastern sky, the boats will be slipping away to sea, while on the market, staff will be laying out the previous day's catch ready for auction. Lorries wanting to load or unload arrive and depart all through the day, keeping a gang of market workers toiling with pallet truck and fork lift. In the packing sheds, fish merchants jabber on their mobile phones, taking orders for their staff to weigh out, pack, ice and dispatch to the customers; filliters with razor sharp knives bone out prime fish for the restaurant trade. In a shed at one end of the market an oilskin-clad figure, indistinct in the billowing vapour, feeds a hissing, rumbling machine with a diet of dirty fish boxes, and in return for their slimy contents, it chucks them out again, clean and ready for reuse.

By mid-afternoon the first mackerel boats will be returning loaded down if they have been lucky enough to locate a good shoal of fish. It's all rush and panic now to try and get the mackerel boats landed and their fish out of the way before the trawlers come in to land, as they might well be loaded down as well. It is just fish, fish, everywhere you look; a team packing and icing mackerel into two stone cartons ready to load onto a waiting lorry; pallets stacked high with boxes of trawl fish such as whiting, squid, plaice, monk and lemon-sole are trundled into the chill rooms to keep them in good condition for the following morning's auction. When a spell of fine weather coincides with a good run of fish, the pace for all concerned is relentless.

Among all the organised chaos of boats, men and fish, two wild animals, one very large and one very small, adopted the harbour as their own.

The large animal was a very fat one-eyed bull seal, later to be named Nelson, while the small animal was a feisty little cormorant that acquired the name of Kevin. Both creatures considered the whole shooting match was organised purely for their benefit, and while Kevin hated Nelson to the point where he would honk in fury at him from the safety of the quay, when the old boy sculled up to the market on the first of the flood tide, Nelson would turn his blind eye, ignoring Kevin completely.

This seal had knocked around the south Cornish coast for several years and was known in Newlyn, Falmouth and Mevagissey. Being a fairly intelligent animal he had obviously come to the conclusion that it was a lot easier to have fish thrown at him than hunt them himself. To this end he became quite tame and would hang around the quays trying to look cute and interesting. How 30 stone of battle-scarred blubber achieved that, I don't know, but he did; he charmed everyone, fishermen, market workers and visitors alike and he never ever went short of a meal. His appetite was prodigious. No matter how much fish was flung his way he never turned it down; any fish would do, but a conger was definitely his favourite. Floating on his back, holding one between his flippers, he would carefully skin it, then devour it with such obvious relish that it made you wonder if you shouldn't try raw conger yourself. 5 stone of mackerel in one session was his record blow out, and he might have eaten more had there been more to give him. He seemed to bask in all the attention that he received and appeared to know his name, turning when called and posing endlessly for visitors to take his photo. Nelson made Looe his headquarters but would holiday at other ports now and then. During the breeding season he would decamp to the rocks around Looe Island, where passengers on the pleasure boats would observe him paying close attention to a lady friend. Skippers calling out to him would be rewarded with a look as if to say, "Bugger off, can't you see I'm busy?"

After a week or two his lust would be sated and a somewhat leaner Nelson would appear back in the harbour to resume gorging on fish and charming the people in equal measure. Once or twice, through mating battles or misjudging boats propellers, he received some nasty looking injuries and the state of Nelson's health would become of widespread concern, the local papers carrying the story. Endless worried well-wishers viewed him from the quayside, a specialist vet from the seal sanctuary at Gweek was summoned who usually prescribed some tablets to be put in his fish. Once or twice, Kevin got hold of these doctored fish first and I often wondered exactly how he felt afterwards, a ½-stone bird swallowing a 30-stone seal's medicine. With an army of adoring fans, both locals and visitors, Nelson became something of a celebrity and his value as a one-animal tourist attraction was probably only rivalled by Fungi, the dolphin of Dingle Bay, Ireland.

But the limelight was not to be entirely his. For a while he had to share it, as well as some of his fish. The story of Kevin the cormorant began during a prolonged and severe winter gale sometime in the mid-1990s, when he was found starving and bedraggled, crouched down sheltering behind a curb on East Looe quay. Terry Puckey, one of the harbour staff, took pity and, scooping him up in his hands, took him down to the fish market and fed him a mackerel. Resting in a fish box out of the wind and weather, with a good meal down his neck, he soon made a recovery and for that he was then rewarded with more fish. And so another bright creature soon realised that here was a whole new way to live, never mind wasting energy swimming around the reefs after fish that really didn't want to be caught. No, waddle around the quay looking cute, and all the fish you can manage will be flung at you. Bingo, got it cracked!

And that is exactly what he did. The cheeky bird charmed the socks off everybody; he was irresistible. Swimming up river, he would hop up the steps by the war memorial and make all haste down to the fish market. With very short legs placed right aft on their bodies and little flippery feet, cormorants aren't built for running, but Kevin always did his very best. Legs going like pistons, feet slap, slap, slapping on the concrete, he would hurry down the quay looking like a portly little gentleman in an evening suit. And if, when the market came into view, somebody waved a mackerel to encourage him, he would try to go faster still, honking loudly in anticipation of a good feed. It was a wonder he didn't blow a gasket.

Kevin became very tame; you could sit down beside him and stroke his feathers which closer examination would reveal were not the dull brown cormorants always seem to look, but were iridescent, each feather edged with a cream-coloured outline. If, upon his arrival at the market each morning, he was ignored because all hands were busy with the auction he would waddle over to Andrew Trust the auctioneer, there to firmly and persistently shake his trouser leg with his beak until eventually, as it becomes very difficult to concentrate or maintain your dignity with a hungry cormorant hanging off your trousers, Andrew had to call a brief halt to the proceedings while Kevin was given his breakfast.

Like Nelson the seal, Kevin the cormorant seemed to relish both the fish and the attention he received, posing with visitors while his photo was taken, but he always had an aura about him that he was your equal and not a pet. I think that both he and Nelson considered they had invested a lot of time and effort in taming and training humans, not the other way about as we thought, and looking back, maybe they were right. Together, but apart, this unlikely duo led the life of Reilly and entertained the public for several years. On one occasion Kevin failed to appear on the market for a week or more and everyone became very concerned for him. And then someone found a dead cormorant in the harbour: it had to be Kevin, and to show respect for his passing, a minute's silence was held in the market. But surprise, surprise, a couple of days later, to everyone's delight, the real Kevin appeared, not dead after all, and ravenous for his breakfast.

When his end did come it was very sad. For a long time he had been pushing his luck with Nelson; he would hover in the water off the seal's blind side, and when people flung him fish, the cocky little cormorant would dart ahead and snatch the fish from right under his nose. This trick drove Nelson to distraction, and on several occasions he caught Kevin by the tail and gave him a good ducking, but the bird just couldn't resist annoying the old seal. Then one day Nelson, ready to explode at the loss of his fish, grabbed Kevin by the wing and gave him one hell of a shaking. In great distress, he hopped up the nearest steps and more or less jumped up into the arms of one of the fish market workers, one wing dangling, broken and all but torn off. Kevin was rushed off to the vet, who declared his wing to be beyond any hope of repair, and as a one-winged cormorant could neither fly nor swim he would never survive. So the vet had to put him down, and a great little character was sadly gone from the harbour.

Nelson carried on as ever, posing for the public and consuming incredible amounts of fish, living many more years than he would have as a wild seal. But with age came infirmity; he started to lose the sight in his one good eye, eventually going blind. And that was his end. He groped around the quays, getting ever thinner, unable to see to feed or to dodge the boats. It was heartrending to witness, and there was nothing anyone could do about it. Nelson starved until he was about half his former size and one day, instead of going out to sea on the ebb tide, he swam up the river to haul out on a sand bank where he died.

But that wasn't the end of the Nelson story. During his years in Looe harbour he had become so well known and loved that a few years after he had passed on, funding was raised and a full-sized statue of him was modelled and cast in bronze. On a rock by the riverside at West Looe, Nelson the seal, in effigy, still charms his public.

21

Wind of Change

By the mid-1980s a chill wind of change was blowing from all points of the compass. The Maritime and Coastguard Agency was starting to introduce new rules and regulations for fishing boat safety, entailing expensive surveys, endless form filling and the buying of over-priced pieces of uselessness that were supposed to make your boat safe at sea. Good seamanship, common sense and years of experience now counted for very little unless your paperwork was in order.

Fish conservation schemes were being introduced, and the issuing of fishing licences had begun, limiting what species you could fish for and where and when, but none of it seemed to make any sense. Fish were not being conserved, just flung back dead if you weren't allowed to land them. Plus, every catch had to be recorded in a log book, and buff envelopes containing letters and forms printed on yellow paper dropped through the letter box on a daily basis, forever informing you of what you were and were not allowed to do. The fishing industry was being driven into a corner to be emasculated by bureaucracy.

Earning a living as a fisherman entailed very long hours and hard work in conditions that shore-side workers could never imagine. But the glory, if glory it was, of our way of life was the freedom and independence that we enjoyed. This made up for everything. The wet, the cold, the pitching rolling deck that was sometimes so bad that you spent the day working on your knees; the winter gales that kept you in harbour for weeks at a time while bills you couldn't pay piled up. It was all accepted as part of the way of life, but that life was ours and we led it as we saw fit. How I loathed and detested this outside interference.

But never mind there was always the summer passenger trade ... or was there? It was around this time that the budget airlines started to make huge inroads into the domestic holiday market, flying millions of people away to exotic sun-filled foreign destinations for less money than it cost to holiday in Cornwall where, unfortunately, grey skies are as likely as blue. The good times were drawing to a close. It was now no longer feasible to employ two crewmen full-time; Nezzer left to work on a trawler, while the Goat got a job ashore. I now worked the *Ibis* by myself in the summer time, taking out whatever sharking trips I could book up, plus the odd weekend taking divers out to the local wrecks and reefs when, for some reason, other skippers were reluctant to take them.

I enjoyed the shark angling. It was easy hours and good money with few expenses, and over the years I had the pleasure of meeting some very interesting people; there were never two days alike. People's experience of a day out sharking varied tremendously, depending on the weather conditions and the success rate with the sharks. Without doubt, venturing out to sea with a gang of novices when the weather was only just about workable was usually a recipe for utter misery. Anglers joining the boat at nine o'clock in the morning would be told that the forecast was not very good, and even though there was a fresh wind blowing it would rarely deter them. Bravado, I think, was the main driving force; nobody wanted to chicken out in front of the others and there was likely to be loads of bluster about how they had fished in a force nine out of Scarborough etc, and anyway, some would say, it was much more exciting when it was a bit rough. So away we would go, rise and fall, roll and plunge, spray flying, taught sheeted mizzen shivering in the breeze, while squally rain showers lashed from solid grey sky as we headed out to the sharking grounds, 12 or 15 miles off the coast.

Inevitably, after an hour of this kind of motion, a few of the intrepid band of anglers would now be quietly studying the horizon, a greenish waxy sheen playing on their rather unhappy faces.

"You feeling okay?" I would enquire.

"Yes, fine skipper, fine," they would lie. A little later, honking and gurgling noises would announce that homage was now being paid to Neptune. Fortunately, most people got to the lee rail in time and made a good clean job of it. But for some, well, vomit went everywhere, over themselves and others, in the deck bucket, in the fish boxes, in carrier bags and the bag that held their packed lunch, or perhaps someone else's. It could be mayhem in the sickbay. By the time we reached the sharking grounds maybe half the passengers would be out for the count. Those remaining would insist that they were okay and wanted to carry on, so the boat would stop and lay broadside to drift to the wind and waves. The shark lines were baited up and streamed away and the fittest of the anglers, braced against the incessant rolling, jigged away with the boat rods to catch a few mackerel. But now came the real test: the 'rubby dubby'.

A dustbin lashed to the port rail, full of salted pilchards and mackerel, all soft and mushy, the crusty top layer seething with maggots. About 2 stone of this vile mixture was then decanted into a mesh bag and hung over the side to attract the sharks. The smell of it could take your breath away. Every time the bag was shaken to lay down the rubby dubby trail of fish oil and bits, a collective groan would go up from the anglers as the dreadful stench proceeded to envelope every corner of the boat. Those building up for a spew, or were spewing or who had just spewed, could well make up three-quarters of the crew at this point, a far cry from the bold lads they had been but a couple of hours before. If they all agreed, then very often a day like that would be terminated with an early return to port, but if a few hard nuts insisted on staying, then so be it.

A shark on the line will buck every one up. Seasickness will be entirely forgotten while the fight lasts, but afterwards the dreaded *mal de mer* creeps back and once again a boatload of misery slowly rolls the hours away. Motoring back to harbour at the end of such a day, once the calm of the bay was reached, even those who hadn't moved all day would come back to life. And by the time we entered harbour, this sea-battered bunch would now be posing on the deck like Viking heroes, and why not? They had certainly earned it.

At the other extreme was the perfect day. There was one I recall on the *Ibis* that could not have been better if it had been scripted for a Walt Disney film. The weather was fine and bright, a light offshore wind ruffled a sea that sparkled in the sunlight and the anglers relaxed around the boat drinking tea and chatting. Never mind jumpers and oilskins, T-shirts were clothing enough on such a day. About 5 miles out we came across the biggest pod of killer whales that I had ever seen, about 60 as near as I could tally them. They seemed to be doing nothing more than sculling idly about with their great dorsal fins out of the water, so I stopped the boat and we watched them for a while. And what a show we had: they swam around the boat, dived under it or just lay alongside to have a look at us. It was a memorable sight, but the atmosphere around a pod of killers could be cut with a knife. It's as if they are saying 'keep your distance, don't annoy us or we will have you and your boat'. And that would be no idle threat; these animals are top predators, 30 to 40 feet long and their weight measured in tons. They are also highly intelligent.

Nudging the boat slowly and respectfully from out of their midst, we cruised away out to the sharking grounds. Once there, the lines were streamed away and the 'rubby' trail was laid. By lunchtime we had caught three good-sized sharks and a box of mackerel on the feather lines. It was then that the dolphins appeared, a big pod of them, leaping, laughing and gambling all around the boat. The atmosphere with them was just so different from the killer whales: it was 'whoopee, what fun we are having, it's just so good to be alive'. For five minutes or so they entertained us royally, and then that was it; the show was over, and away they went, cutting along effortlessly at about 20 knots. Incredible animals.

A little later two more sharks took our bait. I was both surprised and delighted because sharks usually make themselves very scarce when dolphins are about. We arrived back in Looe that evening, everyone suntanned and happy, with many a tale to tell, cameras full of shark, whale and dolphin pictures. In all the years I took people out shark fishing there was never a day to equal that one. It was indeed the perfect day.

One other exceptional day took place in the spring of 1970 when I was relief skipper one Saturday on a little shark boat called the *Guiding Star*. The boat was booked by a gang of students who had never been out angling before. It was a windless day, grey and clammy, and I had intended to fish a good berth at the back of the Eddystone lighthouse but the fog clamped down thick and heavy and I stopped a berth inside of the lighthouse instead. In such conditions the advantage was two-fold: first, we would be safe from any shipping, and secondly, because we had no navigation equipment other than a compass in those days, the foghorn of the lighthouse would give a good bearing for home. The disadvantage was that it was not really an area you would expect to find many sharks, but I wasn't going to tell the students that.

We drifted along in a silent white world, the students entertaining themselves catching mackerel and whiting on the boat rods as the fog wrapped about us like a wet blanket. I was sitting in the wheelhouse enjoying a bite of lunch when a ratchet on one of the shark rods started to go click-click-click in a slow and measured way, indicating that probably a piece of seaweed or a lump of drift wood had caught under the float, for when a shark takes a bait the ratchet fairly screams into life. Handling the rod, I tightened the clutch to wind in and investigate the line when it went bar tight and I had to quickly slacken away again. I shouted to the students that we had a shark and swiftly one of them sat in the shark chair eager to take the rod. And with that, a damn great Mako shark broached the surface and then made off dolphin-like across the water, line screeching from the reel at a terrific rate.

Shouting to the anglers to pull the other lines in as quickly as they could, I started the boat's engine and chased after the shark at full throttle before it ran all the line off the reel. The next minute it was hard to starboard and we went astern as the shark dived. We now lay still on the water, watching the bar-taught vertical line cutting little patterns in the surface. The Mako was hard on the bottom jinking about trying to work out what its next move should be. Immediately the line went slack. The shark was coming up fast, and the angler wound his reel like a demon to retrieve the slack. Then suddenly, about 20 yards from the boat, this huge fish exploded clear out of the water like a Polaris missile. Landing with a mighty splash, it then took off into the fog, leaping and thrashing, desperately trying to escape its tormentors. At full throttle we chased off down the line after it, and again it dived to the bottom. With the engine burbling on tick-over, all eyes were riveted to the line, watching and waiting for the shark's next move. This was a once in a lifetime fish, and even with an experienced angler on the line, the odds of landing one of these monsters was not in our favour. A little bow wave squirted up the line as it cut around in the water, back and forth, in and out. Everyone's nerves were stretched as taught as that line. One mistake and it would be gone. The shark stayed on the bottom doing nothing, probably tired, so I told the lad on the rod to try to lift, drop and reel. This worked, and inch by inch up it came like a dead weight, exhausting work for the angler but he had to keep at it. I made the big flying gaff ready, but all the time I was expecting to dive for the throttle should the thing take off again. And then it was visible down in the water ... up, up it rose, huge and powerful. Bloody hell, I said to myself, had I really got to risk life and limb driving a gaff into that. Laying dead in the water, it came to the surface right alongside the boat and just as I went to make with the gaff it erupted into life once more, an explosion of raw strength and fury.

I slammed the gaff down on the deck and jumped to the wheel and engine controls. It was game on again. The *Guiding Star*'s little cheapo engine was having the guts revved right out of it as we hurtled off after the shark. The battle raged on for nearly 2 hours, the shark diving and broaching and me never knowing from one second to the next which way the wheel would have to go. I had visions of us ramming another fishing boat or yacht as we charged madly about in the fog, looking at nothing but the angle of the line off the bow. Eventually the line was, yet again, up and down in the water, the shark hard on the bottom, resting. Just keeping the line tight I let the angler have a rest as well. He and the Mako were in about the same condition – knackered. Then it was back to business to see if we could bring it to the surface, slowly, lift, drop and reel, lift, drop and reel, inch by inch for an arm-aching 40 fathoms. We were all staring down into the water in a state of nervous anticipation, knowing that there were still plenty of ways of losing this thing yet. And there it was, its great grey outline now visible a couple of fathoms down, she rose, she rose, now on the surface alongside the boat, quiet, and we hoped exhausted. This time it didn't explode back into life, so in went the flying gaff right up under the jaw. I twisted out the handle and pulled hard on the lanyard to bring this monster's head just clear of the water, then made fast. If it had come back to life now it could break the boat up, but no, it thrashed and banged around a bit but the fight seemed to have gone out of it. We had won the battle.

After ten minutes or so it lay still, tethered to the boat by the flying gaff lanyard, but now what were we going to do with it? It was much too big and heavy to get aboard the boat, so four or five lanyards had to be spaced out along its body and inch by inch, pulling on them in turn and making fast to the stringer, the Mako was lifted just clear of the water. When we got back to Looe, this great fish tipped the scales at 326 pounds, not a record breaker by any means, but by far the biggest fish I ever had anything to do with catching.

* * *

By 1988 the writing was on the wall. Because of the activities of the industrial boats, our main winter fishery, hand-lining for mackerel, had become much too precarious to make a season out of; trawling was now the only option. But against the powerful new boats then working out of Looe, the *Ibis* just couldn't compete at that game, so either I had to invest in a purpose-built trawler or get out of fishing. With the right boat and gear a very good living could be earned all year round with the trawl, but I just could not face the mind-numbing boredom of that trade, as well as being hemmed in on all sides by the new rules and regulations.

I used to wake in the mornings always looking forward to the new day, but by now it was all becoming a worry and a chore, and that is no way to lead your life. Come the spring paint up of that year, I retired the *Ibis* from commercial fishing. She had done 58 years on the trot, so maybe she was ready to retire. I had decided instead to concentrate on a more diverse summer trade: previously it had been shark fishing seven days a week, but that, like the winter mackerel fishery, was becoming much less reliable. Foreign holidays were reducing the number of people taking their holidays in the West Country and also, probably due to nature programmes on television, many people were becoming much more conservation-minded. Sharks were no longer viewed as evil monsters of the deep that deserved nothing better than to be fought by heroic anglers, dragged out of the water and killed, for that had been the attitude only a few years before. Now any that were caught were released back into the sea unharmed, and a good job too. The only trouble was that sharks were now being slaughtered in their thousands by large commercial fishing vessels, greatly reducing the numbers that came up the Channel. This meant that instead of being able to catch sharks on a daily basis almost anywhere off the coast, a shark angling boat might now go days without seeing one, so yet another of our seasons was under threat.

It was a similar story for the boats that took anglers out reef and wreck fishing for conger, ling, pollack etc. For now, most of the wrecks and all of the reefs and rough ground were being smothered with fleets' monofilament nets, and they killed just about anything that swam. Many of the more serious-minded fishing clubs from up country and the big angling organisations from Holland, Belgium and Germany that used to make block bookings with the Looe boats began to take their trade elsewhere because results with rod and line off the south Cornish coast had dropped off dramatically. It was all change and unfortunately none of it was for the better.

With the *Ibis* now stripped of all her fishing gear, I employed local shipwright Jeff Lewis to refit her for her new role. I had a deckhouse built over the fish room, inside which was a small galley and comfortable seating for the passengers. Two cabins were fitted in the fore peak, increasing the bunk space from five to eight and, to finish the job, I had her re-rigged with mast and sail. The *Ibis* and I were about to embark on a whole new career. My wife Margaret and I started doing sailing holidays to Brittany, the Channel Islands, the Scilly Isles and Ireland. The *Ibis* was a fine sea boat in any weather, especially with a rig of sail to keep her steady; many is the time we crossed the Channel with a force five to seven blowing. When we weren't on sailing charters, we were booked by diving clubs to explore the wrecks and reefs that lay off shore from Looe, and in addition we still did a certain amount of sharking if other bookings were a bit slack. Within a few years we had built up a very good trade, our customers for the diving and the sailing rebooking with us year after year. A good living could now be earned with the *Ibis* from May to September; the expenses were low and the enjoyment factor most of the time was high and, compared to commercial fishing, it was like being paid to go on holiday.

During the winter months the boat was de-rigged and sheeted down under tarpaulins. But time and tide, as the saying goes, wait for no man, and time was now rapidly overhauling the old *Ibis*. By the mid-1990s a new generation of dive charter craft was coming into service, high speed shiny things made of glass fibre with hydraulic lifts instead of a ladder to get the divers back aboard, while what was left of the shark fishing was now dominated by modern high speed angling boats. Another huge problem for an old vessel was being able to comply with the new rules and regulations that the MCA was then introducing for vessels carrying passengers. If I wanted to keep the *Ibis* working, the only option that I could see was to give her a massive refit overseen by the MCA surveyors to convert her into a charter yacht, and that was an expense that I just could not contemplate.

The 2001 season drew to a close in late September when we returned home to Looe from a boisterous gale of wind charter to Brittany, laying the boat up for the winter as usual but not quite sure what our next move with her would be as a new MCA survey was due. To be honest, the writing was on the wall in capital letters, but I just didn't want to read it. I had now owned and worked the *Ibis* for 23 years, trawling, mackerel fishing, sharking, diving and sailing and she had never let me down, fine weather and foul. But now, after a working life of 71 years, her race was run, her day was done. It was time to retire her as a working boat.

Bob Cann, a friend of mine from Torbay, ended all the pondering with a phone call enquiring if the *Ibis* was for sale, as someone he knew wanted to buy a lugger. I had not said a word to anyone about selling up, so I was quite stunned by Bob's call, but at the same time I knew it was time I faced up to the reality. So I agreed to let this chap come and have a look at her and, to my surprise, within a week a deal had been done, the *Ibis* was sold and the money was in the bank, just as quick as that. My wife Margaret was tearful for days afterwards and I felt as miserable as if I had just betrayed a faithful old friend. It was all very sad and the end of a big part of our lives.

As usual, our customers had booked up their holidays and weekends on the *Ibis* for the following year, so I had to contact them all to tell them the news; it was such a hard thing to have to do because the *Ibis* had been a big part of their lives as well. Nick Jewson and his dive team from Bracknell in Berkshire had booked us for five or six weekends plus a couple of weeks every year for 16 years; even our newest dive club had been with us for over ten. We had been more or less fully booked for the coming summer, so I suppose you could say that we got out while the going was good.

22

Full Circle

Things seem to have gone full circle here in the port of Looe. 45 years ago when I first went to sea, most of the boats that took out angling parties in the summer months were laid up out of season because there was no winter fishery then for them to pursue. The men got jobs ashore painting and decorating, working in the building trade or whatever else might see them through until the following spring. These men were mostly middle-aged to elderly as there were few prospects for the younger men.

Then came the winter mackerel fishery and suddenly there was a good living to be had all year round. These good prospects brought the young men back into the trade. They worked hard, raised their families, bought their homes and new boats, and for over 30 years times were good and they prospered. Those young men are now themselves middle-aged and in the winter time they get jobs ashore painting and decorating, or on the buildings or whatever sees them through until the following spring. The great mackerel fishery that was once 400 boats strong county-wide has ended, and most of the men with the small boats are back where the previous generation had been 45 years ago.

The mighty shoals of fish that were once miles wide and as deep as the sea have now all gone, broken up and slaughtered for fish meal at rock-bottom prices by huge purse seiners and mid-water trawlers. A few boxes of hand-line caught mackerel are landed here and there, now and then, and make very good money, to great acclaim by fishmongers, restaurateurs and food 'ponces' on television. "Wonderful quality fish from a sustainable fishery, bla.. bla.. bla…" they bang on. Meanwhile, out at sea, the industrial fishing ships are still slaughtering the pelagic fish as hard as they can go. The ever-decreasing shoals of herring, pilchard and mackerel are being located and wiped out. In these times of much trumpeted conservation measures, how can these vessels be allowed to continue? Even under the strictest control, they don't fish, they exterminate. Get these sea raping behemoths off the water and give the shoals of pelagic fish a decent chance to recover. And when they have done so, only then can there be such a thing as a sustainable fishery; hand-lining for mackerel and drift netting for herring and pilchards, fleets of small local boats landing good quality fish for human consumption. Then, once again, thousands would be employed as the ports and harbours, coves and quays all around the Cornish coast go from being picturesque and historic tourist traps, to being alive and vital once again, doing the job that they were designed to do, servicing a fishing fleet. Forty years ago, before the arrival of the purse seiners, we witnessed just such a revival, but sadly I doubt that it will happen again. For while the big fishing companies have money and influence, the slaughter will doubtless continue, at least until there is not enough fish left to sustain them, but by then they probably won't care. The big men would have made their fortunes and will have retired somewhere 'completely unspoiled'.

As for the Looe trawlers, for a variety of reasons their numbers have gone into decline, but it is now policy to reduce the fishing effort all around Europe. There used to be grants to build new boats; now there are grants to scrap them. Our fleet has shrunk to a dozen or so far from new boats, and most of the men who work on them, to put it politely, match their boats. Fishing has always been an industry of boom and bust, highs and lows. In my time it held good for a generation, but once again it seems to be in decline. Something has to be done to protect the fish stocks because with today's powerful modern boats and gear technology the assault on them can be relentless. I only hope that when it all balances out that the modern fishing industry doesn't become the sole domain of a few all-powerful fishing companies. Because for so many reasons, the small men operating from the historic coves, ports and harbours all around our shore must survive. There is nothing so sad and soulless as a fishing harbour without any fishing boats. Pay a visit to Mousehole in west Cornwall or Cameret in Brittany and you will understand what I mean. On the walls of the harbour-side pubs and restaurants hang those beautiful black and white photos taken a generation or so ago, showing a busy haven, crowded with working craft plying their many different trades, all now ghosts and echoes from the past, while today's reality is the yachts and pleasure boats that occupy the moorings, their sterile, artificial ambiance only serving to amplify the tragedy that has overtaken these places.

23

The Future

During my lifetime here in Looe, I have seen the fishing fleet change completely three times. From a handful of worn out luggers, plying their age old trade with drift nets and long lines, to a fleet of 40 mackerel boats, and then to a harbour full of trawlers.

The luggers, many of them now well over 100 years old, still exist as much cherished classic sailing craft while the mackerel boats, barring a very few, have all completely disappeared. Where those hundreds of boats went I have no idea. It seems just like a conjuring trick to me; somebody muttered an incantation, waved a wand and hey presto, they were gone. Now, standing more or less alone in every port, are the trawlers, so successful that they were on their way to reducing much of the seabed to a wasteland. But their numbers have been greatly reduced and conservation measures are coming into being, aimed at reversing the damage done and reviving the fish stocks. In the short term, the fishermen are probably going to suffer (yet again) but hopefully, in the long term, providing the conservationists don't insist on making a pet out of every fish, then the fishermen should see some benefits. I certainly hope so.

I think we must be optimistic. High quality fish restaurants have opened up everywhere, cooking fish dishes of all kinds; even the humble pilchard, now remarketed as a Cornish sardine, has found favour. The once despised mackerel is now fussed over for its omega three oils etc, and a couple of fillets of it cooked and served with a bit of salad can cost more than a fisherman would have been paid for a 5-stone box of them not many years ago. To make a living, a fisherman once had to be up to his knees in fish because for most of the time they didn't make very much money but times have changed, thank goodness. The emphasis is now on quality, not quantity; on fish being fresh and locally caught. Nothing boosts the feel-good factor for diners in a restaurant than the sight of a fisherman delivering a box of his day's catch fresh to the kitchen door. It underlines everything that today's chefs stand for and what they are trying to achieve.

Maybe this is the future for the fishermen in our small coves and harbours - not to be lumped in on the market with the big boats' catches as happened years ago, but to be appreciated for being small, being local and landing top quality fish. Whether a diner in a restaurant can tell if his monkfish was landed by a beam trawler or from a small local netter is not the point; people are prepared to pay for the provenance of their food and trust that it is fresh and locally caught. And on this, a whole new branch of the fishing industry is developing. I once asked some of our leading fish merchants if the catch from a sailing fishing vessel would command any premium? They all seemed confident that if such a vessel was working many restaurants would be prepared to pay well over the odds for its fish, simply because of the provenance that it would carry. So, as always the fishing industry is changing, never because it wants to but always because it has to. What the next generation of fishing boats in Looe will look like and how they will operate, only time will tell. A small fleet of trawlers will probably survive if conservation measures and fuel costs don't wipe them out. But if, in time, the measures we are threatened with prove to be successful and the men are allowed to fish these areas again, then maybe we shall see a growing fleet of boats going back to more passive ways of fishing, using hand lines, long lines and static nets, methods that don't smash up the ground or kill spawn and immature fish. But who knows what the future will hold.

Epilogue

Now in retirement, I haven't given up the sea, and while I still enjoy good health I don't intend to. My wife Margaret and I bought the 38-foot lugger *Erin* back from Brittany. She had been built in Mevagissey in 1904 and fished from that port until 1976. Gerard Sey of Lézardrieux then bought her poor worn-out old hull and breathed life back into it, sailing her around the Breton and Cornish coasts for the next 28 years before offering her for sale in 2004.

We gave her a good thorough refit and now, from April to October, we cruise in her all around the coast of the south-west, from Torbay to the Scilly Isles and from the Channel Islands to the Gulf of Morbihan.

Cruising a boat for your own pleasure is such a vastly different experience from operating one to earn a living with. You can take your time, and haven't got to go out when the weather is inclement, but we still do get caught out every now and then, but that's life. We visit many of the ports and harbours that I knew in my fishing days, meeting old friends from those times. But all the hustle and bustle has gone from them. Whether it's commercial or pleasure fishing, where once there were fleets of each, now there are just a few, and the dreaded marina forever encroaches as more harbours turn to the yachtsman for their salvation, for what else can they do? Even Newlyn, the monarch of all Cornish fishing ports, has put out the welcome mat because their once mighty fishing fleet looks to be heading for the buffers.

Will white plastic hulls and smartly attired yachtsmen be the only form of life in our harbours in years to come? Will old photos, framed and hung in the pubs and restaurants, be the only record of what once was? This has been the fate of so many ports in Brittany. I just hope that here in Cornwall a balance can be struck.

Glossary

AMIDSHIPS: Mid section of a vessel.

BACKSTAY: Part of a masts standing rigging.

BAR: The piece of twine that forms one side of a net mesh.

BAULKS: Large beams of timber.

BEAM: Width of a vessel across the deck at her widest point.

BELAYING: Making fast or tying off.

BENDS: Heavy oak timbers to reinforce the hull of a boat.

BIGHT: A loop of rope.

BILGE: Bottom of a boat in the mid section.

BULWARKS: The extension of the hull above the deck to stop fish, gear and crew from going overboard. On a lugger this was set at knee height.

BULKHEAD: A partition on a boat.

BUTT: Formed by two planks meeting end to end on a frame.

CABIN SOLE: Cabin floor.

CAPSTAN: Mechanical device to haul ropes and cables.

CARVEL: Planking method where planks lay edge to edge.

CAULKING: To pack seams of planks with a waterproof material to prevent leaking.

CLINKER: A method of planking a boat where the plank edges overlap.

COAMINGS: The frame around a deck opening, usually 10 or 12 inches higher than the deck itself.

CRAN: A measure of fresh herrings - 37 ½ gallons (about 750 fish)

CRUDDY: Feeling seasick.

DANN: A buoy used to mark the end of a net, a long-line or a fleet of crab pots. A flag is fixed to it.

DEADWOOD: Baulks of oak laid between keel and sternpost and keel and stem to add strength.

DIXIE: A big stew pot.

DRAUGHT: Depth of hull from waterline to keel.

DRUDGING: To control a vessels speed by dragging astern a lump of ballast iron or chain.

FATHOM: 6 feet.

FRAMES: Inside skeleton of vessel that carry the planks, usually made of oak.

GUNNELS OR GUNWHALES: The top outside rail of a boat.

GYPSY: A gear wheel that carries the steering chain at the wheel.

JIB: Triangular sail set between mast head and bowsprit.

JOWTER: Fish seller, usually working from a van or a cart.

KEEL: Heavy elm or oak baulk, forming the backbone of a boat.

KEVEL: A stout oak bar bolted across two stanchions to make a strong point for mooring ropes.

KNOTS: Speed of a vessel through the water, based on a nautical mile of 2000 yards.

LEG: A stout baulk of timber shaped to fit the up and down shape of a boat amidships. This is to prevent a vessel going over on her side at low tide when working from a drying harbour.

MAUND BASKET: A heavy circular two handled wicker basket that held about five stone.

MIZZEN: Aft mast sail on a fore and aft rigged vessel.

PARTING BOARDS: Boards 8 or 10 inches in height set fore and aft on the deck to prevent the catch from sliding about.

PAWL: A ratchet device on the end of the hauling roller.

PEAK: The top most part of a sail.

POLE END BUOY: The very last buoy on a fleet of drift nets.

QUARTERS: The port and starboard aft sections of a boat.

RUDDER: Steering device at stern of boat.

SUANT: The lines of a vessel looking fair and sweet.

SHEAR LINE: The line of a boat running fore and aft at the deck or rail.

SHEET: A tackle to control a sail.

SIDEWINDERS: Trawlers that haul and shoot their gear over the side as against the modern method of over the stern (stern draggers).

SKIRT: The lower section of a drift net.

SPELL: A rest or breather.

STEM: The very front part of the bow, linking the keel to the deck and carrying the plank ends.

STERNPOST: An oak post linking keel to deck, carrying the transom or, if a double ender, the plank ends.

THREE'ERS: Two broken bars requiring three knots to repair.

TRANSOM: The flat stern of a vessel, usually made of oak.

WATERWAYS: The narrow part of the deck between the net room coamings and the rail.

YARN: To talk or tell a story.

The Author

Paul Greenwood was born in Looe in 1947, the eldest of four children. His father Peter was a shipwright by trade, later to become an antique restorer; his mother Pamela was a schoolteacher. Paul went to sea at the age of 16, joining the lugger *Iris* in 1964 as a very seasick 'boy', working drift nets for pilchards and long lines for conger, ray and turbot. In the late 1960s he left the *Iris* to sail as bosun aboard the *Malcolm Miller* before returning to fishing in 1973. He bought his own boat, the lugger *Ibis*, in 1978, which he used for commercial fishing and later charter work with his wife, Maggie, until 2002. His first book, *Once Aboard A Cornish Lugger*, was originally published in 2007; his second book, *More Tales From A Cornish Lugger*, was first published in 2011. Paul and Maggie now live in East Looe and spend their summers cruising in their 1904 lugger *Erin*.